Quality Assurance
for University
Teaching

SRHE and Open University Press Imprint
General Editor: Heather Eggins

Quality Assurance for University Teaching

Edited by
Roger Ellis

The Society for Research into Higher Education
& Open University Press

Open University Press
Celtic Court
22 Ballmoor
Buckingham
MK18 1XW

and
1900 Frost Road, Suite 101
Bristol, PA 19007, USA

First Published 1993
Reprinted 1995

A catalogue record of this book is available from the British Library

ISBN 0 335 19025 1 (pb)   ISBN 0 335 19026 X (hb)

Library of Congress Cataloging-in-Publication Data

Quality assurance for university teaching/[edited by Roger Ellis].
     p.   cm.
  "Society for Research into Higher Education."
  Includes bibliographical references and index.
  ISBN 0–335–19026–X. – ISBN 0–335–19025–1 (pbk.)
  1. College teaching–Great Britain–Evaluation.   I. Ellis, Roger,
1937–
LB2331.Q35   1993
     378.1'25'0941–dc20   92–31746
                                                 CIP

Typeset by Type Study, Scarborough
Printed and bound in Great Britain by
Biddles Ltd, Guildford and King's Lynn

Contents

Notes on Contributors

Jennifer Boore is professor of nursing and head of Department of Nursing at the University of Ulster. Under her leadership the Department offers innovative programmes at degree and diploma level in nursing, professional development in nursing and in community nursing and is developing postgraduate programmes for development of the advanced practitioner. The rapid growth in study and staff numbers has emphasized the importance of actively working to maintain quality in teaching and assessment. The departmental staff have undertaken a number of activities developing assessment schedules for academic and clinical work to enhance reliability of assessment and writing packaged learning materials.

George Brown is a psychologist with a strong interest in the problems of teaching and learning in higher education. He has written over two hundred papers, articles and texts and he has conducted and directed research on many aspects of higher education. He has recently completed an international survey of Research Supervision in the Sciences. His text (written with M. Atkins) *Effective Teaching in Higher Education* (Methuen, 1988) is used widely on staff development courses in this country and abroad. His most recent text is (with M. Pendlebury) *Assessing Active Learning* (USDU/CVCP 1992). Dr Brown was reader in university teaching methods at the University of Nottingham and national co-ordinator of academic staff training for the Committee of Vice-Chancellors and Principals. He has worked as a consultant for UNESCO, WHO and the World Bank. He is currently working as a higher education adviser to the Department of Employment and as a freelance consultant.

John Dallat is senior lecturer in the Department of In-Service Education, University of Ulster at Jordanstown. He lectures mainly in the fields of education policy and the history of education in Ireland and Northern Ireland. His doctoral thesis relates to the latter aspect of his teaching activities. As a member of the Department of In-Service Education, he works mostly with serving teachers, and, in this respect, is senior course tutor of a Master of Education (Professional Development) degree. Dr Dallat is also actively involved in teaching on the University of Ulster's Postgraduate Certificate in Teaching in Higher Education, which course he helped plan and initiate. He is currently researching the effectiveness of video-conferencing in teaching in higher education. He is a graduate of three universities.

Roger Ellis is a professor of psychology and Dean of the Faculty of Social and Health Sciences at the University of Ulster. Having trained as a primary teacher he took an external degree in psychology at the University of London and since then his work has applied psychology to the understanding of professional competence and ways in which this might be acquired and developed. He has been head of departments of educational psychology, social sciences and psychology and throughout has maintained an interest in teaching and learning in higher education. His interests include social skills, professional education and training, and quality assurance and he has published widely on these topics. He is the author (with D. Whittington) of *A Guide to Social Skill Training* (Croom Helm, 1981); *New Directions in Social Skill Training* (Croom Helm, 1983); *Professional Competence and Quality Assurance in the Caring Professions* (Chapman and Hall, 1988); and (with D. Whittington), *Quality Assurance in Health Care: A Handbook* (Edward Arnold, 1993). He is particularly interested in the transfer of ideas regarding quality and its assurance across manufacturing industry, service industries, health care and education. He is an auditor for the Division of Quality Audit.

Lewis Elton is emeritus professor of higher education, University of Surrey, where he had been professor of physics (1964–71), professor of science education (1971–85) and professor of higher education (1985–8). He is a higher education adviser to the Employment Department. His current main research interests are in the improvement of teaching and learning, and in institutional change in higher education.

Catherine Finlay obtained the degree of DPhil from the University of Ulster in 1987. In 1988 she was engaged as a research assistant investigating techniques for student evaluation. Since then she has held part-time lecturing appointments in communication and linguistics at the University of Ulster. Currently she is a part-time lecturer at the Queen's University of Belfast teaching linguistics within the English Department. Dr Finlay's research interests include the study of linguistic variation with particular emphasis on educational linguistics and its assessment.

Norman Gibson is professor of economics at the University of Ulster. He taught economics for some 27 years at the Queen's University of Belfast, the University of Manchester, University of Wisconsin-Madison, The New University of Ulster and the University of Ulster. He was a head of department for fifteen years and a Dean and Pro Vice-Chancellor for sixteen years. For the past eight years as Pro Vice-Chancellor he has had a major responsibility in the development, implementation, monitoring and review of quality assurance procedures for course work at the University of Ulster.

Sandra Griffiths is academic staff development officer at the University of Ulster, on secondment from her post as a lecturer in adult and continuing education. Having begun her career teaching in a further education college she undertook further study in education and was then employed by Queen's University as a community education adviser on one of the first communication education projects in Northern Ireland. In 1978 she joined the University of Ulster as a tutor on the Certificate in Education for further education teachers. Her research and teaching interests are in teacher education, adult education, women's education and staff development in higher education. Recently she established the Staff Development Unit at the University of Ulster and was a founder teacher of the Postgraduate Certificate in Teaching in Higher Education. She has acted as consultant on active learning to the Universities' Staff Development and Training Unit and has worked as a British Council consultant in Pakistan at the University of Punjab.

Jerry M. Lewis is professor of sociology at Kent State University in Kent, Ohio where he has been a member of the faculty since 1966. He was awarded the University's Distinguished Teaching Award in 1983. Dr Lewis received his PhD from the University of Illinois in Urbana in 1970.

Saranne Magennis is administrative officer for the academic audit office at the Queen's University, Belfast. Prior to this she was a research officer for the project on Teaching Effectiveness at the University of Ulster. Dr Magennis is a graduate in philosophy from University College, Dublin and completed an MA in education at Trinity College, Dublin following a period as a primary school teacher.

Gordon Rae is professor of education and Dean of the Faculty of Education at the University of Ulster. He began his career as a physics teacher and moved into teacher training in 1971. In 1978 he was appointed lecturer in education at the New University of Ulster and in the following year completed his doctorate in psychology at the University of Aberdeen. Subsequently he was promoted to senior lecturer in education and appointed head of Department of In-Service Education. His principal interests are in the areas of assessment, statistics, and theories of learning and memory. He has been actively involved in the design and delivery of staff development programmes at the University, including the Postgraduate Certificate in Teaching in Higher Education.

Christine Saunders is senior lecturer in the Department of Communication at the University of Ulster. Her interest in the identification and analyses of professional practice extends across the areas of classroom teaching, speech therapy and most recently university lecturing. In particular she has pioneered means of assisting professionals to reflect upon and articulate effective practice. She is the co-author of *Rewarding People: The Skill of Responding Positively* (Routledge, 1993).

Eric Saunders is professor of education and head of Department of Pre-Service Education in the University of Ulster and has researched and written widely in the fields of teacher education, higher education and sport and leisure studies. He has extensive experience of the assessment and evaluation of courses and students in higher education through membership and chairmanship of committees and boards of studies of the Council for National Academic Awards and external examining appointments in universities, polytechnics and colleges of higher education. His interest in the field of assessment stems from pioneering work started in the late 1970s which led to the validation of the first Bachelor of Education Degree with Honours inclusive of the Assessment of Teaching Practice.

Susan Storey is head of quality assurance at Wolverhampton University and BS 5750 Quality Manager designate. An arts graduate, she began her career as a cathedral music archivist but for fourteen years has pursued the academic administrative route to education management, holding a wide variety of posts in a college of technology, a university and three polytechnics. Since joining Wolverhampton University three years ago, she has been instrumental, together with the University's senior management and her colleagues in the Quality Assurance Unit, in promoting the implementation of a Total Quality Management system. She has a growing reputation on the further and higher education networks as a speaker and workshop leader on TQM and BS 5750.

Maurice Stringer is lecturer in psychology within the Faculty of Social and Health Sciences at the University of Ulster, Coleraine. He is an applied social psychologist who has lectured for over fourteen years to a wide range of professional groups. Dr Stringer has published extensively on intergroup conflict and is co-author of *Rewarding People: The Skill of Responding Positively* (Routledge, 1993), a skill-based analysis of the role of rewards in professional interactions.

Ann Tate is Director of Enterprise in Higher Education at the University of Ulster, and is a sociologist. Her concern with quality in university teaching arises out of a professional interest in the development of sociology curricula for student health professionals. As Enterprise Director she has been active in the promotion of student-centred learning as a means of enhancing the quality of the learning experience. She is currently preparing an introductory sociology textbook for health professionals.

Elaine Thomas is professor of art and design and became Dean of the Faculty of Art and Design at the University of Ulster in 1990. Born in 1950 in Stretford, Lancashire, she took a Foundation Course in art and design, DipAD in fine art, then PGCE at Manchester Polytechnic. She commenced teaching as a lecturer in fine art at the Ulster Polytechnic in 1973, and has lived in Northern Ireland since, becoming head of Department of Fine Art at the University of Ulster in 1980, and head of Department of Fine and Applied Arts in 1988. She is a practising and exhibiting artist.

Dorothy Whittington is senior lecturer in psychology and Director of the Centre for Health and Social Research in the University of Ulster. She has a background in education and has taught in primary and secondary schools as well as in further and higher education. She has published extensively on social skill training, professional competence, and the evaluation of quality and effectiveness in the health and personal social services. She has particular interests in quality assurance in health care and is joint author (with Roger Ellis) of *Quality Assurance in Health Care: a Handbook* (Edward Arnold, 1993) and (with Chris Wright) of *Quality Assurance: a Workbook for Health Professionals* (Churchill Livingstone, 1992). She is a member of the Council of the National Association for Quality Assurance in Health Care.

Roger Woodward after studying psychology at the University of Wales and the University of Stirling, worked as a research psychologist at the Queen's University of Belfast. He became a lecturer, and subsequently senior lecturer, in psychology at the Ulster Polytechnic. When the University of Ulster was founded in 1984, he was appointed to the post of Director of Institutional Research. This was the first such appointment in Europe. He is a regular contributor to the Annual Fora of the European Association for Institutional Research and currently organizer of the Annual Fora of the British and Irish Association for Institutional Research.

Acknowledgements

Thanks are due to: the University of Ulster for sponsorship of the lecture series where several of these chapters originated; and my secretary Valerie Barr for her promptings, pedagogy and patience, all of a high quality.

Part 1
Assuring Quality

1

Quality Assurance for University Teaching: Issues and Approaches

Roger Ellis

Definitions can make tedious beginnings but in this case they are necessary. Quality, quality assurance and, indeed, teaching itself are all open to a range of interpretations. So one purpose of this chapter will be to look at different ways in which the terms have been used. A second aim is to identify some of the key issues in quality assurance for university teaching. A third is to outline the approaches that will be covered in the rest of the book.

In essence quality assurance is about ensuring that standards are specified and met consistently for a product or service. The term is derived partly from manufacturing and service industry, partly from health care. Its adoption for education has been rapid and pervasive. But how appropriate and useful is it for university teaching?

Quality itself is a somewhat ambiguous term since it has connotations of both standards and excellence. Thus to talk of 'the quality of teaching' might refer to high or low standards whereas reference to 'quality teaching' implies excellence. The association of quality assurance with excellence may be misleading. It may also be convenient when it masks the assurance of minimum standards only with the appearance of excellence.

Standards of some kind are essential for quality assurance. But standards, like beauty, are usually in the eyes or perceptions of observers. Who are the observers who would identify quality for university teaching? An important idea is that the consumers of a product or service should be the ultimate arbiters of quality. From this stems the idea that quality is that which satisfies a consumer or customer. In its simplest form quality in university teaching would be that which satisfies the primary customer, the student. This notion is expressed more formally by the British Standards Institute: 'Quality is the totality of features and characteristics of a product or service that bear on its ability to satisfy stated or implied needs.' Thus the needs of students might be stated by them or might be implied on their behalf by the teacher.

Customers or consumers are not always straightforward to identify. Or more usually there are too many of them. For example, who are the consumers of university teaching? In an obvious sense students consume or experience teaching but those who have to be satisfied include colleagues, heads of department, funding bodies, employers, government and society as a whole. All of these may in some sense be identified as customers for the teaching of a university.

A different angle is to conceive quality as fitness for purpose. Hence the quality of a particular machine would be determined by the extent to which it met its stated purpose. Theoretically this kind of quality would exist even if many observers and indeed customers were, at least initially, unable to appreciate it. It is also a more useful definition for situations where there are no obvious customers or where there are multiple customers. Thus the quality of teaching would be determined by its fitness to achieve stated purposes, presumably with regard to learning.

Other definitions include 'conformance to requirements' (Crosby 1984) and 'the predictable degree of uniformity and dependability, at low cost and suited to the market' (Deming 1982). Key concepts here include conformity to standards, and standards that are appropriate for a purpose and satisfy a market. Deming also emphasizes the importance of cost-effectiveness, that is satisfying the market at low or the lowest possible cost.

Of these definitions the notion of fitness for purpose is perhaps the most straightforward. However, the idea of a customer or customers who must be satisfied is too important to lose. So a working definition of quality might be:

> Quality refers to the standards that must be met to achieve specified purposes to the satisfaction of customers.

The purpose of teaching is, of course, learning. So quality of teaching is its fitness for the purpose of promoting learning. Unfortunately there are no laws and precious few theories linking teaching and learning. So standards would be for teaching whose effect on learning is largely conjectural. Or quality may be judged by outcomes or performance indicators, whose cause in teaching is unclear.

If quality refers to standards, what is meant by assurance? First it is important to realize that 'assure' is a transitive verb: the assuring is done by someone who wishes to assure someone else. Thus a box of matches I have just used carries the legend 'Quality Assured'. This is a message from the manufacturer to me the customer. It is intended to reassure me that the standards I expect from a match will be met consistently by each match in the box. Thus *quality assurance* is a process whereby a manufacturer or producer guarantees to a customer or client that the goods or service concerned will meet standards consistently. Who is trying to reassure whom for university teaching? One interpretation is that the university is trying to reassure itself that its teaching is up to standard. Another is that universities, being publicly funded, are trying to reassure society, or at least its representatives, that they are delivering the service they are paid to deliver. At a more basic commercial level universities are trying to assure their customers, whether students, employers or grant awarding bodies, that their service is up to scratch.

While this establishment of confidence is the essence of quality assurance, the term has come to refer to the entire process whereby standards are maintained. It thus subsumes quality control and quality management, both of which will now be considered.

Quality control is the process whereby the product or service, or any part of the process associated with its production or delivery, is checked against a predetermined standard and rejected or recycled if below standard. This is a well known feature at the end of a production line but it is equally important at all stages from the initial acceptance of raw materials. It is more difficult to apply to a service since once a service has been delivered it cannot be retrieved and recycled. But at least a service can be identified as deficient and steps taken to ensure a better performance next time. This is a more complicated notion of quality control than mere rejection of the substandard and begins to shade into the use of feedback as part of quality management.

The total process whereby a particular organization is managed to achieve and hence be able to assure quality is *quality management,* or, less ambiguously, the management of quality. Thus in order to assure quality a manufacturer will have to manage production to achieve quality consistently. This will involve, at key stages, quality control. The management process will be complex and will involve, *inter alia,* specifying standards and procedures; documenting these standards and procedures; regularly checking reality against these standards and remedying any shortfalls; identifying responsibilities; investing in staff training and development and a number of other steps. Central to the whole process will be the identification of a customer's needs and the provision of a product or service to satisfy them. Feedback from customers, whether in detail or, more broadly, through purchase or rejection, will be crucial. If this management of quality is to be effective it can be argued that all aspects of the organization must be covered and all staff involved: a chain is no stronger than its weakest link. It is this, perhaps self-evident, proposition that has led to the expression *Total Quality Management* (TQM), totality referring to the involvement of all (not as is sometimes thought the achievement of ultimate and total perfection).

It is doubtful if any university could claim to have an explicit let alone total management system dedicated to ensuring quality in its teaching. Even if there were agreement about standards for teaching and all teachers were involved, the system would also have to cover all support services since each could be demonstrated to have some effect on teaching and learning, however indirectly.

If a firm claims to have a system for the management of quality, then it can be audited to see whether the system does in fact exist and operate as claimed. Thus there can be a *quality audit.* This is the activity to be carried out by the HEQC Division of Quality Audit (DQA). The Division claims to be auditing the quality assurance mechanisms of universities for teaching. Strictly speaking, if the above definitions are followed, the DQA is auditing the quality management procedures of universities, these being a necessary condition for quality to be assured. These management procedures would be intended to ensure standards in teaching so that the university can assure quality to customers or anyone else who wants to know.

Audit, then, is checking that someone is doing what he says he is doing. It would require a further step to say the organization was aiming to do the wrong thing in the first place. Such an evaluation moves into the area of *quality assessment*, which is judging the standards reached by an organization against external criteria. Thus an external examiner in the present system audits a course's own procedures to check whether the examining system is operating as planned, but also assesses quality in the sense that the standards reached by the students on the course are compared with those obtaining generally in the higher education system.

We now have a number of terms involving the word quality:

- quality assurance;
- quality management;
- quality control;
- quality audit;
- quality assessment.

The quality of teaching is the standards it must meet. Quality assurance is the process whereby customers, producers or any other interested parties are satisfied that standards will be consistently met. To provide such assurance a system of quality management is necessary. Part of this system will be quality control, whereby conformity with standards is checked and steps are taken if conformity is not achieved. The quality management system may be checked to see if it actually exists and works; this is a quality audit. The products or services may be checked externally to see if standards are being met; this is quality assessment. Finally, there might be a commitment to improvement and development; this entails quality improvement or enhancement.

These definitions are derived from the literature on quality assurance in manufacturing and service industries, including health. The terms are still relatively new to education generally and higher education in particular. However, quality assurance has been embraced with almost immoderate enthusiasm by government; this enthusiasm has not been matched by precision of use or, one suspects, any great understanding of its use elsewhere. For example, both the White Paper (1991) and the early pronouncements of the DQA use quality assurance and quality control as if they were interchangeable. It is, therefore, particularly important to be clear at this early stage what is understood by quality assurance and related terms and what kind of activities and procedures might be considered relevant in an educational context. A basic question is whether universities already have procedures that could be described as quality assurance or whether the term implies a radically new approach and practices.

Broadly, responses to quality assurance in higher education fall into one or more of three categories.

First there is the view that quality assurance is just a new label for a set of procedures that are well established in higher education. External examination, course validation, professional commitment, peer review and even examination results have all been put forward as aspects of quality assurance for university teaching. Some of these practices are well established and universal; others, while universal, could be improved; others are established in polytechnics but relatively novel in universities. Quality assurance is thus conceived as more or less *latent* in the university system and just requiring explicit identification to make it manifest.

An opposite view is that quality assurance, as practised elsewhere, represents a novel approach to the establishment and maintenance of standards in universities. Imported from industry or health care, these approaches will give universities a necessary shake-up and in the process make them more accountable, student orientated and cost-effective. Quality assurance will thus involve a *radical* reorientation of the universities' approach to their work. From this comes the great interest in industry-derived approaches, such as total quality management and BS 5750.

An intermediate view is that universities do indeed have much progress to make to assure quality for their teaching and courses but that they should establish systems and approaches that are distinctive and match the special characteristics of the academic endeavour. The basis for many of these procedures already exists in university practices but some imports will be desirable for the growth of the system. A system should thus *develop* which is customized for universities. More ambitiously, it is suggested that the procedures worked out for higher education might, with advantage, be applied in industry.

These three positions I would describe as the 'latent', the 'radical' and the 'developmental'. They are not mutually exclusive: in clarifying existing procedures opportunity might be taken to effect improvement and there might be some borrowing from practices elsewhere.

If there is to be an importation of industrial or public service techniques into universities to assure the quality of teaching it is important to separate essence from accidents. Much of the adverse criticism of BS 5750 has been based on a concern with its surface features and language rather than its basic approach. I would suggest that the following are characteristics of quality assurance wherever it occurs.

1. The specification of standards for whatever is conceived as the product or service.
2. The identification of critical functions and procedures that will be necessary to achieve these standards.

3. Constant recourse to the consumer to set and monitor the accomplishment of standards.
4. Documented clarity with regard to both the standards to be achieved and the procedures that must be followed to achieve these standards.
5. A cybernetic approach to standard and procedure setting, which involves monitoring that standards are being met and procedures followed, and taking action to remedy or rectify shortfalls coupled with a regular review of the appropriateness of standards and procedures.
6. The total involvement of all personnel and a commitment to development and training.

All of this preliminary thinking about quality assurance should now be applied to teaching. Do we have clear standards regarding teaching conceived as a product or service? Do we have constant recourse to, say, the student as consumer to validate the standards of teaching? Are the standards for teaching and the procedures that must be followed to achieve these standards set out clearly? Do we follow a cybernetic approach to setting objectives, monitoring performance and acting on feedback? Are all staff in the university committed to quality in teaching and is there a sustained programme of training and staff development to support this? But the fundamental question is: what do we mean by teaching?

In simple terms teaching is what teachers do. This includes their observable behaviour and the materials they produce. But how observable is the behaviour of university teachers? The majority of their work is carried on in private with more or less consenting adults. How common is it for colleagues, including heads of department, actually to observe lectures, seminars, tutorials or any other form of teaching? Even if such observation does occur, is there general agreement about the events observed and their significance? Further, is there agreement about the standards that should be met?

If teachers produce materials, be they visual aids, handouts or more comprehensive learning packages, then these are more amenable to observation and comment, but to what extent does this take place? Again what are the standards that distinguish the good from the indifferent?

There is, of course, no point in teaching unless somebody, other than the teacher, learns from it. So whatever standards are set for teaching would have to relate in some systematic way to the effect of that teaching on desirable learning in students.

There are two crucial complicating factors here. First, and most important, there is no generally accepted science or technology addressing the relationship between teaching and learning. But there is no point in teaching unless someone learns from it. Such knowledge as there is of the effectiveness of various teaching styles, and George Brown summarizes this convincingly in his chapter, is not widespread among lecturers in universities.

A second problem is the ambiguous professional status of university lecturers. While they spend a large, often the largest, proportion of their time teaching, their professional status and credibility derives not from this central activity but from their knowledge of their subject and their capacity to extend that knowledge. Uniquely among so-called professions, there is no formal requirement of training to be a teacher. Trained teachers are a minority in universities and the recent translation of polytechnics will not affect this proportion dramatically. It is assumed, therefore, that knowledge of the subject and research capability coupled with on-the-job practice and experience are sufficient to ensure professional standards of teaching.

These paradoxes make it extraordinarily difficult to imagine a thorough-going quality assurance approach to teaching, at least in the short term. Clearly there are not generally accepted standards for teaching in either its interpersonal or materially based aspects. While there is a substantial literature, teachers as a whole do not concern themselves with it. In the absence of standards there cannot be procedures to guarantee their achievement. Students, while clearly the recipients of teaching, and indeed its *raison d'être*, are rarely conceived as consumers (or customers or clients). Their contribution to standard setting is patchy and haphazard. The teachers themselves are not trained and there is a pervasive culture which believes that training is, at best, a diversion from more significant activities.

Yet universities do claim that their teaching is of high quality. How is this demonstrated? The answer is in two main ways. First, there are the results that students achieve in their examinations and course work and the consequences of these in degree classifications. Second, there is the much lauded system of external examination. But, of course, both of these mechanisms are in the hands of teachers. Teachers are the stock from which examiners are drawn and teachers are responsible for assessing their own students' achievements. This does seem an unduly inbred and remote system for the identification of teaching quality. Furthermore, even if external examiners are objective and genuinely external, they are concerned primarily with assessment, that is with results and the examining scheme. Their comments on teaching as such are at best based on inference.

Recently universities have begun to discover the formal procedures for course planning validation and review that are so well established in public sector institutions. But how close do these procedures actually get to teaching? Typical documents include statements of aims and objectives bearing upon students' learning, regulations and procedures for admission and assessment of students and lists of content that will be covered. Teaching methods are usually described briefly and in a routine way. It would be rare if not unique to find a course document that contained detailed standards for the teaching activities of staff.

There are, then, numerous problems surrounding quality assurance for university teaching. We don't know much about teaching. Quality assurance is a new term and there is no general agreement on what it might mean for higher education and even how appropriate its techniques might be if imported from other areas. Those ideas and approaches, which are generally accepted as implied by quality assurance, seem difficult or even impossible to apply to teaching. Yet universities are assumed to have some commitment to a quality assurance approach to their teaching. There is now a Division of Quality Audit whose job it is to audit universities' own quality assurance mechanisms for teaching.

It is necessary, therefore, that all universities should have thought through what quality assurance means to them. They must have at least a working definition of teaching and be able to demonstrate that they have standards for it and methods to ensure that the standards are being met. They must have procedures to monitor standards and put things right when there are deficiencies or shortfalls. At this stage they must be open to new ideas and experimental in posture, while able to identify their best existing practice and be committed to its development.

One common theme in all approaches to quality assurance is the central importance of staff. Even when an organization is concerned with manufactured goods the quality of these goods depends ultimately on the activities of the people involved. This truism is even more obvious when the organization offers a service the nature of which is interpersonal. University teaching is the activities of university teachers that aim to bring about desirable learning in students. Supporting this central teaching venture is a complex structure of administrative and service departments. Managing quality for teaching therefore involves, directly or indirectly, the entire staff of the university. If there is to be progress in quality assurance for teaching then we are faced with a massive exercise in staff development and organizational change.

As a start it would be important to identify those activities which already exist in universities and which might form part of a quality assurance system. They include both internal and external mechanisms for assuring quality. These are the latent quality assurance functions referred to above. Examples include:

- existing procedures for the planning, approval and review of courses;
- performance indicators for courses, including the intake characteristics of students, wastage rates and final results, and the follow-up of these statistics;
- feedback from students;
- feedback from employers and sponsors;
- external inspection from, for example, professional bodies;
- reviews undertaken by departmental, faculty and university committees;
- staff appraisal and development, including teaching training.

The university should undertake its own quality assurance audit, first to determine those existing procedures that might contribute to quality assurance and then to assess their effectiveness and ways in which they might be improved.

In the light of its overall concept of quality assurance the university might then consider more innovative approaches, including imports from other universities or organizations. This more radical approach might range from the introduction of a fully fledged total quality management system through the introduction of procedures such as quality circles or local audits to the imitation of best practice from other universities or higher education institutions in the UK or internationally.

A central question should be the extent to which these procedures actually make an impact on teaching, that is the behaviour of teaching staff. It must be recongnised that universities in general are relatively distanced in their procedures from this behaviour. The most significant development in quality assurance for teaching will be the establishment of teaching itself at the centre of the stage. Thus course validation and review, student feedback, appraisal, development and promotion will all have to make specific and detailed reference to the behaviour of teachers, including interaction with students, materials produced by teachers to facilitate learning, and the scholarly output of staff concerning teaching.

The main purpose of this book is to present ideas and initiatives that are relevant to quality assurance for teaching.

One thread running through the book is the description of a number of initiatives that have been introduced at the University of Ulster. They were all aimed in part at giving teaching a higher profile. These include:

- a distinguished teaching award;
- a research project to identify staff perceptions of excellence in teaching;
- a teacher training course;
- a staff development unit;
- an institutional research unit;
- student feedback procedures.

In addition the university has a comprehensive system of course validation and review.

The university is unique in being, so far, the only merger of a polytechnic and a university. In 1984 the Ulster Polytechnic and the New University of Ulster ceased to exist and a new chartered institution came into being: the University of Ulster. The university inherited two quite different systems for course planning and review. The polytechnic was typical of a CNAA validated institution and was well accustomed to course planning and review at course, faculty and polytechnic levels. The New University of Ulster, on the other hand, was typical of most universities, with the primary locus for course planning being at the departmental or individual unit level. Faculty and university scrutiny was concerned mainly with regulations. The developments in the University of Ulster are therefore of great interest in that they represent the merging of two traditions, which is now about to take place nationally.

Another thread is coverage of more radical approaches which universities might follow and which are, in one sense, implied by the new vocabulary. There are thus chapters on quality assurance in industry and in health care and a case study of one polytechnic, now a university, that has followed the total quality management and BS 5750 track.

Three major issues have led to the subdivisions of the book. First is the question of what quality assurance might mean and how it might be practised. Second is the identification of quality in teaching. The third is the development of staff.

In the first section three broad approaches are adopted to the question of what quality assurance might mean in a university. The first is to introduce quality assurance as it is practised in manufacturing and service industry and health care. This is based on the assumption that there could be fruitful transfer from these areas to a university's management of quality for teaching. The second approach is concerned with procedures that already exist to some extent in universities – course validation and review and the use of student feedback – but that might be extended and developed. Finally there are two chapters on approaches that might be developed in universities and would be distinctive to them. To some extent, therefore, the chapters reflect the radical, latent and developmental models outlined above.

Chapter 2 is concerned with quality assurance for university teaching as it might be conceived from the point of view of best industrial practice. This is brought into sharp focus by considering the application of the BS 5750 approach. When the chapter was first written this was no more than a hypothetical possibility. Since then a number of further education colleges have gained BS 5750 for all or part of their operation. Even more significantly, Wolverhampton Polytechnic, now University, is in the process of preparing itself for registration and Susan Storey contributes a case study of progress so far.

Interest in BS 5750 has stimulated strong objections, where it is argued that the standard is fundamentally antipathetic to university practices. Chapters 2 and 3 should enable readers to make up their own minds. It is important to grasp that BS 5750 is a content-free standard for the processes of quality assurance and quality management, whatever goods or services are involved. What is missing is a standard for teaching itself, but BS 5750 is not intended to provide that. However, the emphasis on meeting consumers' needs should at least ensure that the university's approach is student-centred.

There are two main traditions of explicit concern with quality assurance. One is that of manufacturing and service industry; the other is of quality assurance for health care. Arguably health care is closer in a number of respects to education than is manufacturing industry. To begin with, the 'product' is primarily interpersonal and hence psychosocial in nature. Second, the views of customers may be ignored, partly through the absence of a market and partly on the basis of the assumed superior knowledge of practitioners In Chapter 4 Dorothy Whittington and I review approaches to quality assurance in health care and consider their possible applications to teaching.

Inasmuch as quality assurance for University teaching might claim a tradition, two approaches are the most widespread. One is the planning, validation and review of courses; the other is the use of feedback from students on the perceived quality of teaching. Polytechnics and institutes of higher education are well used to course validation, which was brought to a fine art by the CNAA; in established universities the approach is more novel. There is, therefore, particular interest in Norman Gibson's chapter, where he describes and reflects on the first eight years of such a system in a university. As described above, the University of Ulster was in 1984 a unique trans-binary merger and since that date it has operated a comprehensive system of course validation and review, involving at several points external advisers. Significantly, the new university severed its connections with CNAA and the system is therefore entirely generated from within the university. This should be of interest both to universities who want to develop a system and to new universities who wish to demonstrate their independence.

The systematic and widespread use of feedback from students is almost universal in North American universities but still relatively novel in the UK. Maurice Stringer and Catherine Finlay review the extensive literature and describe an experimental scheme in a faculty. Their review of the literature and case study should be of value to those intending to introduce or develop such schemes.

Roger Woodward outlines the functions of an institutional research unit as an aspect of quality assurance and links with the preceding chapter in showing how it might operate to sample students' views. All quality assurance schemes require a highly developed internal intelligence function to develop measuring instruments and to gather relevant data to inform decisions. While all universities no doubt have staff dedicated to such functions the idea of an institutional research unit has the merit of explicit in-house intelligence that is objective in stance but committed in purpose.

Despite the absence of teacher training for its practitioners, a lack commented on in several chapters, it is often asserted that the best assurance of quality for university teaching rests with the dedication and professionalism of university teachers. In his chapter, Lewis Elton reflects on the nature of professionalism in university teachers and how this might contribute to quality in teaching. Less than impressed with what he finds, he sets out a unique model for improved practice and comprehensive quality assurance.

The second major section addresses quality in teaching. The chapters are concerned to identify what is known about effectiveness and hence quality in teaching, but also to outline ways in which standards might be identified at a local level.

An interesting starting point is the distinguished teaching awards that are well established in the USA. There, at least, staff, students and ex-students (alumni) believe they can recognize quality sufficiently well to make prestigious annual awards to a small number of outstanding teachers. What can we learn from this practice? In his chapter, Jerry Lewis of Kent State University, Ohio, describes the well established award at his university. In addition to describing the award and its history he reflects on the characteristics of those who have received it. Lest it be thought that such awards are entirely culture-specific, Elaine Thomas describes the introduction of a comparable award in a UK university. There is sufficient information and evaluation in these two chapters to enable any university to introduce a similar scheme and benefit from the undoubted effect it has on raising the general profile of teaching.

While there is a body of knowledge regarding styles, methods and techniques of university teaching it is largely ignored by practitioners. It is particularly important that any descriptions, categorizations and criteria applied to teaching should be intelligible and acceptable to the teachers themselves. Christine and Eric Saunders give an account of a research project that uses the perceptions of acknowledged expert teachers to furnish a description and categorization of effective teaching. Their chapter describes a method that could be widely applied for local standard setting.

Similarly, Jennifer Boore describes the use of quality circles to identify standards for a range of teaching methods. However, her circles were made up of staff and students. Her method could be extended to establish various cross-sectional groups of those involved, whether as suppliers, recipients or support staff.

Finally George Brown, an international authority, summarizes the research-based knowledge available on effective teaching. His chapter should be required reading for all teachers and could be linked with in-service courses where teachers would have an opportunity to develop and practise the various techniques he describes.

Following on from this, the last section of the book addresses steps that might be taken to develop staff as high quality teachers.

All universities now have some form of staff appraisal in place. How useful is this for quality in teaching? To what extent does it enable staff and their appraisers to initiate staff development that will enhance the quality of teaching? Saranne Magennis considers appraisal and its place in ensuring quality in teaching. Her chapter is a most useful summary of ideas and evidence concerning appraisal and should be of great value to all involved in the new schemes, whether as providers or recipients.

Whatever form quality assurance takes the commitment and capabilities of staff are fundamental to its success. Recognizing this, organizations must invest in staff training, retraining and development. Sandra Griffiths describes the establishment of a staff development unit in a university. This she sees as a necessary condition for quality assurance, but she also identifies the value of a quality assurance for the staff development function itself.

Teacher training, or the lack of it, is a recurrent theme. Gordon Rae and John Dallat consider this missing ingredient. They reflect on the history of teacher training for university teaching as a succession of missed opportunities but then, more positively, describe a unit-based course of teacher training for university teachers which they have introduced.

Finally Ann Tate considers the contribution that the enterprise initiative can make to the enhancement of quality in teaching and learning. At its worst the tradition of amateurism and relative indifference which characterizes university teaching needs a radical initiative to change its direction towards explicit quality assurance. The enterprise initiative can provide this in that it encourages a new look at learning objectives for students and teaching approaches for lecturers.

The book is, then, a series of perspectives on quality assurance, teaching and the development of teachers. It is not, and could not be, given the state of the art, a comprehensive and definitive handbook. However, it is hoped that it will stimulate thought and action in this vital area.

References

BS 5750 (1987 and 1990) *Quality Systems, Parts 0–4*. London: British Standards Institution.

Crosby, P. (1984) *Quality without Tears*. New York: McGraw-Hill.

Deming, W. E. (1982) *Quality, Productivity and Competitive Position*. Cambridge, MA: MIT Press.

White Paper (1991) *Higher Education: a New Framework*, Cmnd 1541. London: HMSO.

2

A British Standard for University Teaching?

Roger Ellis

Introduction

Two years ago the idea of a British Standard for University Teaching would have been dismissed as an extreme case of Jarrett's disease or a reject from the jottings of Laurie Taylor. But now there is a Higher Education Quality Council with a Division of Quality Audit dedicated to ensuring that universities have quality assurance mechanisms in place. In education generally the rhetoric of equality has yielded to that of quality. So there is some point in looking at quality assurance in general and British Standard 5750, the industrial quality standard, in particular. University teachers should get a grip on quality assurance before it gets a grip on them.

I must admit to some responsibility for all this. I suggested (Ellis 1988) that there might be merit in applying quality assurance techniques from manufacturing and service industries to education. I had managed to convince myself and at least five co-authors that there were common issues and problems across service industry, health care, social services and education. In particular there was the central and crucial question of what professionals did and how their behaviour, once we knew what it was, related to outcomes and satisfaction.

My argument in essence was this. It is important to be able to specify standards for products, whether these be material objects or services, and to be able to manage the production process to ensure that these standards are met. In the case of service industries, health care and education, the product and the production line are based largely on the actions of qualified professionals. Yet the behaviour, whether effective or not, of professionals is largely hidden from objective scrutiny. A crucial step in quality assurance would therefore be to make more explicit the actions of professionals and to study their cost-effectiveness in relation to outcomes. Given the importance of professional motivation I commended an approach that would involve them in specifying their standards, in describing and evaluating their actions and in improving the service they offered.

Having advocated this approach I am nevertheless feeling as much apprehension as approbation at the speed with which the CNAA and now CVCP have adopted at least the language of quality assurance. At worst, quality assurance could become another stick to beat the professional back. We cannot afford another initiative that alienates teachers. I say this not out of any desire to sustain professional power for its own sake but in simple recognition that there can be no progress in education at any level without the whole-hearted support of teachers. Education as a product is essentially what teachers do. One vital lesson we can learn from quality in industry and health care is that assurance requires a commitment to quality throughout the organization and works best when all play their part. In the current jargon there must be perceived ownership of quality assurance by teachers. This is not to say, however, that they should be the sole judges of quality. Their involvement is in satisfying the consumer and their responsibility is to consumers at several levels, starting with students but including industry, government and, if this is not too nebulous, society as a whole. Furthermore, quality assurance does require management and organiz-ation, and ownership includes recognizing responsibilities and divisions of labour within the system.

In this chapter I want to look at what quality assurance means in industry, with a view to identifying its essential features. During this review I want to consider how these features might translate to university teaching if it is conceived as a product or service.

As a preliminary it is important to stress that there is no single set of principles and procedures that constitutes the industrial approach to quality assurance. Rather there are a number of approaches and tech-niques whose common ground is a commitment to quality and its assurance. We should therefore select from this patchwork those tech-niques and procedures that seem to fit our objectives and mission. There may also be some features of university teaching and its approach to quality that might with profit transfer to health and industry.

Quality assurance

What does quality assurance mean? Quality is one of those interesting words that has both a neutral and positive interpretation. In a neutral sense quality refers to the standard achieved. It is thus acceptable to talk of poor as well as good quality. On the other hand, the label 'quality' is usually associated with high standards and so-called quality goods are assumed to be the best available. Whether employed neutrally or positively, quality carries with it the notion of standards that must be met. Assurance then adds the notion that these standards can be ensured or guaranteed. Thus quality assurance is the process whereby standards are specified for a product or service and steps are taken to ensure that these standards are consistently met.

In industry, quality effectively means giving satisfaction to a customer. This requires a partnership between customers and supplier to ensure that the needs of the customer are adequately defined and that the supplier designs and produces a product or service that can meet these needs. In this sense the ultimate test of the quality of a product is whether anyone wants to buy it. The market serves to validate fitness for purpose. The object of quality assurance is thus to ensure that the product consistently achieves customer satisfaction. The British Standards Institute defines quality as 'the totality of features or characteristics of a product or service that bear on its ability to satisfy a given need.'

This emphasis on consumer satisfaction is crucial and is a useful touchstone when quality assurance is complicated and obscured by its application to that elusive service called education. Obviously the producer is the originator of quality but his standards have to be tested out against a consumer, at least when a market is in operation. Many contracts are set as a negotiation between supplier and customer to agree standards. Quality assurance is then concerned with ensuring that these agreed standards are met consistently. But in education, where a straightforward market is less likely, standards may remain the prerogative of the producer: teachers, like doctors, know best. For much professional activity the producer plays the role of consumer in judging the quality of his actions. The external examiner system is an extension of this.

Of course, consumption is more complicated than a simple individual consumer and his satisfaction. My consumption of a Balkan Sobrani or a Maserati involves secondary consumers of the products of combustion: every individual act has a multiplicity of consequences, many of which may operate to the longer-term disadvantage of the initially satisfied consumer. No doubt the ideal green consumer has a complex view of needs and satisfaction that goes beyond his immediate gratification.

Quality assurance and teaching

Education certainly has a number of consumers beyond the individual student. There is the potential employer of the student, and the society that may benefit from his skills. There are the short-term monitors of the teacher, including her head of department, external examiner and colleagues. There is the critical self-monitoring that charactizes pro-fessional action, (or so we are told). Without becoming too metaphysical, the student may be conceived as a multiplicity of consumers stretching into the future: the product may not appeal to him today but eventually he will see the point of it. Despite all this there is value in recognizing the student as a consumer here and now, and one who is unlikely to operate in a market with purchasing power and for whom, therefore, special steps must be taken. It is not so much that the student as consumer determines what is of quality in *knowledge* but that he or she should be the judge of quality in *teaching methods*.

While quality assurance is not just about consumer satisfaction, meeting the needs of consumers is central and vital. It is therefore worth looking at seven steps followed in manufacturing industry to assure quality. They include:

1. Knowing the customers' needs.
2. Designing a product or service to meet the needs.
3. Guaranteeing the performance of the product.
4. Providing clear instructions for the use of the product.
5. Delivering the product punctually.
6. Providing a back-up service for the product.
7. Using customer feedback to improve the product.

How would a typical university programme, course or unit measure up to these requirements? Remember we are not trying to reinvent the substance of a discipline or field of study, but to determine the best way or ways for a student to learn it as a result of our actions as teachers. Pedagogy is the product.

What do we know of our student needs? How do we find out? To what extent have the course as a whole and the individual teaching sessions in it been designed to meet these needs? To what extent can we guarantee that doing the things we prescribe, including attending our lectures and undertaking the assignments we set, will guarantee learning? Do we provide clear instructions to help students make the best use of the course? Do we deliver the product, including, for example, not only our direct teaching but feedback on assignments, punctually? Do we provide a back-up service if the planned features of the course are not achieving the learning objectives anticipated? Do we make use of student feedback to improve the course?

So quality is about satisfying the consumer. But assurance implies that quality can be maintained consistently unit after unit. Standards must be met not just in the handmade prototype but also in the everyday production run. At this point it is worth making the distinction between quality control and quality assurance. Quality control means checking a particular product against standards and rejecting any products that do not measure up to these standards. This is, of course, a necessary step but could prove impossibly expensive if most of the products have to be rejected. Quality assurance is about attending to all features of production in such a way as to minimize the number of rejects necessary at the final stage of quality control. Thus quality control is about the product, whereas quality assurance is concerned with the whole process of production. Quality assurance is about managing the entire process of design and production to minimize rejection by quality control.

We now have several key terms. One is product; another is consumer and another satisfaction. Then we have quality; standards; control and assurance. The potential for confusion of these in their application to education is considerable. First the product: is it the actions of the teacher, the actions of the students in response to the teacher, the learning achieved by the students, the students at the end of their course, the course document or the written materials distributed during a course? All of these can properly be considered products with consumers. For the purposes of this exercise I would suggest that we concentrate on the teacher's behaviour and call this the product. This would include: teachers' plans, including course documents, syllabuses, schemes of work and lesson notes; teachers' behaviour, including lecturing, chairing or leading seminars, supervising, tutoring; products generated by the teacher for consumption by students, including blackboard work, transparencies, slides, posters, handouts, workbooks; and materials produced by the teachers for assessment and feedback, including course work and examination questions, and written feedback on performance. This collection of actions and artifacts constitutes the product of which students are consumers. Consumption of these products is intended to produce a result desired by the student, and as consumer he or she will be more or less satisfied with these products.

Quality is the general term for a set of standards for these products. Thus the judgements that are made to differentiate a good example from a bad example would have to be specified as standards. Ideally these should be measurable but at the least they should be amenable to reliable identification by informed judges. Quality control would then be a process whereby products were tested and rejected if they fell below the standards. Quality assurance, on the other hand, would be concerned with controlling the entire process that led to the products. It would be intended to guarantee as far as possible that the products were not rejected at the quality control stage.

A simple example might be an overhead project transparency produced as a visual aid for a statistics lecture. Standards could be specified regarding the overall dimensions of the slide, the size of numerals, colour contrasts and perhaps the optimum or maximum amount of information that should be included. A transparency produced for the lecture could be rejected if it failed to meet these standards and this would be quality control. However, the whole production sequence for the item could be analysed and standards specified for it with a view to ensuring that few, if any, transparencies would be rejected at the quality control stage. Even such an apparently uncontroversial item might pose problems, first in agreeing standards and subsequently in controlling production. More complex teaching products would be considerably more problematic. But standard setting and quality control are essential elements in the quality assurance approach. In the production of the OHP the attitudes and skills of the teacher are crucial. So quality assurance immediately raises questions about the selection, training, monitoring and development of teachers.

In manufacturing industry, the specification of standards for material objects and quality control at the end of the production line are well established and indeed essential. Quality assurance as set out, for example, in BS 5750 is a detailed description of the steps that must be taken to achieve quality assurance. In broad terms this requires an analysis of the production line in terms of input, process, output and outcome. The input is the resources required for the manufacturing process, the process is the transformation of those raw materials into the product, the output is the number of products produced and the outcome is the detailed character- istics of these products and their effects on the consumer. Quality assurance is about identifying and specifying the standards that must obtain for each part of this model and then further specifying procedures that must be followed to ensure that standards are met, problems are identified and solved, and the system maintains quality in the end product. This in its turn requires the establishment of checking procedures, documentation and job descriptions for key operatives. Further along the line it raises questions about the competencies of operatives and the training procedures necessary to ensure, maintain and develop those competencies.

For a manufacturing firm to be certified as meeting BS 5750 a com- prehensive audit is undertaken to make sure these various procedures are in place and can be guaranteed to remain in place. There are several key assumptions underpinning this approach. First, and obviously, it is assumed that these various procedures are related to the input and process and that they thus have a direct bearing on the output and outcome. Furthermore, a level of knowledge must exist to allow there to be a confidence regarding the cause and effect relationship between one activity and another. In manufacturing industry, where the primary area of knowledge is derived from the science and technology of materials, this is a reasonable assumption. However, as soon as the human operative is taken into account scientific laws and associated technologies are harder to come by. When the process is primarily interpersonal, albeit mediated through materials, the task is infinitely more complex.

BS 5750

Returning to industry, what is BS 5750? In 1982 a White Paper, *Standards Quality and International Competitiveness*, was issued which identified four broad areas in which the government could help to increase the efficiency of industry and commerce by promoting the importance of quality and encouraging the use of standards. First was the encouragement of independent certification schemes for products, including the develop- ment of national accreditation marks and the launching of a quality awareness campaign. BS 5750 is a kind of meta-accreditation against which firms are assessed to determine whether they have an adequate quality assurance scheme in operation and are thus able to manage consistent and consumer-satisfying quality. Second was closer cooperation between government and the British Standards Institution (BSI) to develop relevant and up-to-date standards that could form the basis of public purchasing specifications and be used by British industry to enhance its position in domestic and world markets. Third was a greater commitment by government to adapt these standards into statutory rules and regulations. Fourth was a greater effort by public purchasers to examine how far products built to existing standards could fulfil their requirements as effectively as their own specifications.

There is an important distinction to be made here between standards for a product and standards for the management of design and production. The BSI approach is to specify standards for a whole range of products, from petrol to electric blankets. Coupled with each of these standards, for a particular firm, is the standard for quality management, BS 5750. Thus if I were going into business to produce electric fires and I wished to gain BSI approval, I would have to pass two tests, first that my product met the appropriate standard for electric fires and second that my management of design and production met BS 5750. One problem with applying BS 5750 to education is that there is no product or service standard that covers teaching. Thus institutions are being judged for design and production alone. However, this is not totally inappropriate since BS 5750 requires procedures to be followed to identify consumers' needs and gauge their satisfaction with the product or service in question.

BS 5750 is the most common general quality assurance standard in the United Kingdom and comes in booklet form in five parts. Part 0 is concerned with principal concepts and applications and comes in two sections, the first of which is a guide to selection and use, and the second of which is a guide to quality management and quality system elements. Part 1 is a specification for design and development, including production, installation and servicing. Part 2 is a specification for production and installation. Part 3 is a specification for final inspection and test. Part 4 is described as a guide to the use of BS 5750 and is divided into three parts: first, a specification for design and development; second, a specification for production and installation; third, a specification for final inspection and test. This is not the most user-friendly publication. While Parts 0 and 4 are intended as guides to the central material in Parts 1, 2 and 3, they are not that intelligible in themselves.

Further publications that sketch in important background include BS 4891, which is a guide to quality assurance, and BS 4778, which covers quality vocabulary (or perhaps more accurately the vocabulary of quality). It is not easy to identify the essence of all this nor for that matter to trace the exact steps that must be followed. It is not surprising that a whole industry of quality consultants and a range of government assistance schemes have grown up to help companies along the path of virtue. However, it is in my view worth the effort since there are key procedures that have demonstrated their effectiveness in industry and could be applied in universities. (Interestingly, the embryonic Academic Audit Unit gave up the struggle and turned instead to the Reynolds report.)

Having been daunted by the sheer opacity of BS 5750 I turned to the British Standards Institute for help. This proved a fascinating inquiry. The apparent irrelevance of BS 5750 for service industry is recognized and attributed to three main factors. First is its origins in military procurement: the standard was produced as a procurement aid to NATO to ensure that suppliers of expensive military hardware kept to specification. Thus its language is oriented towards large-scale hardware rather than services. Second, the standard was produced by an international committee to satisfy the member nations of NATO and is thus couched in a kind of 'Euroese' which stems from a succession of transliterations. Finally, the standard is concerned primarily with ensuring that a number of management techniques should be in place and can often seem at several removes from specific problems.

I learned that there has been widespread interest in the applicability of BS 5750 to services in two senses. First, there is an interest in extending the approach from material products to services provided to consumers. Second, there is a recognition that in any manufacturing organization many of the activities are services rather than direct manufacture. Within a factory the majority of activity is a series of human services to ensure that the production line is operating. Further, the manufacturer offers not only a product but a service to the purchaser, including delivery and maintenance.

So it is recognized that a new standard may be required to cover *service*. A draft standard 90/97100 has been prepared for public comment and some sections of the present BS 5750 have been rewritten with a view to making them more intelligible to service industry, health and even education. (Interestingly there is no record of CVCP contacting BSI, so maybe they gave up more quickly than I did.)

Armed with all this I felt that the most useful thing I could do for this chapter was to concentrate on those parts of BS 5750 which had been revised in a service direction. In particular I concentrated on Part 4, which is described as dealing 'with products and services and attempting to redress some of the unintended residual ambiguities of BS 5750'.

First it is useful to remind ourselves what BS 5750 is trying to do. It is to help an organization to ensure that the way it is managed will guarantee that its products will consistently be up to standard. It is expected that potential purchasers should make two judgements: first whether the product is what they want; second, whether the manufacturer can consistently produce to that standard. These are, as any purchaser of a British car in the 1960s would testify, quite different issues. Brilliant design in, for example, the Mini, the Triumph Herald and the Rover 2000 were regularly let down by poor management of consistent quality. Rover's recent resurgence is attributed directly to quality assurance.

Part 4 identifies, somewhat dauntingly, 20 elements of a quality assurance system.

Management responsibility
Quality system
Contract review
Design control
Document control
Purchasing
Purchaser supplied product
Product identification and traceability
Process control
Inspection and testing
Inspection, measuring and test equipment
Inspection and test status
Control of non-conforming product
Corrective action
Handling, storage, packaging and delivery
Quality records
Internal quality audits
Training
Servicing
Statistical techniques

Each of these is given an explanatory paragraph. The provenance of the list in the procurement of machinery is obvious but several of the elements translate to university teaching without any difficulty. Others appear at first sight to be quite inappropriate. There are some that can be applied but more metaphorically than literally, and their vocabulary can be off-putting.

Two preliminary points are worth making before a translation is attempted. First, quality assurance should not be conceived as a disciplinary measure being applied to one part of an organization by another. Specifically it is not 'management' keeping an unruly and incompetent workforce in line. Quality is in everybody's interest since it makes for a successful organization. This applies as much to a university as to a manufacturing company. Second, quality is about the entire organization and thus applies as much to those parts which service the producers as to the direct producers. In university terms this means that quality assurance applies as much to central services as to the faculties and the teachers who are in the front line. Standards and quality assurance are every bit as important for staffing and finance departments as course teams.

BS 5750 for university teaching

The first element, *management responsibility*, includes responsibility for a clearly articulated quality policy, including a mission statement, objectives and a commitment to standards in a recorded statement. This statement should be published throughout the organization and be seen to be supported by management. All employees throughout the organization should be able to understand, or should be trained to be able to understand, these objectives and the commitment required by them to achieve these objectives. Universities have a head start in this collective understanding of objectives through the collegial system, but efforts must be made to ensure that this embraces all employees. Management is responsible for ensuring that new employees are trained. It is considered important that customers should be aware that the organization has this training policy. In university terms there would be value in our customers, whether they be students consuming our teaching or employers consuming our qualified students, knowing of the university's commitment to quality and training.

Second, management must ensure that there is a clearly understood and effective *structure of responsibility and authority* to achieve the policy objectives. In particular it is stressed that the personnel having the responsibility and authority to control the key elements in the quality system and processes should be identified, and the job requirements should be defined. Of these key elements emphasis is laid on: the prevention of quality deficiencies as defined by explicit standards; the control of corrective action systems to prevent recurrence of quality deficiencies; control to ensure that corrective actions are effective; and, finally, ensuring that the quality system is regularly reviewed to keep it relevant to the organization's objectives. So a key role for responsible individuals is to monitor output against agreed standards, pick up any shortfall, find out why there is this shortfall and do something about it. Whatever system is used to do this should itself be subject to regular review. If our product is, in part at least, face-to-face teaching, how might these ideas apply? There is an assumption, not always made explicit, that lecturers do have standards for their teaching, that they monitor their performance against these standards and take corrective action if they are falling short. But as a university can we be sure of this? Have we actually documented what these standards are? Are there any persons in the organization, other than the teachers themselves, who can claim to fulfil the functions set out in this element? Without this can we claim to ourselves or the Higher Education Funding Council (HEFC) that we have a quality assurance system?

This leads on to the next management responsibility, which is for *verification* and the resources and personnel needed to achieve this. Verification is the systematic inspection, checking and testing of products or outputs of all departments to ensure that they are meeting standards, and the testing of the satisfaction of consumers with these products and services. Consumers in this sense include both the customers of the organization and the customers within the organization. It is stressed that reviews and quality audits need to be performed by persons independent of those producing the particular output under review. So management (including the collective if that is the style) must ensure that there are verification or quality control procedures for all identified products and services and that these are conducted by persons other than those who directly produce or provide.

In this section on management responsibilities it is suggested that within the organization there must be a representative who is responsible for the quality system. This might be the sole responsibility of this person or there might be other functions that he or she has to perform. If there are other functions then there must be no conflict of interest.

Finally, management is responsible for a review of the quality system, including two activities: a regular review of documented policies and procedures that define the system, and a review of internal audit results.

This first element addressing the responsibilities of management touches on most of the crucial elements in quality assurance, which are then spelled out in greater detail in the remaining 19 elements. The notion that quality assurance must be managed is a crucial one for universities but should not be confused with questions of the provenance and tenure of the managers. Whoever assumes these responsibilities will have to address the issue of managing an essentially private and autonomous activity, university teaching, together with support activities that are more obviously amenable to industrial practices, for example estates and purchasing. Whoever performs them and however the control and verification of teaching is tackled, the key elements are the definition of a quality policy, the identification of responsibility and authority for its implementation, the verification of activities against agreed standards and the separation of the reviewers from the reviewed.

The second element is described as the *quality system* and elaborates the detail of the organization required to achieve the objectives set out as management responsibilities. The idea of the system is that it should at every stage ensure that it meets agreed customer requirements. Standards should be arrived at as either an anticipatory or a negotiated response to customer need. This quality system should have two interrelated aspects: (a) the supplier's needs and interests; (b) the customer's needs and expectations. This is a crucial point since it balances the meeting of customers' needs with the necessity to do this in the most economical way. Customers' needs must be met by the planned and efficient utilization of the technological, human and material resources available to the organization. The customer needs assurance and confidence that the supplier has the ability to provide the product or service consistently to the defined quality. As already stated, he makes two judgements: first, does he like the product and, second, does he trust the supplier to produce it?

As a part of this quality system it is suggested that a *quality plan*, which identifies the key elements in a product or service and the means by which they are provided and verified, and a quality manual, which brings all documentation together, would be valuable.

The next element is described as *contract review*. This assumes that at some point a contract will be drawn up between the supplier and the customer and that this will be reviewed through the following steps.

Requirements should be clearly understood and agreed by both parties and properly recorded. Both parties should go through a defined process to ensure that they have the necessary resources, organization and facilities to fulfil all the requirements of the contract.

This is an interesting way of looking at the student–lecturer relationship and suggests that a more explicit analysis of what both are expected to bring to the teaching–learning relationship might be of value. This is not the same as, but is related to, the contract that the student has with the university. Certainly the contract with the university is cast in the broadest terms and falls far short of the kind of detail anticipated here; at present the contract with the lecturer is likely to be implicit and half understood, with the exception of certain areas of work and no doubt individuals whose disposition is to be more forthright.

The next element, *design control*, emphasizes the importance of taking the customer's needs and translating these in a systematic and controlled way into a specification that defines a product or service. This specification should be such that the product is producible, verifiable and controllable in the operating environment available. The organizational structure, responsibility and authority during the management of design should be clearly defined.

The standard then goes on to spell out in detail the characteristics that should be aimed for in a good design specification and the procedures that should be followed to ensure that it meets customer requirements and that it is consistent with available resources. While this section is obviously written with the design of a product in mind, it does raise interesting questions about the kind of course plans with which most of us are familiar or becoming familiar. The kind of discipline that must attend a plan which is to be translated into a functioning and economical production line is easily lost in a plan for a series of teaching sessions and subsequent unobservable learning activities. Furthermore, there is rarely an initial contract with a customer to refer to, or the expectation of regular verification of the details of the plan.

Within a university course, documents are one kind of design plan. Departments of the university that serve internal customers also need to design the service they will provide, and in their case the customers are easier to consult. For both groups the key quality activities identified in the standard are:

1. The design specification should comply with the agreed customer requirements and should contain all the necessary information from which a design can be created.
2. The specification should take into account all the problems identified in a full assessment of any hazards associated with the product and include statutory regulations relating to its use, including, for example, safety, environmental issues and liability.
3. During the process of design, acceptance criteria for its required

performance should be continually evaluated and means for verification should be provided.
4. Changes in design should be anticipated and carefully evaluated against the original contract, fitness for purpose and amenability to verification.

The next element is *document control*, which emphasizes the importance of a formal and defined system indicating the format of documentation, who produces it, how and by whom it is reviewed and approved and the method of its review and updating. It is stressed that the key to effective quality documentation is to ensure that it is brief while covering the essential points. It is essential that the documented procedures reflect the actual working practices and needs of the organization. The implications of this for course documents are obvious.

The next element covers *purchasing* and the procurement of materials or external services, whether for inclusion in the product or service or to contribute to the quality system. Again emphasis is placed on ensuring that the materials or services meet an appropriate standard, with the implication that standards will have been specified and verification procedures established. This element also emphasizes the importance of subcontractors being assessed to ensure that they are capable of supplying materials or services of a consistent quality.

The next element, *purchaser supplied product*, covers those situations where the purchaser provides elements that are then built in to the product supplied. At first, it is difficult to see any direct relevance here to higher education. However, it could be taken as pointing to the key part active involvement by the learner plays in effective teaching. It does point out that the responsibility for non-conforming parts supplied by the customer rests with the customer!

The eighth standard, described as *product identification* and *traceability*, identifies the importance of being able to trace back from a problem to its cause at an earlier point in the production process. This is described as fundamental to the achievement of good quality in a service or product. Product identification refers to the importance of discriminating clearly between products that may appear the same but where there are crucial differences. Specific reference is made to the transfer of responsibility from component parts to personnel when the root cause of a problem is being identified. The basic point here is that when problems arise, presumably in products or services not meeting an agreed standard, it should be possible to trace back to the root cause in order that remedial action might be taken. This root cause is likely to have both human and material elements even in manufacturing industry. In service industry and education, personnel issues will be paramount.

The ninth element is central to quality assurance as opposed to quality control and concerns *process control*. Whether the process is concerned with manufacturing a product or performing a service, it is necessary to specify standards and process limits for each stage leading to the product or service. The features that closely affect the quality of the product or service should be identified from the quality plan where this exists. The standard emphasizes that written procedures or work instructions at each stage of the process should be employed as useful tools for the successful control of the enterprise. It is suggested that inadequate or non-existent work instructions may be a frequent cause of poor quality performance. The standard goes on to detail the precise specifications and control that are necessary for the materials used at each stage of the production process. Traceability and identification apply, of course, throughout the process. The standard refers to special processes where control is particularly important to quality.

Again this standard has obviously been written with material products in mind. A brief sentence at the end suggests that the performance of services may require planned control during execution and that consideration may have to be given to the levels of skill required and to process checks. University teaching does involve the provision of material products of various kinds to students and here the standard is of direct relevance. Clearly teaching requires skilled performance, whether this is learned on the job, trained for, or, as some seem to assume, innate or a necessary consequence of subject knowledge. What is interesting is the extent to which standards have been specified and verification and control introduced for this service. If shortfalls can be identified, can they then be traced back to their root cause? Can improvements then be implemented and the problem eliminated?

The next element addresses *inspection and testing*. Three phases are identified in which inspection, verification or testing may take place. The first is on receipt of any purchased or subcontracted items or services. The second is during the manufacturing or service preparation stage. The third is prior to final release to the customer. Presumably in the case of a service there could also be checks during the actual service delivery. Records of all checks should be kept in order to aid traceability. Again the message, as in so many of these elements, is that they could be applied exactly as stated to material features of teaching. In the case of the behaviour of the teacher careful, and sensitive, translation would be necessary and the role of the teacher in self-monitoring should be balanced against the need for independent assessment.

The eleventh element covers the *specialist measuring and test equipment* that might be required and the need to control and calibrate that equipment. It is pointed out that the control of measurement consistency must apply to more intangible quality testing measures, such as questionnaires used to guage customer satisfaction. In effect this element is concerned with the reliability and validity of, and testing procedures used during, the quality assurance process.

Element 12 covers the *inspection and test status* of products and services at all times during the design to delivery stage. The idea is that it should be clearly planned and documented when a product or service is to be inspected and hence there should be no doubt as to its status at particular times in relation to that system. It is not difficult to see the relevance of this consideration to, for example, the status of a syllabus in the validation procedures of a university.

Element 13 deals with what are described as *non-conforming products*, that is suspect or defective items or aspects of a service. Methods are required to prevent further processing, installation or delivery of such items. This element has been written with clear reference to material objects but in principle applies to any element in a service or the process of production for a service where the element is identified as failing to meet a standard.

It is emphasized that once a non-conforming item is identified this identification should stay in place until some documented action is taken. This action might include scrapping or aborting the item, using it under concession from an appropriate authority, reworking it or repairing it. Repaired or reworked items should be subject to reinspection. It is important that there should be clearly documented procedures for dealing with a non-conforming item, including the identification of who is responsible for particular actions. The item having been identified and dealt with *per se*, procedures must be initiated to trace the cause of the non-conformity and remedial action taken and checked. The entire process should be documented.

The next element elaborates on the *corrective action* that should be taken when a non-conforming item is identified. The quality system should include a defined method to eliminate the causes of non-conforming products or services by initiating appropriate corrective action designed to remove the root cause of the problem. Corrective action may be immediate or more long term.

It is recognized in this section that a key source of information regarding product non-conformity will be *customer complaint*. All such complaints must be recorded and dealt with and the complaint and subsequent action fully documented. In the longer term there must be regular analyses of customer complaints to identify any trends and to trace these to problems. These problems, if they have not been addressed earlier, should have their causes identified and action taken to eliminate them.

The fifteenth element recognizes the importance of storage packing and delivery in maintaining the quality of a material product. For a service it is suggested that the recording, labelling and identification of its delivery or completion is an important factor in providing evidence that the service has been performed.

The sixteenth element is *quality records*. These records are described as the objective evidence that the quality system is operating. The records should be clearly identified as dealing with a particular product or service, readily retrievable and stored for an agreed period. The type and extent of the records should reflect the nature of the processes or products involved but they should be designed to demonstrate the achievement of the required quality.

The seventeenth element refers to *internal quality audits*. These are planned and documented checks aimed at ensuring that the defined quality system is being operated correctly and effectively. They are designed to ensure:

- that the quality system documentation adequately defines the needs of the business;
- that the documented procedures are practical, understood and followed;
- that training is adequate to ensure that personnel can undertake their allotted tasks.

The timing and frequency of these audits will depend on the importance of a particular part of the system but should be predetermined and recorded. The results of audits should be documented and the records should cover the following:

- the deficiencies found;
- the corrective action required;
- the time agreed for corrective action to be carried out;
- the person responsible for carrying out the corrective action.

The eighteenth element identifies the central importance of *training* to the achievement of quality. This includes specific training to enable personnel to carry out specific tasks and also general training to heighten quality awareness and to develop attitudes. It is suggested that the following steps should be followed. Those tasks and operations which influence quality should be identified. The training needs of individuals who perform these tasks should be identified. Appropriate training should be planned and implemented to cover both specific needs and general awareness. Training and achievement should be recorded so that updating and the filling of gaps can be attended to.

The central issue of teacher training for university lecturers is the most obvious application of this requirement. It is difficult to sustain an argument that quality can be assured for a service that depends primarily on the activities of teachers when there is no formal identification of their necessary skills and the training needed to develop them. There are obviously training implications for all personnel of the university whose functions effect the delivery of teaching.

The nineteenth element is described as *servicing* and is intended to cover what is normally referred to as after-sales service. This is set out entirely with reference to material products and covers such items as special purpose servicing tools, measuring and testing equipment for field installation, instructions for installation and use, the logistics of back-up, and the training of service personnel. As we have found throughout this analysis, the standards apply most obviously to materials and equipment that are provided by the university to its students. For teaching itself servicing would have to be translated into the follow-up that is often necessary to ensure that the first presentation has had its desired effect, and the provision of additional or even remedial help.

The final element covered is described as *statistical techniques*. Statistical methods are advocated as a very powerful tool within the quality process. By statistical methods the standard appears to mean systematic approaches to data collection, analysis and application and covers techniques such as:

- design of experiments or surveys;
- tests of significance, including analysis of variance, regression analysis and factor analysis;
- safety evaluation and risk analysis;
- quality control charts;
- inspection based on statistical sampling.

I have summarized the elements set out in BS 5750 as central to a quality assurance system. As I have stated and the BSI recognizes, these standards were devised to suit manufacturing industry. Specifically they were meant to aid the government purchasing departments to judge whether a supplier managed his affairs well enough to guarantee that standards would be maintained in the goods supplied. The BSI does, however, believe that the system necessary to manage quality in that context can be applied *mutatis mutandis* to the manufacture of any product and, further, to the provision of services. The procedures required by the standard have been distilled from analyses of good managerial practice.

There is thus an essence to the standard which it is important to grasp. It is that effective management of production or delivery requires an explicit approach to the activities of the organization. Standards must be specified in a form that makes it possible to ascertain whether or not they are being met. Critical functions must be identified for all parts of the organization and these must be set out as procedures that describe clearly who does what for or to whom when. These standards must be clearly documented so that everybody knows what they are supposed to do and who is responsible for what. It is then necessary to monitor reality regularly in order to detect any discrepancies from these agreed standards and procedures. If discrepancies are found there must be procedures for remedial action. Furthermore, standards and procedures must be regularly reviewed to ensure that they are still appropriate. There must be procedures to do this.

All this may sound daunting if applied to the elusive process that is face-to-face teaching. But what about learning materials and, more specifically, the support services necessary to produce such materials? Surely BS 5750 could be appropriate for these? At a more general level, what about the entire infrastructure of administrative and service departments in a university, including finance, staffing, estates and the registry. If academic staff are, in large part, their customers, could a BS 5750 approach improve their activities? It is possible to argue that this would be the best focus for new quality assurance procedures. Such as there are at present tend to be concentrated entirely on course and hence academic staff: what about support services?

How intelligible is the standard? Does it simply lack face validity or is it just inappropriate?

Some effort has clearly been made to modify the standard to cover services as well as products, but this is usually in the form of obvious additions to a text that addresses material products and the production line for them. Often this is just a matter of the examples chosen but sometimes, as with test equipment and packaging, the element has no meaning outside the manufacture of products. Apart from these occasional sins of commission there is a conspicuous lack of detailed attention to human factors. These are important in manufacturing, where the production line, if not operated by humans, is certainly served at some staged by them. Furthermore, customers and suppliers will interact at crucial stages and the management function, which is given prior place in the list of 20 elements, is in large part concerned with human resources. It is not that human factors are ignored in the Standard but one is left with the feeling that more could have been made in substance and expression of such issues as motivation, attitudes, interpersonal skills and indeed the problems of reliable and valid measurement of human factors, including customer and supplier characteristics.

Nevertheless, there is much to be learned from the direct or modified application of the standard to services generally and education in particular. Certainly the obviously inappropriate aspects of the standard should not be used as an excuse to avoid the central principles.

While I have commented on the standard while setting it out I would now like to summarize what seem to me to be some of the main lessons to be learned from it. First is the idea that there should be *standards* associated with any product or service and these should be agreed between supplier and customer. Second is the recognition that keeping to these standards will require an *explicit and managed effort* by the supplier, as will delivering the product or service in a cost-effective and profitable fashion.

In order to achieve the successful management of consistent customer satisfaction that is quality assurance, certain steps will be necessary. I have covered the 20 elements specified for BS 5750. Here they are rephrased to suit a university conceived as a firm wishing to assure quality for its teaching service.

1. The university must produce a statement of its policy for quality in teaching and learning and ensure that it is understood by all employees of the University, including, but not only, academic staff.
2. The university must identify those responsible for key elements in the assurance of quality in teaching, the range of their authority and their interrelationships.
3. The university must decide how its quality standards will be described and how their accomplishment will be verified and by whom, bearing

in mind that there should be some involvement of people independent of the particular output being verified.

4. The university must identify a particular senior person and associated committee responsible for its quality assurance operations.
5. The university must regularly review its management of quality in teaching and learning.
6. The university must set out in detail its system to assure quality in teaching and learning, including its organization and plan for a specified period. The policy, organization, system and plan should be set out in a quality manual or manuals.
7. The university should determine the nature of the contracts that will be established in general and particular with its students. The specific contract at course level should cover the expectations that teacher and students have of each other's contribution to the students' learning.
8. The university must identify the procedure that will be followed for the planning of courses and the validation of these plans against agreed standards. *Inter alia*, attention should be given to the consumers' contribution to design, the precise responsibilities of individuals and groups in planning and validation, the relation between design and implementation and the status of plans at each stage of the process of planning and validation.
9. The university should specify the documentation required for the assurance of quality with a view to brevity and direct relevance.
10. The university should set and monitor standards for suppliers and subcontractors associated with their teaching service, including both external and internal suppliers.
11. The university should ensure that key elements in teaching and their primary causes are identified in such a way that problems may be traced back to their roots and appropriate action taken.
12. The university should address in detail the process that characterizes teaching and learning and the process that supports teaching in order that those features affecting quality can be controlled, standards can be set and monitored and problems can be identified and solved.
13. The university should devise reliable and valid measures that might be used to test and verify key elements in teaching, planning for teaching, and student response to teaching.
14. The university should identify external inputs that will be necessary to verify the validity of internal quality assurance.
15. The university should devise procedures for identifying teaching that is sub-standard and take steps to remedy sub-standards elements.
16. The university should have established procedures with designated responsibilities to take short-term and long-term corrective action in response to complaints from students.
17. The university should keep such records as will allow objective assessment of the quality assurance system.
18. The university should devise a planned and documented system for

internal quality audits of key features of the quality system, including, for example, course validation, staff training and educational services in support of teaching.

19. The university should identify the skills required of teachers to deliver teaching to agreed quality standards and ensure that all staff receive appropriate training.

20. The university should identify the contribution made by its various non-academic staff and associated resources to the meeting of standards in teaching, identify the standards necessary for those services and the skills necessary for personnel involved, and ensure that all staff receive appropriate training.

21. The university should offer training to all staff to encourage positive attitudes towards a comprehensible quality system.

22. The university should ensure that there is a follow-up to all its teaching to assess its acceptability and effectiveness to students, and that appropriate follow-up action is taken when teaching has not achieved its objectives.

23. The university should systematically gather data relevant to its quality objectives and subject this to appropriate statistical analysis, the results of which then play a part in its review and planning.

This is by no means an exhaustive list but it does represent a direct translation of BS 5750 that is sufficient, I hope, to demonstrate its relevance to our work. When teaching and learning is associated with materials and equipment then the standard is applicable in its present form. It is entirely appropriate to support services in the university that are no different from similar activities in manufacturing and service industries.

The British Standards Institution has recently produced a draft document that is explicity directed at service industry and is intended to be relevant to health care and education. This document is issued for comment and I hope this consideration of the present standard will enable universities to contribute to the refinement of something suited to their pursuit of quality in their teaching. My own view is that the discipline of preparation for BS 5750 registration will focus on a university's attention on the steps that must be taken to assure quality for teaching. However, it does require considerable effort to translate an apparently alien vocabulary into terms and procedures that are relevant to university practice. Critics would argue that this translation is not worth the effort and that universities would do better to start from their own procedures, refining these and adding to them to produce an appropriate management standard for an educational institution.

There remains the fundamental problem that there is no comprehensive standard for teaching itself and this the universities must produce. That standard should then be combined with an appropriate standard for managing the consistent accomplishment of these standards. BS 5750 provides an option for the latter.

Until a standard exists for teaching itself, management standards such as BS 5750 will be most obviously applicable to the support services of a university. There is no difference in principle or indeed practice between such functions as finance, personnel, estates, accommodation or catering in a university and any other large organization. Such activities would undoubtedly benefit from the customer-oriented, standard setting and monitoring approach of BS 5750. The same could be said of educational support services, such as the library, computing and audio-visual services, which, while more likely to be found in educational institutions, nevertheless should be amenable to more general approaches. As will be seen from Susan Storey's case study, procedures have tended to concentrate on support for teaching rather than teaching itself.

References

BS 5750 (1987 and 1990) *Quality Systems, Parts 0–4*. London: British Standards Institution.
Ellis, R. (ed.) (1988) *Professional Competence and Quality Assurance in the Caring Professions*. London: Chapman and Hall.

3

Total Quality Management through BS 5750: a Case Study

Susan Storey

Organizational preamble

Throughout this case study I have used the first person plural: this is variously the corporate 'we' and the 'we' of the core implementation group. It can be taken as read that decisions on the policy, approach and implementation of total quality management and BS 5750/ISO 9000 have been taken by the Director, the Directorate or the Senior Quality Management Team, and the detail of implementation has been worked out and recommendations have been made to the Director/Directorate by the core implementation group. The structure of the Senior Quality Management Team is set out in Appendix 3.1.

The writer is Head of Quality Assurance at Wolverhampton University. In addition to her post there are designated quality managers, a Quality Assurance Unit and a Quality Assurance Committee. The Committee reports to the Academic Board and the Quality Assurance Unit to the Senior Quality Management Team. If quality management is to have the desired effect then it must be taken seriously and built in to the structure at individual executive, corporate management and representative committee levels.

Introduction

Wolverhampton University has embarked on a journey that has no ultimate destination: we are travelling towards total quality management.

It is part of the lore of total quality management (TQM) or continuous quality improvement (call it what you will) that you never reach the position where you can say, 'This is it! This is quality! We have arrived!' So, mindful of the need to provide people with a visible and achievable goal and of the need to provide a solid systematic foundation for TQM, the Directorate of Wolverhampton University has decided to apply BS 5750, the British

Standards Institution's Quality Assurance Standard, to all its operations and to register to Part 1 of the standard during 1993. The scope of the university's application for registration is all activities concerned with the delivery of the product, defined as learning experiences, and delivered through courses, research and consultancy.

To understand the appeal of TQM, and BS 5750, for Wolverhampton University, and why we see them as concomitant, it is necessary to know something of our history and our vision: where we are coming from and where we are going to.

Where we are coming from

Without going too far into West Midlands politics, it is probably fair to say that Wolverhampton University was more tightly controlled by, and dependent on, its local authority than most other universities. This control manifested itself not so much in any direct restrictions on the institution from without but more in terms of attitudes within, particularly those of the service departments of the university. Notions of power to take decisions and of taking responsibility were conspicuously absent. The net result of this was that the rapidly developing, innovative, expanding academic portfolio of the polytechnic was laid on top of, not supported in any sense by, a monolithic infrastructure that was obsessively hierarchical, obstructive through fear, staffed by people who were at one and the same time deeply loyal to the university and overtly cynical about its management. Indeed it was a typical public sector culture of the 1970s, but in 1989.

So there we were, with an academic structure in transition, rapid growth, an inappropriate quality assurance system and, following incorporation, the freedom to go bankrupt.

Where we are going to

The university's VISION 2000 is to be 'the best university in the UK for mass higher education'. This vision has determined the way the university has developed, and continues to develop, into a fully modular, client-responsive institution, growing steadily at around 5 per cent per year, multi-site and with some 3000 plus students, currently, studying 'off campus' i.e. by distance learning, in franchised colleges or on in-company schemes. This profiles raises major quality issues.

In the first place there are those who equate mass with poor, or at best mediocre, quality. So we have a built-in market disadvantage unless we can demonstrate quality convincingly. A major performance indicator for quality in both the university and (formerly) public sectors has been the input indicator, normally 'A' level 'points' scores. The inference was that a high average score for your incoming students meant both that your 'raw material' was of high quality and that you had a high standing in the market place because you attracted 'high quality' applicants. This indicator is irrelevant to open access, continuing education and mass higher education. How, then, do we demonstrate quality? The output indicator, results, is to a great extent under our own control and therefore suspect in a suspicious world. We operate in a context that views the award of more first class honours degrees than anyone else as an indicator of funny business rather than excellence. The process indicator, 'drop out rate' (gentle souls call this the completion rate), is an important indicator of student satisfaction and a variety of other issues to do with fitness for purpose and counselling, but progression rate loses much of its relevance outside the full-time three-year degree pattern. The most significant performance indicator for mass higher education will probably be 'value added' (a measurement of the enhancement to the student as a result of having followed a programme of study), over which the debate continues to rage. Various bodies believe they have cracked the value added formula. They are all still arguing about it.

The larger, the more complex and the more flexible the institution, the harder it is to manage, especially in the context of high student to staff ratios (SSR) and a low, and getting lower, unit of resource. For the lay reader this means that there are huge classes, not enough teachers and the amount that the government paymasters allow per head of the student population (the 'unit of resource') is being squeezed to invisibility. We cannot throw resources at a problem these days: we have to prevent the problem occurring in the first place.

The growing number of off-site students creates its own set of quality control problems. It has proved difficult to manage the monitoring of the student experience at a distance. University staff have found it time consuming and college or company staff have found the exercise bureau-cratic. Our model for the future is based much more on an assessment of the out-centre's own quality assurance systems than on imposing our own. There would need to be a defined and understood framework, however, and we are looking to BS 5750 to provide the basis for that framework.

We find the CNAA criteria for academic quality assurance useful and, among all the performance indicators, the concept of peer review continues to have a place. The *practice* of academic quality assurance CNAA style, however, has been inspection-based, retrospectively focused and norm-referenced. The whole system was founded upon the notion of equivalence. Equivalence comes a bit unstuck when you are breaking new ground, as we have found repeatedly and sometimes painfully. It was also founded upon the concept of a *course* being an entity with a unity, life and management structure of its own. It is not a concept 'fitted to the purpose' of a mass higher education environment. In a fully modular system (sometimes affectionately called 'cafeteria' or 'pick-n-mix') there is a need to find different ways of looking after the *whole* student and the totality of the student experience.

Taking all these issues into account, the Directorate formed the view that effective quality control could only take place if responsibility for delivering quality was located at the point of delivery, and quality assurance as near the point of delivery as possible. This implied a total quality management system. The conventional wisdom among practitioners of TQM is that it takes a crisis to get you going. I think we probably agree with that. TQM is not a soft option: why do it unless you have to? We think we had to.

The great debate

Once the Director had decided that the quality management approach was the only way to take Wolverhampton University into the twenty-first century a number of key questions needed to be asked, and answered, before even a strategy could be determined. These were:

● What do we mean by quality?
● What do we mean by management?
● What do we mean by total?
● What is our corporate starting point – what do 'they' think of 'us'?

What do we mean by quality?

Ask that question anywhere and you will get a variety of responses. Ask it in an academic institution and it could take you 18 months to get an answer you can all live with. That is how long it took us. The encouraging thing was that everybody had a view on what quality was, believed in it and believed they delivered it (or would do if only . . . here followed various wish lists). The problem was that definitions varied enormously, 'excellence' and 'high standards' featuring prominently, as you might expect.

The 'quality debate' was conducted at various levels. The first act of commission was to expand the terms of reference of the Reviews Committee (the academic standards committee) to include responsibility for monitoring the quality of *everything* that impacted on the student experience. To reflect this the committee was renamed the Quality Assurance Committee (QAC) and it was in this forum that the debate began. As the debate progressed, contributions were invited from HMI and CNAA and the committee held open meetings in order to widen the debate. At the same time, faculties, schools and departments held their own discussions, some holding seminars and workshops, and made their views known to the chair of the QAC or to myself. Finally, we arrived at the following definition.

A quality service shall meet three criteria. It shall be:

- fitted to purpose;
- satisfactory to the client;
- of a quality grade equivalent to other suppliers.

This applied to 'in-house' as well as external services and/or products.

What do we mean by management?

Well, we teach management. We understand the theory. Is quality management management of the institution for a quality result or 'high quality' management? Or both? We did not debate this one at great length (although perhaps we should have) since the first review of a service department, the Academic Registry, in November 1990 had revealed such major managerial and structural issues for the whole organization, not just the Registry, that discussion seemed a luxury. Urgent and radical action was required.

The outcome of the review of the Registry was that, across the university, responsibilities within cross-functional activities *were not clear*. On the one hand there was a tendency to think that everything at the interface between the Registry and schools or faculties was someone else's job and on the other there were staff assuming responsibility for activities over which they had no control whatsoever, with all the consequent anxiety and stress.

An example of this occurred in the area of student debtors. Debts of all sorts, you would think, would be the province of the Finance Department, but, naturally, the Finance Department would rely on the Student Records section to provide accurate information on the status of student enrolments and registrations. Equally, the Central Records section would rely on the staff who enrolled students in the first place to do this correctly and input accurate data. What happened in reality was that because it was not clear who was responsible for the various aspects of enrolment, registration, the database etc., staff in the Student Records section were generally assumed to be responsible for everything and, because they once helped out the Finance Department in a crisis, this included chasing student debts. They spent much of their time doing this. Because the management information system left something to be desired and was not updated as quickly or as accurately as it should have been, information coming off the database was frequently wrong. Students were sometimes pursued who were not debtors and debtors frequently escaped. It was *not* the responsibility of the Records section to sort this out but the staff *felt* responsible, and they felt the failure of the system.

This general dysfunction was described by the Chair of QAC as an 'unclear model of devolution'; meaning that the management structure, lines of responsibility and accountability were ill defined, responsibility was devolved to and within departments without the necessary authority to discharge that responsibility, and authority was sometimes assumed without the associated accountability.

Before any responsibility for the *quality* of any functional area could be assumed, therefore, the Directorate had to clarify the institutional management model:

- who is responsible for what;
- who is responsible to whom;
- extent and limits, of managerial and functional responsibility;
- key accountabilities.

Observable outcomes have been:

- formal devolution of much student and academic administration to faculties (and associated new posts in faculties);
- disaggregation of former Academic Registry sections into functional central units;
- publication of the university's management map;
- implementation of a new standard job description format, requiring the specification of limits of responsibility and key accountabilities.

Having defined the system and the location of responsibility for quality within the system, the Directorate confirmed its stance that quality assurance must operate outside the delivery system. The Quality Assurance Unit and Committee are shown on the management map, therefore, as separate: their function is to monitor delivery not to deliver.

What do we mean by total?

We mean the whole university, all staff, all functions and (although we have barely started on this) all students.

I have come across instances of departments within large corporations initiating TQM in advance of the rest of the company, or without any real expectation that the rest will follow. There is a lot that can be done but it depends very significantly on the degree of financial and managerial autonomy given to the department: the more of both, the better are the chances of effecting continuous quality improvement in isolation from the rest of the corporation.

It seemed important to us that *all* staff were involved from the outset for two main reasons: most of the hassle (our word for the absence of quality) was happening at the interfaces between schools and departments; support staff perceived, and deeply resented, a gulf between the academic staff and themselves in the way they were treated and in their sense of contributing to the university's primary function.

What do they think of us?

Total quality management necessitates culture change. All change is difficult: culture change is very difficult. Before we could begin to initiate any moves towards the culture that supports total quality management, which is open, respectful, responsible, committed, task-oriented and non-hierarchical, it was necessary to find out what the culture was at the outset and how the various tiers of management were perceived by the staff. To this end, the Directorate commissioned an *attitude survey*, in the form of a questionnaire sent to a random stratified sample of academic, support and manual staff. It had a 95 per cent confidence level.

The results were remarkably uniform from all parts of the university. Whereas staff experience of middle management varied, the top management were perceived across the board as remote, uncaring and without any interest in or understanding of what was going on at 'grass roots' level. This came as no surprise and similar results would be achieved in most traditionally managed large corporations but, although anticipated, it did shock. To quote our Director: 'It is one thing to suspect they hate you; it's another to know.'

Clearly, some form of major communications exercise was needed if Directorate commitment to total quality management was to have the credibility that all practitioners agree is indispensable.

The total quality management strategy

Choosing the model

For six months before any public declaration was made the Chair of QAC researched the quality literature. This preparation enabled him to feed pertinent quality definitions and quality management models into the great debate as it progressed. What came out of the debate and the review of the Registry was that the primary aim of our quality management system needed to be the removal of hassle. Hassle was costing the institution untold sums in wasted staff time, lost opportunities and general wear and tear on individuals. In order to remove hassle the first step had to be that everybody should be clear about the requirements; that is, the corporate requirements and the requirements of their particular job.

Thus it came about that the TQM model which has most informed our model was one that tackled these points directly and straightforwardly. It was Crosby's (1984) 'four quality absolutes':

- the definition of quality is conformance to requirements.
- the system of quality is prevention.
- the performance standard is zero defects
- the measurement of quality is the price of non-conformance.

The Wolverhampton University key factors are:

- Know the requirements.
- Error-free delivery.
- Error prevention.
- Count the cost.
- Recognize your client.

The quality statement

We had our corporate vision, our corporate mission and, now, our definition of quality and quality management key factors. We needed a quality statement, short and to the point, that somehow encapsulated all these. TQM firms the world over have their quality statement printed on a plastic, or laminated, card, credit card size, that employees carry around with them. It has been known for employees in these companies to 'show the card' to members of the senior management (rather like the football 'red card') if they felt that the manager was not facilitating quality improvement.

Our Quality Statement includes the undertaking: 'We will foster a cost-effective, do-it-right-first-time culture by understanding and conforming to the requirements of our tasks at all times.' (See Appendix 3.2 for the full statement.)

The code of practice

To focus attention on what we would consider to be a quality service, rather than on quality in the abstract, all constituent groups within the university ('family groups' in TQM parlance) were asked to produce their own code of practice focusing on what they considered to be the quality characteristics of their functions, the standards they considered appropriate (and achievable) and the measured or performance indicators for those standards. Departments entered into this exercise with varying degrees of enthusiasm: some put in a great deal of effort. Results ranged from short statements of general goodwill, through sky-high aspirations to something (from the Quality Assurance Unit I am sorry to say) rather like a National Vocational Qualification (NVQ) assessment grid. Somewhere in between there were one or two model codes of practice (that of the Estates Department was one) that augured well for the procedures we were shortly to ask people to write.

Despite the variety of presentations, there was a remarkable degree of unanimity on important issues that enabled the Chair of QAC to extract the common themes and produce a generic code of practice for the university. This was circulated to *all* full-time and permanent part-time staff (in their pay packets) in final draft, for a last chance to comment, and has now been published.

Communications

Directorate walkabout
The methodology was quite formal: the eight members of the Directorate and Deans group paired off and held specially convened meetings with groups of staff, normally one school or department or a group of smaller units. It was organized to some extent, pragmatically, on a building by building basis.

The good things that can be said about the Directorate Walkabout are that:

- it made the Director in particular visible and 'real' to staff;
- people are *still* talking about it;
- the Directorate members learned a great deal about their organization;
- it symbolized Directorate commitment to TQM.

Magazines and broadsheets
Our in-house magazine, *Polyspective*, is issued monthly to all staff on the payroll and since the beginning of the quality debate has been carrying a series of 'quality' articles and correspondence. The tone of some of the articles has, of necessity, been rather academic or technical for general consumption so we are now intending to issue regular 'hot news' broadsheets from the Quality Assurance Unit to let people know what is going on.

Training
We have found training activities to be the most fruitful vehicle for effective communications, whether major training events taking place over one or two days, the informal visits members of the core implementation group have made to schools and departments as a follow-up to the Directorate walkabout, or the one-to-one training given to our procedure writers.

'Spread the word'
We are very much relying on the quite large (over 100) number of people who have been actively involved in developing the university's generic procedures to act as the quality missionaries in their own schools and departments. Many, if not all, of these people are being trained as BS 5750 internal auditors and will also be trained as facilitators.

BS 5750 as the launch pad for TQM

To quote Roger Sugden, Chair of the Quality Methods Association Quality Management Study Group and Manager, Total Quality Consulting, Rank Xerox (Xerox is ten years into a TQM programme and its Business Product Systems Group is a Baldridge Award winner): 'In an inspection based quality assurance system BS 5750 is a liability. In a prevention based quality assurance system it is a necessity.' We think this is about right.

BS 5750 can, if you set it up that way, be bureaucratic, cumbersome and inflexible. This tends to happen when external consultants are brought in to install a quality assurance system – quickly – because a company has been told by a major client to get BS 5750 or else. Typically, a consultant in that context might start by writing the quality manual and then fit procedures into the structure. We have approached it entirely differently.

We started from the question: 'what procedures do we have and what do we need?' Only after we had considered the university, its functions and structures, did we attempt, seriously, to relate procedures to the clauses of the Standard.

We had decided before the start to attempt to involve as many of the staff who would be managing, operating and expected to comply with the procedures as possible in their creation (where new procedures were needed), improvement (where procedures existed but were not working well) or, simply, recording in BS 5750 format (where there were sound procedures already in place and adequately documented). To this end we convened groups of 'users' and 'doers' (or internal suppliers and customers if you prefer) to critique, refine and recommend for approval procedures that had been drafted by a nominated procedure writer. We called the groups 'quality circles', although this was somewhat wishful. The staff swiftly renamed them 'magic circles'. The first procedure writers and some of the initial membership of the magic circles were drawn from the staff who were invited, by the core group on the recommendation of heads, to the initial BS 5750 awareness and procedure writing training days. We have since called upon many more 'volunteers' to participate and the magic circles have started to regulate their own membership.

As an act of commission we asked some people to write a procedure with which they were notorious for non-compliance. We did not do this irresponsibly: these 'poachers turned gamekeepers' were all people of energy and intelligence who we were confident would do a good job. We reasoned that their participation in this way would increase their sense of ownership and encourage them to comply with the procedure in future; furthermore, since they were neither ill-intentioned nor stupid, if they were not complying there must be something that could be improved about the existing procedure. The briefing given to procedure writers was to start with the currently approved procedure, but if there was no procedure, no documentation, conflicting versions or evidence of system failure, they were to write down whatever people were doing that seemed to work.

Even where procedures existed and were documented, most procedure writers and magic circles have been unable to resist the temptation to effect rationalizations and improvements. This has resulted in some slippage in the timescale. We had intended to follow our external consultant's advice to 'get the procedures written down *quickly*, don't try to perfect them, then spend your time *auditing*.' It is only through the audit process that you really find out whether the procedures work. However, we were reluctant to hassle our volunteers, especially as their zeal for improvement was so commendable, as long as some progress was being made.

There is some distaste for BS 5750 in higher education because it does not, of itself, set standards. As pointed out in Chapter 2, there is no standard for educational delivery itself. You can, if you wish, devise a quality assurance system to manage for minimal standards. What you cannot do, by definition, within the Standard, is set up a system for *unsatisfactory* standards. It is built into the clauses of the Standard that the product or service you provide must meet the customer's specification, not only at the stage of initial discussions but following updates and reviews ('contract review'). It is also incumbent upon the supplier to make sure that the customer's specification meets the customer's 'stated and implied needs', not just what he or she says he or she wants. For example, if you are buying a table you might specify that it should be square, of certain dimensions, made of pine, costing no more than so much and with a bevelled edge. What you would not normally feel it necessary to specify is that it should have a leg at each corner equal in length, a level top and not collapse during normal use. These last are your 'implied' needs.

If you take it that your customers, in higher education, are students, parents, employers, sponsors, validating and professional bodies, government paymasters and society at large, you begin to see that BS 5750 is not some simplistic mechanism for regression to the mediocre. All these customers have their part to play in determining the specification for the 'product' (for us, learning experiences), so that not only what the student might say he or she wants (which might be quite simply 'a qualification and quickly') is taken into account but also the standards of the validating body, the needs of industry, commerce and the profession, expectations that society has of people educated to a certain level, ethical considerations, and so on. What we thought was:

- BS 5750 was developed out of *real* good practice in *real* companies;
- it is, quite simply, a blueprint for good management;
- it has certain attractive features that harmonize with TQM;
- it is a *discipline* that we sorely need;
- if our procedures are sound they can easily be put into BS 5750 format so we may as well apply for the standard, and if they are not we need to go through the process.

We knew perfectly well that the number one benefit for us, initially, would be going through the process.

The features that harmonize with our preferred model for TQM are:

- responsibility must be specified at every point of a procedure;
- error must be traceable;
- error and system failure must be corrected;
- the system is open and known;
- everyone must understand the requirements;
- training is a key factor.

The emphasis throughout is on:

- understanding the requirements;
- getting it right first time;
- cutting out the hassle.

Why Part 1?

There is a continuing debate over the design function of educational institutions, which I will not get into. As far as Wolverhampton University is concerned, we are quite clear that we design learning experiences. Having defined our product (or service) as learning experiences, we considered it appropriate, not to say mandatory, to apply for Part 1. That is the logic. On a pragmatic level, we wished to include as many of the university's functional areas in the scope as possible (not just those directly concerned with teaching) in order to progress *total* quality management, and we found that this worked most effectively if we defined our product as learning experiences, rather than as some kind of enhancement of the student, and went for Part 1.

Summary of progress so far

We have:

- published the university's quality management map;
- obtained draft procedures for most functions;
- made the connection between procedures and clauses of the standard;
- outlined the quality and procedural manuals;
- established groups that have mutated (or will mutate) into genuine quality circles;
- identified critical training needs, e.g. facilitator training;
- effected many small, 'by the way', improvements.

Relationship of procedures to the clauses of BS 5750 Part 1

Appendix 3.3 shows the BS 5750 Part 1 system requirements. We have established procedures for the various critical functions of the university. These relate to the BS 5750 requirements as shown in Appendix 3.4. In that appendix I have set out the procedures, by category, and shown how they relate to the requirements by reference number. This may not be particularly intelligible to an outsider but it does show that real statements about university procedures, produced by staff of the university, can meet the requirements of BS 5750. Sceptics say that it can't be done, is not worth doing or distorts reality. We have done it and are convinced that it is relevant and helpful.

What have been the benefits of BS 5750 implementation so far?

Communications
The principal benefit has been in the area of communications. People have been operating for a long time on what they believed to be shared assumptions, which have turned out not to be shared at all. The most frequently heard remark during the quality circle meetings has been, 'Well, I never knew that!' People didn't know that something was done, or why it was done, or why it was done that way.

Ownership, participation and empowerment
In many cases, participation in the magic circles has been the first opportunity for some staff to contribute to the systems they were required to operate or comply with. In others, beleaguered managers who have felt that they have been running a Cinderella operation have suddenly realized that the system will, in future, *require* compliance with all approved procedures, including theirs. They are beginning to feel supported.

There is a dawning sense of power to get things changed for the better: 'Do you mean to say that we can approve this and *they* can't stop us?' (a magic circle member). Well, not quite. Although the procedure for approving and changing procedures has the magic circles as the main forum, final power of approval resides with the Director (or nominee). Were the Director's exercise of that authority to lead to system failure, however, our continued registration would be seriously threatened. He and those to whom he delegates are hardly going to exercise power of veto for the sake of it, having invested so heavily in the quality management system.

System improvements
We are not yet in a position to prove categorically that things are running more smoothly: it is my impression that they are but impressions are worth very little in quality management. As the BS 5750 auditors are reputed to say, 'In God we trust: from all others we require objective evidence.' We will not have objective evidence of any credible kind until we have carried out and recorded at least one, and preferably two, internal BS 5750 audit cycles. It is the audit process, we are told, that brings the greatest system and communications benefits.

Lessons we have learned

Prepare thoroughly or get started?
We have come to the conclusion that you need a bit of both. The message from companies well down the TQM road is: 'prepare – resist the temptation to get stuck in.'

It is very important that those charged with spearheading the effort, whether for TQM, BS 5750 or both, inspire confidence in all other members of the company, *especially the executive*. It is not enough to appear confident: we have to make others feel comfortable that we know what we are doing. They may not like what we are doing but at least they should feel that they are not in the hands of incompetents.

It is critical, therefore, to have a plan; better any plan than no plan at all. You may deviate from it and your eventual implementation strategy may bear no resemblance to it whatsoever, but that does not matter. Just the fact that you have a plan will enable you to proceed with confidence and give you a default position when you might otherwise be casting about for a direction. But *be flexible*. When common sense or a golden opportunity tell you to ditch the plan, temporarily, and go for it, then go for it!

Communicate effectively
The thing that makes everyone uneasy, especially the executive, is not knowing what is going on, or perhaps more accurately not understanding what is going on.

It is not enough to report progress in terms of 'we have done this and this' and 'such and such has happened'. It is even less adequate to report, 'Everything is proceeding wonderfully well, you have nothing to worry about.' Nothing to worry about? With a huge corporation to manage *and* implementing this new quality system: nothing to worry about? They will think they have entrusted this crucial and difficult matter to idiots.

Give them chapter and verse, hard evidence, cases, examples. Start a report with the particular and extrapolate the general. Minutiae (provided they are not too detailed and time consuming) make people (even top people) feel secure. Then you can hit them with the abstract and general.

Of course, once you are operating in an environment of mutual trust it is exactly the same. People are people.

So much for the bosses: what about the 'poor bloody infantry'? The message there is: keep it live, keep it involving, keep it interesting and *demonstrate the advantages at every possible opportunity*. What the PBI want to know is 'what's in it for us?' The cynics do not want there to be anything in it for them because they are protecting their position as court fools, but the PBI, who want to do a good job but are always in the front line (and in most HE institutions are thoroughly worn out) will give the implementation effort all they have got (just as they have given all they have got and then some to every other initiative) if they really believe it will do some good. It is up to you (and me) to show them some real results, pay-offs, to persuade them. Talk is cheap – we need some results.

The final message is: the most effective communication is through pay-offs.

Any model can be made to work
It has been worth our while spending some time and effort researching the various TQM approaches and models, but not too much time. Popular wisdom in TQM circles says, 'read some; talk little; take action.' This is, of course, somewhat contrary to the advice to prepare thoroughly, which gives you an indication of what it is like in the quality jungle. You have to hack out your own path. What is much more important than the model you choose is *how* you put it into practice.

The crucial role of the executive
The approach that any organization takes to quality improvement will depend on the following factors:

- the degree of commitment of its top management;
- the prevailing culture of the organization;
- the forces at work within the organization and its power and influence systems;
- the resources available – human and fiscal – to pump-prime quality improvement;
- the previous track record of the company or institution;
- the credibility of the top management with the staff.

In the context of higher education these factors may seem unreasonably biased towards seeing the performance of the senior managers as the single most important determinant of the quality improvement model or approach. After all, a university is a community of peers who operate by consensus: a community of professionals committed to improvement by the very nature of their profession. I believe there is a large measure of truth in this and, certainly, in at least two other HE institutions that I am aware of the total quality improvement initiative has originated with the staff and spread sideways. It makes progress with the encouragement, or acquiescence, of the executive. That in itself may say something about the nature of 'government' of those institutions. Like it or not, quality improvement cannot be the institutional aim unless those in power allow it to happen.

Define your terms but avoid jargon

We have found, the hard way, that quality jargon is a real turn-off for all but the enthusiastic quality manager. Rallying cries have their place but you need to judge carefully when your institution is ready for them and it is much more likely that they will have the desired effect if they evolve by more or less common consent, or people at least get a chance to become familiar and comfortable with them before they are posted on every notice board.

It is *very, very* important to choose appropriate descriptors for what you are trying to do, explain *clearly* what you mean by them and *use them consistently*. If you use 'quality assurance' and 'quality control' interchangeably, that's fine, as long as you explain that as far as you are concerned they mean the same thing. If you think there is some distinction between the two then define it. We have been in considerable bother over the definition of a 'procedure' despite the fact that this is quite precise in BS 5750 'speak' and we thought we had explained it fairly unambiguously as: 'What is done; in what sequence; who is responsible for making sure that it (or each stage of it) is done; when (where appropriate).' Intellectual athletes on the staff became involved in the semantics: many just did not know what we were on about.

The procedural map

When we came to try to relate our procedures to the clauses of the Standard we found two very interesting phenomena. The first was that, as our existing academic quality assurance procedures were comprehensive, well established and focused very firmly on our product (learning experiences), they answered, wholly or in part, most of the requirements of the Standard. There were fewer areas in which other university academic and student-related procedures were strictly *required* than we had anticipated. We were a little exercised about this, as we wanted to include these activities in the scope, until we made our second discovery: if there is nowhere else for a procedure to go and you want it in, it will almost certainly fit nicely under Clause 4.9, process control.

The quality assurance strategic plan – what next for TQM?

It is an indicator of Wolverhampton University's senior management's commitment to total quality management that we have retained a quality strand in our institutional strategic plan, notwithstanding that this was no longer required by the Polytechnics and Colleges Funding Council (PCFC). The quality assurance strategic plan moves forward, on a five-year cycle, to continued functional and developmental training, quality measurement and costing, the use of TQM tools and methods and the establishment of quality networks. Appendix 3.5 shows the implementation diary of our strategy. We haven't finished – we never will – but we are well on the way to the target of registration. When you see us parading BS 5750 you will have a good idea how we got there.

Appendix 3.1   The senior quality management team, 1992

Director[a,b]
Deputy Director[a,b]
Assistant Director (Academic Planning)[a,b]
Assistant Director (Marketing)[a,b]
Assistant Director (Information)[a,b]
Assistant Director (Administration)[a,b]
Dean (Quality)/Chair of QAC[a,b,c]
Dean (Continuing Education)[a,b]
Personnel Manager[a]
Finance Manager[a]
Head of Quality Assurance/Quality Manager[c]
Internal Quality Consultant[c]

[a] The polytechnic executive. [b] Directorate and deans' group. [c] Core implementation group (plus external consultant as required).

Quality management accountability/reporting structure

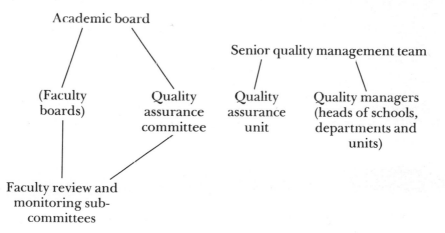

Appendix 3.2   Full quality statement

The staff of Wolverhampton University are committed to providing high quality services – regionally, nationally and internationally – to its wide range of student and other clients regardless of their gender, creed or nationality. This provision is aimed at developing the relevant knowledge, skills and competences to meet the future needs of industry, commerce and society.

We will foster a cost-effective, do-it-right-first-time culture by understanding and conforming to the requirements of our tasks at all times.

Appendix 3.3   BS 5750 Part 1 system requirements

4.1   Management responsibility
4.2   Quality system
4.3   Contract review
4.4   Design control
4.5   Document control
4.6   Purchasing
4.7   Purchaser supplied product
4.8   Product identification and traceability
4.9   Process control
4.10 Inspection and testing
4.11 Inspection, measuring and test equipment
4.12 Inspection and test status
4.13 Control of non-conforming product
4.14 Corrective action
4.15 Handling, storage, packaging and delivery
4.16 Quality records
4.17 Internal quality audits
4.18 Training
4.19 Servicing
4.20 Statistical techniques

Appendix 3.4   University procedures related to BS 5750 Part 1 requirements

University	BS 5750 system requirements
Policy control	4.1, 4.4, 4.10
Management review	4.1
Document control	4.1, 4.5, 4.4
Approval and change of procedures	4.1, 4.4, 4.5

Quality assurance:	Almost every clause
• validation	especially 4.2, 4.16 and 4.17
• review	
• monitoring	
• audit	
Planning permission (for new courses etc.)	4.4, 4.5, 4.8, 4.10
Strategic planning and management	4.4, 4.10, 4.11, 4.13
Resource allocation	4.4., 4.10
Academic policy and regulations	4.4, 4.10
Course development	4.4, 4.10
Teaching delivery	4.9, 4.15
Delivery methods	4.9, 4.15
Learning support	4.9, 4.15
Contacts	4.3, 4.6
Total environment	4.3, 4.6, 4.15
• inventories	
• approved supplier evaluation	
• ordering	
• inter-site travel	
• repairs and maintenance	
• cleaning	
• conference room hire	
• residences	
• purchasing	
Timetabling	4.15
Accreditation of in-company and other	4.10
Recruitment and admissions	4.3, 4.7
Enrolment	4.3
Module registration	4.3, 4.15
Accreditation of prior learning	4.7
Franchising and associated colleges	4.6, 4.7
Staff recruitment/appointment	4.1, 4.18
Appointment of visiting lecturers/ consultants	4.6
Induction	4.18
Training	4.1, 4.18
Advertising and marketing	4.3
Consultancy	Almost every clause
Short courses, approval	Almost every clause
Research degrees	Almost every clause
Research	Almost every clause
Assessment	4.9, 4.10, 4.13, 4.20
Assessment boards	4.9, 4.10, 4.13
Conferment of awards	4.10

Equipment inspection	4.6, 4.9, 4.11, 4.15
Calibration	4.11
Information systems	4.4, 4.8, 4.10, 4.15
Complaints/appeals	4.3, 4.14
Counselling	4.9

Notes: Clause 4.14, Corrective action, applies to most procedures. Clause 4.15, Servicing, does not apply in any sensible way to our product.

Appendix 3.5   Implementation diary

December 1991
● Core implementation group brain strain to match procedures to clauses of the Standard and identify overlaps and gaps.
● First round of internal auditor training.
● Informal approach to BSI Quality Assurance.

January to February 1992
● Detailed progress report, with completed procedures to Senior Quality Management Team and, subsequently, to heads.
● Mid-sessional senior staff seminar to introduce procedures in BS 5750 format and prepare managers to facilitate the writing of work instructions.
● Launch of pilot suggestion scheme.

Remains to be done
● Formal involvement of *students* (our major client group).
● Involvement of franchised colleges and companies.
● Formal consultation with board of governors.
● 'Filling the procedural gaps'.
● Publication of approved procedures.
● Training in writing work instructions for the procedures.
● Writing work instructions.
● Training in the operation of the procedures and work instructions (where appropriate).
● Two complete BS 5750 audit cycles.
● Compilation and printing of the quality and procedural manuals.
● Application to BSI Quality Assurance.
● Assessment by BSI QA auditors.
● Registration to the Standard.
● Evaluation.

Reference

Crosby, P. (1984) *Quality without Tears*. New York: McGraw-Hill.

4

Quality Assurance in Health Care: the Implications for University Teaching

Dorothy Whittington and Roger Ellis

Introduction

Those attempting to ensure quality in higher education are often referred to techniques and procedures first developed in industry and commerce. In fact there is an equally important and separate tradition of quality assurance in health care which might provide models.

Quality has become topical in health care and higher education for somewhat similar reasons. In both contexts demographic and technological changes have led to increased demand for the service. Satisfaction of this increased demand leads to the expenditure of additional resources but in periods of recession both areas are targets for economic scrutiny and cost cutting. In both contexts consumers are now more aware of their rights and more generally knowledgeable. They are therefore less likely to defer to professionals and more likely to have views on service standards. Professionals themselves have responded to these pressures by clarifying and reasserting their claims to special knowledge and competence.

This chapter will begin by outlining the development of health care quality assurance. It will then identify some health care themes that are relevant in educational quality assurance and describe techniques that could be adapted for education. It will conclude by suggesting that mutual benefit would accrue from regular dialogue between health care and educational quality assurance specialists.

The development of health care quality assurance

Concern for quality and recognition that practitioners have a duty to uphold standards have a long history. Quality assurance in health care is innovative only in so far as it involves explication and systematization of *methods* of setting standards and maintaining or improving quality.

From the 1930s onwards this concern for the quality of health care extended from attention to standards in the education and training of professionals to more general interest in outcomes. A number of studies ensued in both the USA and the UK, including, for example, investigations of preventable maternal death, anaesthetic deaths, deaths in people under 50 and perioperative deaths. National and international statistics on mortality and incidence of diseases have been published for the past 50 years. At a much less formal level many hospitals and clinical units have a long-standing tradition of holding clinical meetings at which unusual or problematic cases are considered.

By the beginning of the 1980s quality assurance in health care was a topic of national and international discussion among health care professionals. In UK community medicine, for example, the Royal College of General Practitioners launched a quality initiative in 1983 (RCGP 1983, 1985a,b) and by 1990 GPs were involved in many quality activities ranging from large scale patient and practitioner surveys (Health Care Research Unit, Newcastle upon Tyne University 1990) to informal practice meetings reviewing care in individual cases (Irvine 1990). In hospital medicine also many quality schemes were initiated. In the UK these are sometimes referred to as 'medical audit' (HMSO 1990a,b; Shaw 1990) but the activities themselves are essentially those of observation, review and improvement, which characterize quality assurance. There has been great variation in the enthusiasm and commitment evinced by hospital consultants and physicians, but active opposition has been tempered by the perception that failure to participate may result in a system imposed by less well informed managerial or government forces.

The UK professional bodies for non-physician health care groups have been particularly active in encouraging quality assurance. In the USA too there has been substantial activity in the development of quality assurance systems by and for non-physician groups. Indeed, major surveys of health care quality assurance activities in the UK (Dalley *et al.* 1991) and in the USA (Casanova 1990) have demonstrated that the professions most heavily involved are nursing and the rehabilitation professions.

Increased demand for expensive health care has coincided with international recession. This has naturally led to public and governmental concern over the costs of care and to widespread discussion of relationships between costs and quality. Specifically, the US government Medicare/Medicaid systems of public health insurance have been criticized for encouraging the provision of unnecessary care. This has led to the establishment of systems of cost containment and 'utilization review', and of the Peer Review Organization. PRO employs physicians to review the practice of other physicians (Webber 1988). Specific sanctions are employed if facilities or physicians have failed to meet standards. These various systems have been far reaching in their influence and have been the stimulus for several other quality initiatives. It has been widely suggested, however, that their impact on the actual quality of delivered care is limited (US Committee on Government Operations 1989; US General Accounting Office 1990).

Despite its substantial history and despite these recent excursions into government control, the formal US system of health care quality review is diverse and in some respects fragmentary. Many commentators have observed that the various systems that have evolved do little to examine the impact of provision on the health of communities or regions.

In the UK, concern for quality of care was a primary factor in the genesis of the NHS. Thus Aneurin Bevan, introducing his Bill to the House of Commons in July 1948, said that the proposed service was designed to 'universalise the best' and 'to provide the people of Britain, no matter where they may be, with the same level of service.' Each of these statements of intent implies a system for identifying, developing and maintaining quality.

Government interest in specific systems of health care quality assurance can be detected from as early as the 1950s. The Guillebaud Committee (HMSO 1956), when given the remit of examining costs in the NHS, commented, 'it is one of the problems of management to find the right indices for efficiency.' They went on to propose comparisons between health authorities in respect of 'average occupancy of beds, length of stay of patients, bed turnover interval, waiting time etc.' Both the Merrison Committee (HMSO 1975) and the Alment Committee (HMSO 1976) were set up to enquire into the nature of medical training and competence but took it upon themselves to comment on the importance of assessment of quality of practice. The 1979 Report of the Royal Commission on the Health Service contains substantial sections on quality of care in both hospital and community settings. Its recommendation 63 is that there should be 'a planned programme of peer review of standards of care and treatment . . . set up for the health professions by their professional bodies and progress monitored by the health departments.'

The Financial Management Initiative (HMSO 1982) led to the production of a long series of 'performance indicators' for the health service, which regional and district authorities were expected to use for internal and external comparisons. However, these indicators were restricted to 'input/output' measures, such as staff, beds, length of stay etc., and were widely regarded as confusing, irrelevant and intrusive by both practitioners and local managers. Despite this their use and development continues to be recommended (HMSO 1990b).

Finally, the *Working for Patients* White Paper (HMSO 1989) and the subsequent Health Service Reform Bill confronted the issue of quality assurance directly. One of the central proposals was that all doctors and other health professionals in hospital, primary care and community settings should be involved in some form of 'medical audit'. Working papers associated with the reforms and the recent Report of the Standing

Medical Advisory Committee (HMSO 1990b) have subsequently filled in details of the roles of local health authorities and medical audit committees and of the extended remit of medical postgraduate education committees.

Quality assurance in the National Health Service has thus become not just a matter of professional concern or enthusiasm but a mandatory part of service provision. There is considerable activity at all levels in the service (and indeed in private UK health care) in discussing, piloting and establishing procedures.

Teachers in higher education, in contrast to health care professionals, have never been as clearly 'professionalized'. Their training has never been formalized and (as is discussed in detail in other chapters of this book) the standards to which they refer in the various systems of external refereeing, course evaluation and external examination have until very recently been largely unarticulated. While national statistics and institutional 'league tables' of degree classifications, failure rates and graduate employment have been produced it is difficult to know how they are related to the processes of provision. Without such a link action for improvement is a risky venture. Finally, there is no subject-by-subject equivalent in higher education of the various quality initiatives pursued by the Royal Colleges and other health care professional bodies, and thus little or no tradition upon which to build.

Themes in the health care quality assurance literature

Alongside the proliferation of practical initiatives in health care quality assurance, there has developed a substantial literature. Common themes can be discerned, many of which are equally relevant in quality assurance for university teaching. Those explored here are as follows:

● the definition of quality and quality assurance;
● measurement and methodology in quality assurance;
● the organizational contexts of quality assurance;
● the relationship between costs and quality.

The definition of quality and quality assurance

Several authors have suggested that 'health care quality is in the eye of the beholder'. Thus Anderson (1986) suggests that 'employers define health care quality in terms of value obtained for their health care dollars. . . . For the patients quality means feeling better . . . and for the hospitals quality means care that they can get paid for.' In university teaching it would also be possible to derive definitions of quality dependent upon perspectives. Thus 'curriculum relevance' might be defined by teachers as 'bearing upon recent debates within the discipline', by university managers as 'likely to attract students', by graduate employers as 'likely to lessen the need for expensive induction and retraining of graduate recruits' and by students themselves as 'interesting and related to personal experience and aspiration'. Conscious of such differences in perspective, Rodriguez (1988: 4) notes that 'quality may be ideal, adequate or normative, depending on who is assessing it – and what values and consensus are used in evaluation – and by what implicit or explicit standards or gauges it is being objectively or subjectively evaluated.'

Faced with such a moving target for definition several authors in health care quality assurance have had recourse to analysis and the naming of parts. Thus Avedis Donabedian (1966, 1980, 1985) distinguishes between *technical* and *interpersonal* aspects of quality health care, and between quality of structure, process and outcome with respect to each aspect. The technical aspects of care involve the physical manipulation of material things. Thus the orthopaedic surgeon replacing a hip joint remains in the realm of the technical just as long as his patient is under anaesthetic. When providing pre-operational information and reassurance or post-operational advice on recovery he has entered the interpersonal arena. His interpersonal interventions are just as important but much less predictable in their impact, and many health care quality assurance initiatives are restricted to the technical aspects of care.

In recent publications, Donabedian (1987, 1989, 1991) has hinted at a third aspect of quality health care, namely the moral aspect. Here choices must be made between types of provision and judgements undertaken about levels of access within attainable resources. These, as he rightly implies, are issues of social justice and political philosophy. Standard setting for these aspects of quality is even more difficult.

Each of Donabedian's aspects of health care quality has an analogue in university teaching, although it is clear that the interpersonal aspect occupies a more central place and that the technical aspect may be less significant. One consequence is that quality in university teaching may be inherently more difficult to appraise.

Donabedian's other categorization of quality dimensions – structure, process, outcome – is more frequently quoted. Structure is often taken to mean simply the human and material resources available for care, but is more properly defined as 'the nature of the resources that, assembled, provide health care, including for example, the mix of manpower . . . and the rules of procedure' (Berwick and Knapp 1987). Process is more readily defined: it refers to the delivery of care from the point of patients' first signalling a desire to be considered for potential treatment (or indeed to be kept well) to the point at which they can be declared either fit or beyond further care. Finally, outcomes can be defined as the 'end results' of care. They include health status, improvement of function, longevity, comfort and, possibly, quality of life.

Equivalents of these for university teaching can readily be identified.

Thus quality for structure is determined by both resources and organizational procedures. Process quality comprises quality of selection, admission, curriculum design, teaching and examination. Arguably it also includes quality of pastoral care, social and sporting activities, careers advice and other necessary 'services' in support of teaching. Outcome quality is a function of the effects of teaching, including changes in students' knowledge, skills, attitudes and values.

In university teaching as in health care there is long-standing and fundamental debate as to the identification and specification of outcome quality. Early health care systems limited their aims to the reduction of mortality and the prevention of disease. If more people lived longer and virulent diseases were wiped out or controlled then health care was of high quality. Increasingly, however, health care systems aim to deliver more subtle benefits associated with maximization of function, positive health, perceptions of personal well-being and capacity to 'enjoy life'. Setting standards in these areas is naturally more difficult. In university teaching too, the aims of the enterprise have increased in both subtlety and complexity.

Despite the popularity of Donabedian's categorizations it can be argued that they are in fact categories of care rather than of quality itself. Somewhat closer to quality criteria as such are Maxwell's (1984) dimensions of health care quality. They are as follows.

● access to services;
● relevance to need (for the whole community);
● effectiveness (for individual patients);
● equity (fairness);
● social acceptability;
● efficiency and economy.

These dimensions of quality translate very readily to university teaching. Thus high quality higher education might be expected to arrange a sufficiently flexible pattern of study modes and course locations to enable normally under-represented groups (e.g. women, the disabled) to obtain appropriate access. Most university teachers would acknowledge the significance of community relevance, and all would agree that their courses should be effective in producing intended learning outcomes. Equity is an obvious characteristic of high quality selection and examining, and few would disagree that efficient use of resources was desirable. In health care, social acceptability refers partly to prioritization decisions (e.g. deciding whether to buy a body scanner or to fund additional geriatric care) and partly to the acceptability of individual treatments. High quality higher education might also be expected to acknowledge the legitimacy of wider social opinion in establishing priorities (e.g. between longer and more ambitious professional courses and the preservation of 'threatened' traditional disciplines).

Being able to define, or at least recognize, instances of quality is not the

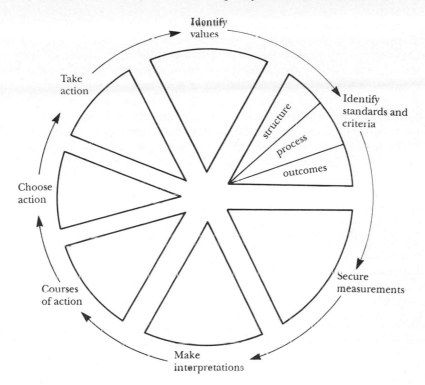

Figure 4.1 The American Nurses' Association model for quality assurance in nursing (*source*: ANA 1982).

same as being able to assure quality. The simplest definition of quality assurance in any setting is that it is the consequence of procedures established for making sure and being able to guarantee that high levels of quality will be maintained. What these procedures should be, however, is as much a matter of debate as is the definition of quality itself.

In health care there is increasing use of models of quality assurance that depict it as a cyclical process of *setting standards*, for care, *carrying out* care, *reviewing* that care to see how far it matched the standards and, finally, *improving* care so that the match between standards and performance can be increasingly close. The American Nurses' Association model (see Figure 4.1) is one of the very many diagrammatic representations of such a cycle. The implication of representing the process cyclically is that the cycle (or sections of it) will be repeated in an ongoing, dynamic 'quest for quality'.

Measurement and methodology in quality assurance

Both health care and education are essentially services − collections of things that people do to, for and with other people. Evaluation is thus fraught with the problems associated with measurement of relatively intangible phenomena ranging from non-verbal features of interactional behaviour to attitudes, perceptions and values. Fortunately these are problems familiar from many areas of enquiry in the social and behavioural sciences, and many of the techniques of health care quality appraisal have their origins in these disciplines. Thus the measurement of patient satisfaction as an index of the quality of care frequently involves survey methodology; and appraisal of doctor–patient interaction quality generally involves techniques familiar from the social psychology of interpersonal behaviour. Other aspects of the methodology debate in health care quality assurance are more specific to health care itself.

Unfortunately, the most intractable area has proved to be the measurement of treatment outcomes. As many authors have observed, these are difficult to disentangle from the confounding influences of broader societal variables, such as diet, housing, poverty, and health-related knowledge, attitudes and expectations (Klein 1980; Donabedian 1986; Whittington 1989). In education the assessment of teaching outcomes is similarly confounded by variables such as student ability, motivation, family support and personal organization. In both areas there is a sense in which outcomes can only be measured over a substantial timespan.

The problems of outcome measurement have led many health care quality assurance systems to rely heavily on the assessment of input or output variables that can often be expressed in straightforward numerical form. If outcome quality is considered it is on a restricted set of indicators thought to be short term and specific to the programme of care being assessed. Thus, if the delivery of care is conceived as including input, process, output and outcome variables, input and output are much easier to measure than process and outcome. This is directly analogous to higher education. It is relatively easy to measure input in terms of staff and other costs and output in terms of the number of students completing the course. The difficult parts are the process, when the input is applied through teaching, and the outcome, which is the relatively long term learning of students.

Two general methods of health care quality assurance can be identified. First there are systems that evaluate and try to improve the quality of care without being particularly concerned about the articulation of standards. They are often known as systems of *implicit* review. Then there are systems in which a great deal of emphasis is placed on the determination of clear and appropriate standards before review is undertaken. These are often called *explicit* review systems.

Implicit review systems stress the value of professional judgement. Groups of acknowledged professional 'experts' are used either to scrutinize episodes of care, as in the clinical meetings upon which medical audit procedures are often based, or to examine records, systems or whole organizations, as in many of the hospital accreditation procedures. Review can be of past patients and events (when records are the basis of the assessment) or of current patients and events (when reference to records can be supplemented by direct observation). The 'expert' review groups may be internal or external to the organization or care setting being scrutinized.

In implicit review groups the 'experts' may attach numbers and values to the judgements they make but the standards on which they base them remain unarticulated and a high degree of inference is employed in moving from observation to evaluation. In higher education the Universities Funding Council's scrutiny of research productivity and the institutional review activities of the sometime Council for National Academic Awards are analogous. There are clear guidelines for the information to be supplied to the expert group and for the way it is to conduct itself, but much of the basis for the eventual 'grade' awarded is not available for public scrutiny.

Explicit review, on the other hand, involves careful specification of standards before the review of care. Standards are set by groups of acknowledged experts who may or may not be associated with the organization or care setting under review. Simple lists of standards may be developed or they may be grouped algorithmically to reflect clinical decision-making or patient progress through care, in what has come to be known as a 'criteria map' (Greenfield *et al.* 1975; Greenfield *et al.* 1981) or a 'process flow chart' (Dagher and Lloyd 1991). Standards are often susceptible to simple yes/no recording or to the use of very straightforward scales of measurement. Thus the recently published UK Patient's Charter sets simple unambiguous standards for the length of time patients may remain on waiting lists. Many of the standards developed by the various professional bodies can be assessed through use of simple checklists or tallies. Thus records are checked for the presence or absence of entries, or for the pattern of referrals. Even the simplest of tallies of patients failing to return for outpatients appointments or suffering post-operative complications can yield useful information.

In education the determination of explicit quality standards for teaching or even of indicators of poor quality is a relatively novel exercise. Several of the initiatives described elsewhere in this book are attempts to move from implicit to explicit standards and criteria.

A further methodological issue concerns the frequency and timing of reviews and the sampling of patients whose treatment is to be the subject of scrutiny. It is impractical and unnecessary to monitor all aspects of all care all of the time so selection must be made. There are numerous approaches and a variety of selection criteria have been adopted.

The organizational contexts of quality assurance

The crux of all quality assurance activities is the extent to which they have an impact on the improvement of products or services. There is, however, a strong vein of criticism in the health care literature which suggests that there is not as much impact on care as there might be. Thus the briefing report to the US Bipartisan Commission (US General Accounting Office 1990) states categorically:

> Quality assurance systems typically concentrate on quality assessment and on the identification of the relatively small number of providers whose care is obviously unacceptable. They do comparatively little to directly improve the overall levels of quality provided by the majority of health professionals.

This unease about the outcomes of health care quality assurance in the USA has led to increasing emphasis on the notion that quality action is *organizational development* and that it must therefore be explicitly *managed*. A number of authors recommend adoption of models and approaches to quality assurance current in industrial contexts. There is much discussion of, for example, the relative merits of centralized, standardized and regulatory, 'top-down' models as opposed to distributed, diverse, self-monitoring, 'bottom-up' models.

Particular themes in the quality management literature include the importance of: senior management commitment and hands-on involvement; clear delegation and designation of responsibilities; effective communication channels; and staff development and training (Ellis and Whittington 1993: Chapter 6). Several authors also comment on the importance of initiating quality assurance schemes gradually and with due recognition of existing quality and evaluation expertise within the organization (Wilson 1987; Øvretveit 1992). This is particularly important in professional settings (like health care and education) where reflection on personal practice is an integral part of working life. Suggestions that concern for quality is new or that professional judgement is worthless are unlikely to encourage acceptance of new quality assurance systems.

The relationship between costs and quality

In both health care and higher education the combination of demographic change and rising costs is a significant generator of increased interest in quality assurance. All are agreed that resources must be stewarded and there is increasing discussion of techniques for limiting or reducing costs while maintaining quality. In the UK the recent NHS reforms are in large part an attempt to introduce market forces as a stimulus to improvement of cost/quality relationships at all levels.

It is often pointed out that the techniques of quality assurance themselves have costs. Thus Wong (1989) identifies four categories of health care quality costs. In this analysis costs are associated with: outcome failure (the costs of additional treatment, community support for disabled patients etc.); process failure (costs associated with communication failures, unnecessarily bureaucratic procedures, phantom waiting lists etc.); monitoring outcome and process quality (costs of establishing and maintaining quality assurance procedures); and prevention of outcome or process failure (costs of the more proactive aspects of quality assurance, usually known as quality management or continuous quality improvement). A similar categorization could readily be derived for university teaching.

Quality assurance is only successful when the costs of monitoring quality and preventing failure are substantially less than the costs of failure. In industry there is substantial evidence that they can be made to be so. Public service quality assurance is premised on the assumption that however difficult the cost benefit calculations may be, a similar effectiveness can in the end be demonstrated.

Quality assurance techniques

Many of the techniques of health care quality assurance are obvious imports from the social and behavioural sciences and several are likely to be adopted in quality assurance in university teaching. Ellis and Whittington (1993) discuss the health care quality assurance applications of social science techniques in full detail. They also present a compendium of techniques that have been developed specifically for use in health care quality assurance. The techniques that are discussed here are a small selection from that compendium, chosen both for their representativeness and for their apparent relevance to quality assurance in university teaching. Many of the others might also be useful and interested readers are referred to Ellis and Whittington (1993). The techniques that will be discussed here are grouped as follows:

- techniques based on implicit standards;
- techniques based on explicit standards;
- local problem-solving techniques;
- process measurement techniques;
- outcome measurement techniques;
- consumer-oriented techniques.

Techniques based on implicit standards

Much early health care quality assurance consisted of 'experts' making judgements about quality of care or, typically, of facilities in settings where they were not themselves professionally involved.

In the USA an early landmark study was carried out by Peterson *et al.* (1956), who assessed quality in a group of general practices in North Carolina by employing trained visitors who undertook direct observation of doctor–patient transactions and consultations and, using their own implicit standards, arrived at judgements about care. Very similar procedures are currently employed in the Royal College of General Practitioners' (1985b) *What Sort of Doctor?* initiative. In this scheme GPs visit each other's practices on a voluntary and reciprocal basis. Visitors have guidelines in which it is suggested that they engage in observation and discussion, view videotaped consultations, and inspect medical records. They are also recommended to bear professional values, accessibility, clinical competence and communication skills in mind. Otherwise they are expected to make up their own minds about appropriate standards of care. Group reports are only available to group members and to the members of the practice visited. Some groups also involve non-medical members of the primary care team or even outsiders to act as facilitators.

Throughout the practice review meetings members do not refer to predetermined standards but to implicit standards thought to have been internalized in the training and experience of participants. Essentially these processes of peer review are analogous to external examining in universities.

Techniques based on explicit standards

Standard setting and monitoring are central to all forms of quality assurance. However, innovators can choose whether to develop standards of their own, to adopt or modify standards that have been articulated elsewhere, or to develop a system with elements of both. The Royal Colleges and other professional bodies have involved themselves either in setting high level guideline standards or in encouraging and facilitating the development of local standards. The accreditation organizations, on the other hand, have tended to move away from specification of standards for practice to specification of standards for quality assurance systems – in other words to providing health care equivalents of BS 5750 (it should also be noted that several health authorities and units of management are in the process of registering for BS 5750 itself).

It is quite likely that a similar division of function will emerge in the establishment of quality assurance for university teaching. Thus the Division of Quality Audit of the HEQC is intended to address quality systems and institutional structures and processes rather than the quality of teaching itself, which will be subject to a separate assessment exercise. There is no precise higher education equivalent of the professional bodies in health care, although some professionally oriented subject groupings, such as engineering, are moving in that direction.

Since the recent NHS reforms all UK health professions have recognized that they are about to be involved in formal quality assurance. Several have responded by setting up working parties or research groups to develop standards. Standards have currently been published by the College of

Occupational Therapists, the Chartered Society of Physiotherapy and the College of Speech and Language Therapists. Each of these bodies suggests that its central standards should be used as a framework for more local exercises in specific and detailed standard setting. Some professional bodies adopt the opposite strategy and provide guidelines for a process of local standard setting, on the assumption that at some later date general standards may grow from the local and specific. The Royal College of Nursing, for example, has published the Dynamic Standard Setting System (Kitson 1990; RCN 1990). DySSSy, as it is known, is a system for local standard setting and quality assurance that is typically carried out at ward level. It can be used in any area of nursing and lays particular emphasis upon local relevance and specificity.

DySSSy is based upon a cyclical approach to quality assurance reminiscent of the ANA cycle detailed above. The DySSSy cycle is divided into three phases characterized as describing, measuring and taking action. The phases are subdivided to give twelve steps in all, as follows:

Describing
- select topic for quality improvement;
- identify care group;
- identify criteria (structure, process, outcome);
- agree standard.

Measuring
- refine criteria;
- select or construct measurement tool;
- collect data;
- evaluate results.

Taking action
- consider course of action;
- plan action;
- take action;
- re-evaluate results.

DySSSy is simple to use and has had very wide take-up in the UK. It places considerable emphasis on the use of measurement in the appraisal of standards and encourages the setting of very specific standards for all activities on all wards. With appropriate modifications it could be used fairly easily by course or unit teaching teams in higher education.

Local problem-solving techniques

In much US health care quality assurance, patient records are screened retrospectively to generate the maximum possible number of instances of poor care. These cases are subsequently reviewed and underlying problems are identified. Since the early 1980s a number of commentators have thought the procedure a top-heavy, ritualistic and time-wasting way of identifying opportunities for quality improvement. In their view, a quicker route to problem identification and quality improvement consists of simply asking local groups to identify and track likely issues. This also has the advantage that practitioners themselves feel less threatened by the procedure and are motivated to seek out problems rather than to hide them for fear of subsequent sanctions. As Skillicorn (1981: 21) suggests,

> staff physicians are in fact the best equipped to review the problems of their peers. They know their colleagues, they know the institution, and they know the idiosyncrasies of both. And when significant things in patient care go wrong they are tough on their peers, tougher than any external group.

A number of techniques have been developed for such 'looking for trouble', including positive solicitation of patient and employee complaints, records monitoring systems, and scrutiny of a range of other data sources, such as committee minutes, liability proceedings and hospital or unit log books. This philosophy of 'shop floor' initiation of quality improvement is also the basis of the 'quality circles' movement referred to by Boore in Chapter 12.

Quality circles are small groups of people from a common background whose purpose is the improvement of quality in a specified area of care. The group usually has a membership of between six and twelve people but the precise details of membership can vary. Thus some quality circles consist entirely of volunteers (as in Ishikawa's original (1982) model) while others are based upon the 'natural work group' principle, which in the health care context might be all staff on a ward, all staff in a given professional department, or all staff in a multiprofessional team.

One further variation in membership is the inclusion of a group 'facilitator' who is particularly skilled in the operation of quality circles. This facilitator might be brought in from an outside consultancy or be a hospital-wide quality coordinator or member of a hospital or district quality committee. Alternatively the facilitator might be selected by a more senior coordinating group but still be a member of the work group upon which the circle is based.

Quality circles have had considerable impact throughout health care quality assurance and, as Boore shows in Chapter 12, have great potential for the improvement of university teaching.

Other approaches to local problem-solving in health care quality assurance involve tracking and monitoring the occurrence and solution of quality problems in the various departments of the health care organization. Thus Brown *et al.* (1984) describe a system of 'issue logs'. These are simple documents available for completion by any member of staff in any hospital department on their own behalf or on behalf of patients. They have space for a brief description of the problem identified, the patient's (or patients') name(s), the name of the attending physician, and the date of completion. The logs can be signed by their initiator or completed anonymously. They are then passed to a central quality assurance committee. The committee considers the logs alongside other quality assurance data and information and quality profiles are prepared for each department. Problem solutions are then determined in the light of overall profiles and trends and are passed to appropriate groups or individuals for implementation.

Issue logging could easily be used in higher education, where staff and students would both have access to logs. The identification of problems and suggestions for their solution would expedite the normal processes of departmental and faculty consultation.

Process measurement techniques

Where explicit local process standards are in place the appropriate strategy for appraising them may be the design of local recording or measuring instruments. Thus if the standard suggests that all lecturers should return assignments within three weeks of submission all that is needed is a way of recording the time actually taken. Simple low-level measurements of this kind are useful when what is sought is an indication of local problems and of opportunities for immediate quality improvement. Where detailed standards do not exist or where the assessment of process that is required is a broad overall measure for comparison between different settings, more sophisticated measurement may be necessary. Several relevant techniques have been developed in health care.

The health care professions vary in the extent to which they have developed instruments for the measurement of the process of care and as in so many areas of health care quality assurance nursing is in the forefront. Many of the instruments developed for nursing could be adapted for other professions and, with creativity, for university teaching.

Estimates of the quality of care process can be made retrospectively from records of recently discharged patients or concurrently from records of patients still undergoing care. The Phaneuf audit (Phaneuf 1976) assesses nursing process quality entirely from retrospective records. Many process measures, however, involve concurrent appraisal of quality and in some cases this includes direct observation of the delivery of care as well as scrutiny of records.

Records of university teaching are far less comprehensive than the records typically available in health care settings but written evidence could be made available in the form of course documents, teaching hand-outs, student work and course evaluations. They could thus afford a basis for retrospective records-based audit. Concurrent appraisal might supplement such scrutiny with direct observation of teaching interactions, consultation with students and so on.

As several authors note in other chapters of this book, examination of the process of university teaching is a relative novelty. School teaching, by contrast, has developed a considerable tradition which stretches back to the early years of this century (Medley and Mitzel 1963; Flanders 1970). Interestingly, the analysis of interpersonal process typical of that tradition is considerably more sophisticated than that which can be found in the various nursing process measures. Indeed, Ellis and Whittington (1988) argue forcefully for the adoption of techniques derived from the observation and analysis of teaching behaviour in the development of measures of health care competence and quality. University teaching might therefore be well placed to develop superior systems for the appraisal of process quality by combining techniques from the two sources.

Outcome measurement techniques

The existence of sound techniques for the measurement and analysis of outcomes might be thought to be the *sine qua non* of health care quality assurance. Regrettably, however, the literature reflects the extreme difficulties encountered by researchers, clinicians and quality assurance specialists in: (a) agreeing what appropriate indicators of good and bad outcomes are; (b) disentangling the results of health care interventions from the confounding effects of other variables; and (c) demonstrating relationships between measures of the process of care and measures of notionally related outcomes.

Despite the difficulties, outcome measures do have several advantages. First, they reflect the totality of care received from the point of first admission or request for treatment to final discharge or death; second, they are readily understood and accepted as valid by both patients and practitioners; finally, they can also be used to indicate not just the quality of care received but also needs for further or compensatory care.

Published accounts of medical audits, as described by Shaw (1990), have included: local outcome evaluations as means to the improvement of quality in X-ray identification of carcinoma of the colon; follow-up procedures in respect of women with abnormal cervical smears; management of acute myocardial infarction patients; prescribing of anti-microbial drugs to maternity cases; use of blood fractions; notification to GPs of hospital deaths; identification of fractures; and prevention of deaths from asthma. The 'Lothian Audit' (Gruer *et al.* 1986), which is the longest standing systematic local audit in the UK, also makes substantial use of outcome evaluation. In nursing a number of specific local initiatives have developed and used outcome standards and many of the general systems developed for local nursing quality assurance give explicit guidance on so doing (Mayers *et al.* 1977; Daugherty and Mason 1987; Pearson 1987; Kemp and Richardson 1990; Kitson 1990).

The measurement and appraisal of outcomes in university teaching is likely to present problems very similar to those encountered in health care quality assurance. They are equally long term, equally susceptible to the confounding influences of contextual variables and equally vaguely related to process variables. Fortunately, however, there is a long tradition of educational evaluation in which relationships between long-term aims and much more explicit short-term objectives have been examined (Scriven 1967; Bloom *et al.* 1971). Specification and appraisal of outcome standards for university teaching in the light of that tradition as well as of the health care experience could yield methodological advances that would benefit both areas of quality assurance.

Consumer-oriented techniques

Patient satisfaction surveys are among the most frequently used techniques in health care quality assurance. There is a substantial literature and several extensive reviews can be found (e.g. Evason and Whittington 1991). There is a separate but related literature on the use of questionnaire and survey techniques for the assessment of patient compliance with instructions and treatment regimens (Ley 1988; Sbarbaro 1990).

Patient satisfaction scales and questionnaires have been used for a variety of purposes and in a wide range of settings. Some are designed to identify problems and potential improvements, some provide an overall estimate of satisfaction with a given service or episode of care and some are used as part of an overall evaluation of service quality. Almost all specialties have been the subject of patient satisfaction measures although the Dalley *et al.* (1991) survey of NHS patient satisfaction activities showed that maternity care was the most frequent setting.

The measures themselves vary in reflection of the wide variety of purposes and settings for which they are designed. Thus some are substantial documents providing a structure for hour-long interviews while others are extremely simple instruments with half a dozen closed or even yes/no questions targeted at very specific groups of patients. Some scales are detailed, multidimensional measures of the overall construct of satisfaction and have been tested for reliability and validity, while others are simpler one-off measures designed for specific settings and do not aspire to such sophistication.

A number of problems have been identified in the measurement of patient satisfaction. Each of these methodological considerations would also be relevant in the development of student evaluation instruments. Thus the concept of student 'satisfaction' is likely to vary, its measurement may well be confounded by other variables, students still involved in courses will have a vested interest in not offending their tutors, and the designers of scales may be tempted to avoid the difficult issues. These problems are addressed in detail in Stringer and Finlay's chapter (Chapter 6).

Students are not the only consumers of university teaching. Employers would certainly see themselves in that light and given that universities have a role in the general education of citizens it can be argued that everyone is an indirect consumer. Employment-oriented courses have developed a variety of means of 'market consultation' through advisory panels or even the involvement of representatives in course management committees. The most substantial schemes are the various 'validation' procedures developed in areas of professional education. Notable among these is the *partnership* approach currently being developed by the Central Council for the Education and Training of Social Workers for the courses it validates. Here both managers and field workers are involved in all aspects of course design, validation, delivery and evaluation and partnerships of education institutions and agencies are expected to meet local and national needs for pre-service and in-service education, training and research as and when they arise.

Conclusion

This chapter began by noting that while the industrial origins of quality assurance were commonly cited, parallel developments in health care were much less frequently acknowledged. In fact quality assurance in university teaching may have as much, if not more, to learn from health care quality assurance as it has from its industrial counterpart.

A number of problems have been shown to be particularly challenging in both sectors. These include difficulties associated with the identification and measurement of outcome quality and with teasing out relationships between the processes of care or teaching and desirable outcomes. Measurement of process quality is itself made difficult by the relative centrality of interpersonal behaviour in both teaching and health care. While none of these problems has been finally resolved in health care they have at least been refined and quality innovators in university teaching should find the discussion enlightening.

Health care and university teaching quality assurance have also been shown to share an advantage. In both sectors concern for quality can be taken as axiomatic. Professionals, managers, government and consumers may debate procedures for quality appraisal and improvement but all are fundamentally committed to it. Even where provision is organized through free market systems (as in much US health care) the profit motive is at least theoretically subordinate to the desire to provide a high quality service. The problem for quality innovators is not so much demonstration of the importance of quality as demonstration of the effectiveness of specific techniques and systems in fostering its improvement. Quality assurance in university teaching and in health care have much in common, and quality specialists and innovators in both sectors would benefit from the promotion of increased dialogue.

References

American Nurses' Association (1982) *Nursing Quality Assurance Management Learning System*. Kansas City: American Nurses' Association.

Anderson, W. G. (1986) Definitions of quality. *American Medical News 12*, December: 24.

Berwick, D. M. and Knapp, M. G. (1987) Theory and practice for measuring health care quality. *Health Care Financing Review*, Annual Supplement: 49–55.

Bloom, B., Hastings, J. and Madaus, G. (1971) *Handbook on Formative and Summative Evaluation of Student Learning*. New York: McGraw-Hill.

Brown, D. E., Levy, D. and Sarmiento, M. (1984) Patient-oriented quality assurance activities. *Quality Review Bulletin*, 10(1): 19–22.

Casanova, J. E. (1990) Status of quality assurance programmes in American hospitals. *Medical Care*, 28(11): 1105–9.

Dagher, D. O. and Lloyd, R. J. (1991) Managing negative outcome by reducing variances in the emergency department. *Quality Review Bulletin*, 17(1): 15–21.

Dalley, G., Baldwin, S., Carr-Hill, R. *et al.* (1991) *Quality Management Initiatives in the NHS. No. 3: Strategic Approaches to Improving Quality*. York: Centre for Health Economics, University of York.

Daugherty, J. and Mason, E. (1987) *Excelcare Nursing System*. London: Price Waterhouse.

Donabedian, A. (1966) Evaluating the quality of medical care. *Milbank Memorial Fund Quarterly*, 44: 166–203.

Donabedian, A. (1980) *Explorations in Quality Assessment and Monitoring, Volume One*. Ann Arbor, MI: Health Administration Press.

Donabedian, A. (1985) Twenty years of research on the quality of medical care. *Evaluation and the Health Professions*, 8(3): 243–65.

Donabedian, A. (1986) Quality assurance: corporate responsibility for multi-hospital systems. *Quality Review Bulletin*, 12(1): 3–7.

Donabedian, A. (1987) Commentary on some studies of the quality of care. *Health Care Financing Review*, Supplement: 75–85.

Donabedian, A. (1989) The quest for quality health care: whose choice? Whose responsibility? *Mount Sinai Journal of Medicine*, 56(5): 406–22.

Donabedian, A. (1991) Reflections on the effectiveness of quality assurance. In Donabedian, A. and Povar, G. J. (eds) *Striving for Quality in Health Care*. Ann Arbor, MI: Health Administration Press.

Ellis, R. and Whittington, D. (1988) Social skills, competence and quality. In Ellis, R. (ed.) *Professional Competence and Quality Assurance in the Caring Professions*. Beckenham: Croom Helm.

Ellis, R. and Whittington, D. (1993) *Quality Assurance for Health Care: A Handbook*. London: Edward Arnold.

Evason, E. and Whittington, D. (1991) Patient satisfaction studies: problems and implications explored in a pilot study in Northern Ireland. *Health Education Journal*, 50(2): 73–87.

Flanders, N. (1970) *Analyzing Teaching Behavior*. Reading, MA: Addison Wesley.

Greenfield, S., Lewis, C., Kaplan, S. and Davidson, M. (1975) Peer review by criteria mapping: criteria for diabetes mellitus, the use of decision making in chart audit. *Annals of Internal Medicine*, 83: 761–70.

Greenfield, S., Cretin, S., Worthman, L. *et al.* (1981) Comparison of a criteria map to a criteria list in quality of care assessment for patients with chest pain: the relation of each to outcome. *Medical Care*, 19(3): 255–72.

Gruer, R., Gordon, D., Gunn, A. and Ruckley, C. (1986) Audit of surgical audit. *Lancet*, 1: 23–6.

Health Care Research Unit, Newcastle upon Tyne University (1990) *North of England Study of Standards and Performance in General Practice*. Newcastle upon Tyne: HCRU, Newcastle upon Tyne University.

HMSO (1956) *Committee of Enquiry into the Cost of the National Health Service: The Guillebaud Report*, Cmnd 663. London: HMSO.

HMSO (1975) *Committee of Enquiry into the Regulation of the Medical Profession (Merrison Report)*, Cmnd 6018. London: HMSO.

HMSO (1976) *Competence to Practise: The Alment Report*. London: HMSO.

HMSO (1979) *Report of the Royal Commission on the National Health Service*, Cmnd 7615. London: HMSO.

HMSO (1982) *Efficiency and Effectiveness in the Civil Service: The Financial Management Initiative*. London: HMSO.

HMSO (1989) *Working for Patients*, Cmnd 555. London: HMSO.

HMSO (1990a) *Medical Audit*. Working for patients. Working paper no. 6, Department of Health. London: HMSO.

HMSO (1990b) *The Quality of Medical Care*. Report of the Standing Medical Advisory Committee, Department of Health. London: HMSO.

Irvine, D. H. (1990) *Managing for Quality in General Practice*. London: King's Fund Centre.

Ishikawa, K. (1982) *A Guide to Quality Control*, 2nd edn. Tokyo: Asian Productivity Organisation.

Kemp, N. and Richardson, E. (1990) *Quality Assurance in Nursing Practice*. Oxford: Butterworth-Heinemann.

Kitson, A. (1990) Quality matters and standard setting. *Nursing Standard*, 4(44): 32–3.

Klein, R. (1980) *The Politics of the National Health Service*. Harlow: Longman.

Ley, P. (1988) *Communicating with Patients: Improving Communication, Satisfaction and Compliance*. London: Chapman and Hall.

Maxwell, R. J. (1984) Quality assessment in health. *British Medical Journal*, 228: 1470–7.

Mayers, M., Norby, R. and Watson, A. (1977) *Quality Assurance for Patient Care: Nursing Perspectives*. New York: Appleton-Century Crofts.

Medley, D. and Mitzel, H. (1963) Measuring classroom behaviour by systematic observation. In Gage, N. (ed.) *A Handbook of Research on Teaching*. Chicago: Rand McNally.

Øvretveit, J. (1992) *Health Service Quality*. Oxford: Blackwell.

Pearson, A. (1987) *Nursing Quality Measurement*. Chichester: Wiley.

Peterson, O., Andrews, L., Spain, R. and Greenberg, B. (1956) An analytical study of North Carolina general practice, 1953–4. *Journal of Medical Education*, 31(2): 1–165.

Phaneuf, M. C. (1976) *The Nursing Audit – Self-regulation in Nursing Practice*. New York: Appleton-Century Crofts.

Rodriguez, A. R. (1988) An introduction to quality assurance in mental health. In Stricker, G. and Rodriguez, A. R. (eds) *Handbook of Quality Assurance in Mental Health*. New York: Plenum.

Royal College of General Practitioners (1989) The quality Initiative. *Journal of the Royal College of General Practitioners*, 33: 523–4.

Royal College of General Practitioners (1985a) *Assessing Quality of Care in General Practice*. London: Royal College of General Practitioners.

Royal College of General Practitioners (1985b) *What Sort of Doctor?* Report from General Practice, 23. London: Royal College of General Practitioners.

Royal College of Nursing (1990) *Dynamic Standard Setting System*. London: Royal College of Nursing, London.

Sbarbaro, J. A. (1990) The patient physician relationship: compliance revisited. *Annals of Allergy*, 64: 325–31.

Scriven, M. (1967) The methodology of evaluation. In Tyler, R., Gagné, R. and Scriven, M. (eds) *Perspectives on Curriculum Evaluation*. Chicago: Rand McNally.

Shaw, C. D. (1990) *Medical Audit: A Hospital Handbook*. London: King's Fund Centre.

Skillicorn, S. A. (1981) A conversation with Dr. Stanley A. Skillicorn. A leading proponent of integrated problem-oriented quality assurance. *Quality Review Bulletin*, 7(4): 20–3.

United States Committee on Government Operations (1989) *Quicker and Sicker: Substandard Treatment of Medicare Patients, 7th Report*. Washington, DC: US Government Printing Office.

United States General Accounting Office (1990) *Quality Assurance – a Comprehensive National Strategy for Health Care Is Needed*. Briefing report to the Chairman, United States Bipartisan Commission on Comprehensive Health Care, GAO/PEMD-90-14BR. Washington, DC: GAO.

Webber, A. (1988) History and mission of quality assurance in the public sector. In Hughes, E. (ed.) *Perspectives on Quality in American Health Care*. New York: McGraw-Hill.

Whittington, D. (1989) Performance indicators and quality assurance in the NHS. Paper delivered to the European Group for Public Administration Study Group on Quality Assurance and Productivity, Chester.

Wilson, C. R. M. (1987) *Hospital-wide Quality Assurance: Models for Implementation and Development*. Toronto: W. B. Saunders.

Wong, H. (1989) Quality measurement and customer service. In Spath, P. (ed.) *Innovations in Health Care Quality Measurement*. Chicago: American Hospital Publishing.

5

Quality Assurance through Course Validation and Review

Norman Gibson

Introduction

The type and quality of course provision in the United Kingdom have become a major preoccupation within and outside higher education. There are various reasons for this. It seems to be a commonly held view, among some members of government and the public service, and also certain employers, that higher education, and especially universities, have not served society as well as they should; in particular, they have not contributed as much as might be expected to economic growth, which has lagged behind that of major competitors. The implicit proposition seems to be that the 'right kind' of higher education, provided it is on a sufficient scale and properly integrated with the rest of the education system – which it must not distort – can contribute greatly to the creation of wealth. A second reason is clearly the cost of higher education to the tax-payer, currently some £5 billion per year or about 1 per cent of gross domestic product.

These views, strongly emphasizing economic aspects of higher education, are in danger of diminishing its wider role and significance to society: the cultivation of openness to new ideas, of intellectual adventure, detachment and integrity in reflecting upon and analysing complex social, scientific and technical problems, the nurturing of creative imagination, the exploration of value systems and the heroic attempt to form a view of the whole. There is no suggestion that these pursuits can be independent of resource considerations or the contribution higher education makes to wealth creation, but society will be the poorer if the wider purposes get subordinated to overly narrow goals.

While I do not ignore these wider purposes, the primary aim of this chapter is to discuss the validation, monitoring and review of course provision by the University of Ulster within the context of the national approach to quality assurance. The origins, operation and other aspects of the procedures, including the development of course budgeting, are briefly described, followed by consideration of the debate on quality assurance and the important issues it raises; finally some conclusions are drawn.

Origins

The merger in 1984 of The New University of Ulster and the Ulster Polytechnic to form the University of Ulster brought together institutions from each side of the binary divide with very different approaches to course planning and approval. Those of The New University of Ulster were typical of universities at the time. New award-bearing courses – almost entirely at undergraduate or postgraduate degree level – were generally planned within academic departments, with or without informal external advice, and approved by Senate on the basis of an outline course description. The monitoring of standards related almost exclusively to the performance of students in examinations and relied heavily on the external examiner system. The Ulster Polytechnic, by contrast, had long experience of more formalized course planning and validation procedures, through offering courses leading to awards of bodies such as BTEC and CNAA.

The charter of the merged institution reflects both university and polytechnic backgrounds and requires it

> To provide a range of courses of study, academic, professional, technical or other, at higher Degree, Degree and non-Degree levels, leading as appropriate to qualifications awarded by the University or by national or professional bodies. (Article 4 (I))

The university, except for transitional arrangements for students who were already studying for awards of the CNAA, decided to terminate the previous links between the latter and the Ulster Polytechnic. But the university felt it desirable to maintain and, indeed, develop its links with BTEC so that students of the new institution would have the opportunity to study for Higher National awards.

The university inherited from the two merging institutions more than three hundred courses, some of which overlapped and needed to be rationalized. It was decided, building in part on CNAA practice, that the university should have its own formalized system of course planning, evaluation and review for both existing and new courses. The exercise was designed to give assurance on the quality of courses on offer and to ensure that they were consistent with the overall objectives of the university as expressed in the charter, mission statement, policy documents and development plans for each of the four campuses. It also had the incidental advantage of bringing together staff from similar academic areas in the previous institutions to work on a shared task of course and curriculum development. This assisted the process of merging, though a small number of staff objected to the whole course evaluation procedure. But the opposition was short-lived as the benefits of open discussion and analysis of detailed course proposals became apparent.

Course providers had to produce evidence that courses were and would continue to be in demand, had clear educational and learning objectives, were designed to meet the requirements of students for intellectual and personal development, would offer career opportunities, reflect perceived needs for graduates and diplomates, satisfy quality standards in terms of structure – including as necessary work placement experience – syllabuses, organization and achievement goals, and could be properly resourced. An almost identical approach continues to be applied to new courses and to substantial revisions of existing ones.

Operation

The Senate, working through two main committees, the Development Committee and the Academic Policy Committee, has overall responsibility for the evaluation, monitoring and review of courses. The procedures distinguish between new courses, periodic major reviews of existing courses, annual reviews and minor revisions.

New courses

Proposals for new courses are usually initiated at departmental level and then submitted through the faculty board to the Development Committee, which, if it supports the proposal, establishes a Course Planning Committee. The membership of this committee includes those who are to teach on the course and, depending on its proposed academic content, may be drawn from any department or faculty. Commonly the committee is augmented by members with particular expertise or knowledge drawn from industry, commerce, the professions and other academic institutions. The Course Planning Committee is required to produce a comprehensive course document (guidelines are provided), which should explain the reasons for the proposal, describe the objectives, outcomes and structure of the course, demonstrate academic progression and internal coherence, specify the syllabuses and reading, name the staff who are responsible for each syllabus, state teaching, learning, assessment and examination methods, and set out course regulations. A section of the document should contain brief curricula vitae of participating staff, and describe the other resources, library, laboratory and computing, available for the course.

Despite the guidelines for the form and content of the course document problems do arise. The structure and academic progression of the course may not be well conceived, syllabuses may be out of date, contact hours may be too high or too low, regulations may not meet university requirements, reading references may not be at the appropriate level, distinguish sufficiently clearly between recommended and indicative reading or be properly presented and, where sandwich placements are involved, the arrangements for their organization and monitoring may be vague and incomplete. Many of these and other shortcomings are recognized and corrected at faculty level or by assistance from the Academic Registry – which has responsibility from Senate in these matters – in advance of the formal university evaluation of the course proposal. If this is not done the latter may be less beneficial than it should be.

Evaluation meeting

Once the document for a new course is complete an Evaluation Panel, established by the Academic Policy Committee, and chaired by a Pro-Vice-Chancellor, with at least two members of staff from departments not directly associated with the proposal but who have relevant knowledge or experience and two external members with expertise in the fields it covers, meets with the Course Planning Committee to discuss the proposal. External members may come from other higher education institutions, industry, business, professional organizations and government agencies. Where the course requires or is seeking recognition by a professional body, university procedures allow for joint evaluation, with parties reporting to their respective parent bodies. This has been a particularly useful and important development but is not universally accepted by professional and similar bodies.

Evaluation panels are invited to undertake an independent, thorough and constructively critical assessment of the proposal; at its best the exercise becomes an informative and rewarding seminar. Guidelines are issued to panels which indicate that courses of study should encourage rigorous and imaginative thinking and an understanding of intellectual detachment, allow where possible a problem-solving approach to learning, explore the basis for and develop the capacity to make thoughtful and responsible value judgements, alert the student or participant to the interdependencies and social implications of fields of study, and provide opportunities for acquiring communication skills (oral, written, numerative and artistic, as appropriate) and other personal and social skills. They should also introduce a knowledge of the methods and techniques of computer usage relevant to the particular course, meet the requirements of students in preparing for and furthering their careers, including the acquisition of technical and practical knowledge at a suitable level and as may be required by professional bodies, commercial, industrial and other interests, and incorporate an understanding of resource management issues and enterprising skills.

Following discussions with the Course Planning Committee, a report with recommendations is prepared by staff of the Academic Registry and forwarded to the Academic Policy Committee. The recommendations state whether or not the course should be approved, on what conditions and for how long. If necessary the original course document is revised in response to the report. A detailed comparison is made of the original and revised document to check that the requirements of the Evaluation Panel are met. This is usually decided by the chairperson unless the panel is to reconvene or members are to see the revised document. Copies of the approved document, but without the curricula vitae of staff, are deposited in the university library and are available to readers. External examiners also receive copies as background information for their examining responsibilities.

Annual reviews

Annual reviews monitor the operation of each course on a year-to-year basis. The Course Committee, the analogue of the Course Planning Committee and with a similar internal membership, chaired by the course director (frequently the head of department) or by the senior course tutor, is responsible for the completion of a course report form which records student applications, enrolments and performance, gives comments from staff–student committees and, especially important, responds to external examiners' reports, detailing as may be necessary remedial or other actions that should be taken. A panel, drawn from the Faculty Board and with representatives of the Academic Policy Committee, meets course directors and senior course tutors to consider the reports. The reports from the panels are collated and presented to a special meeting of the Academic Policy Committee to determine what further action may be necessary.

Periodic reviews

Periodic major reviews of existing courses generally take place after four or five years' experience of their operation. A course document is produced with similar content to that for new courses but, in addition, must provide a careful appraisal of the course, giving information about student admissions, examination results, career outcomes, external examiners' reports, annual course reviews, responses to the latter and students' views.

An evaluation panel, similar to that described for new courses, is established to consider the course document. Alternatively, the Academic Policy Committee may decide on the basis of annual reviews and other information that a major review is not required and delegate responsibility to the faculty to carry out the periodic review, but with representatives drawn from the Committee. The faculty forwards a report to the Academic Policy Committee for its consideration.

There is also a procedure for handling minor revisions to courses that may be desirable but do not justify a major review. The revisions are considered by the faculty and reported to the Academic Policy Committee, which may note them or specify conditions to be satisfied for them to be accepted.

Review of course evaluation

How well has the system worked? The broad consensus within the university is that it has worked well and led to substantial improvements in the structure, content and presentation of courses, and has encouraged interdisciplinary collaboration. This view is also widely supported by those from outside the university who have participated in evaluation panels and by those professional and other bodies who have engaged in joint validation procedures.

A successful evaluation meeting depends on many factors. A well thought out and clearly presented document, in terms of objectives, structure, content, academic progression, organizational arrangements, teaching, learning, assessment and examination methods, is of critical importance, as is close liaison with the Academic Registry about course regulations. All this depends particularly on the chairperson of the Course Planning Committee and his or her skill in eliciting and presenting written materials and contributions from other members in a coherent and integrated form. This requires editorial and organizational abilities of a high order – a fact that deserves due recognition.

The composition of the evaluation panel is also very important. Members should be well prepared, having studied the document and supporting papers carefully and have, or be able to earn because of their specialist knowledge or experience, the respect of the Course Planning Committee. They should have the generosity to commend where it is deserved and the capacity to criticize constructively without being pedantic or patronizing.

The chairperson of the evaluation panel should also be well prepared and thoroughly briefed by the support staff. A preliminary discussion with other members of the panel in advance of the meeting with the Course Planning Committee can be of great assistance. It enables the panel members to exchange views about the course proposal and gives the chairperson the opportunity to plan the discussion in a way that allows for a systematic and coherent approach to the consideration of the proposal. During the full meeting it is essential that all members of the Course Planning Committee have an opportunity to contribute and that there is genuine and constructive dialogue.

Course evaluation procedures as described do not guarantee good teaching by the individual member of staff, although they may assist in this direction by emphasizing and articulating teaching and assessment methods; more specific attention is given to the quality of teaching in a later section.

The system of course evaluation will clearly have to change to accommo-
date course modularization, including the freer choice of modules by
students, and to take account of credit accumulation and transfer both
within and between institutions. Notions of course structure and progression will come into question, as will the time over which course credits
may be accumulated to lead to an award. But it can hardly be doubted that
higher education will still need to ensure that the quality of its educational
services, whether in the form of modules, combinations of them or courses,
can stand open and constructive scrutiny.

Other aspects

Validation elsewhere

Increasingly the university is involved in validation of courses offered in
other institutions which lead to university awards. Agreements exist with
further education colleges to offer special courses for teachers and access
courses leading to the award of a certificate; with nursing colleges leading
to diplomas, and negotiated as part of the evolving arrangements under
Project 2000; and with a limited number of institutions outside the United
Kingdom. In addition, there is an arrangement with BTEC by which
certain Higher National courses are offered in part or in some instances
completely in selected further education colleges under 'franchise' procedures.

The validation process is essentially similar to that followed for courses
that operate within the university. It requires the production of a course
document and a careful evaluation of the academic and other resources
available to support the course in the proposing institution, generally
involves a visit to that institution, and results in a formal agreement
between the other party and the university. Assessors are appointed from
the staff of the university to participate in the Course Committee, which
oversees the operation of the course; the university also appoints external
examiners. Monitoring and reviews of such courses are carried out under
the procedures described earlier for internal courses. A system of charges
is levied to reimburse the university for the costs involved.

Quality of teaching

As well as attention being given to the standard of courses offered by or
under the auspices of the university growing emphasis is placed on the
quality of teaching. Applicants for academic appointments are required at
interview to give a brief presentation on a suggested topic. Staff who do not
have a relevant teaching qualification or whose practical experience is
considered insufficient are encouraged to undertake a Postgraduate

Certificate in Teaching in Higher Education designed to improve peda-gogic and related skills. In 1990–1 a pilot study was carried out in which questionnaires were issued to students to collect their views on lectures. They were invited to comment on the clarity, organization and integration of material, the punctuality, audibility and style of delivery of the lecturer, the use of teaching aids, the guidance given on course reading and other forms of learning assistance, the interaction in class between lecturer and students, the instructiveness of lecture assignments and their timing, speed of return and quality of written comment. The practice is to be extended and maintained on a regular basis. The information will be made available to the individual lecturer and to the head of department so that good performance is encouraged and where necessary remedial action is taken. A similar approach is planned for tutorials, seminars, practical work and for the teaching and learning environment generally. A Distinguished Teaching Awards Scheme acknowledges quality in teaching on the basis of nomination by students and others. Up to three awards are offered annually, with the successful candidates receiving a certificate and monet-ary prize. A research project is seeking to refine methods of teaching appraisal.

Heads of department are required to report annually on the teaching and examining performance of staff on probation, making use of reports from staff/student committees, external examiners' reports and other information. Performance in teaching is one of the criteria in considering staff for promotion.

Course budgeting

It is evident that measures to ensure quality of course provision and delivery give rise to substantial costs. Clearly in the interests of good management it is important to be aware of these relative to the correspond-ing benefits that accrue or are assumed to accrue. Costs and especially benefits are notoriously difficult to determine accurately, although this is not a sufficient reason to give up the attempt.

The university has embarked on a course budgeting exercise that necessarily encompasses the costs of evaluating, monitoring and reviewing course provision as well as course delivery. In time it is expected that the approach will generate notional trading and perhaps eventually profit and loss accounts for individual courses as an aid to efficient management. Central to the approach is the allocation of academic staff time on a percentage, not hourly, basis to activities related to teaching, research, consultancy and one other aggregate category. Revenue is to be allocated correspondingly; student course enrolment is obviously a major source.

Non-academic departments identify, generally, not more than six main activities, and as far as possible allocate staff time and other costs to each of these. For example, quality assurance is one of the key activities of the

Academic Registry. The cost of this is in turn attributed to particular academic departments. All such activity costs will similarly be allocated unless non-academic departments actually sell services to other parties, as does the Sport and Recreation Department. Further consideration is to be given to how it can be ensured that non-academic departments operate efficiently.

The preliminary evidence indicates that there is substantial variation in the costs and overall financial viability of courses, but that this is not simply related to student numbers. There is no suggestion that the continued provision of particular courses should be decided exclusively on the basis of financial considerations. But these must feature in the approach to course provision and, indeed, quality assurance might stimulate innovative thinking and encourage the adoption of new forms of education and learning as the system responds to the requirements of mass higher education.

Public debate on quality assurance

Quality assurance in higher education has received much attention since the early 1980s. The CVCP has produced codes of practice on academic standards, staff training and university validation of courses for the public sector, and more recently established an Academic Audit Unit. The PCFC has also investigated teaching quality. The CNAA and HMI have for many years, and long before the 1980s, exercised certain responsibilities for quality assurance in the public sector; the HMI also has a role in relation to teacher education in universities. A Committee of Enquiry, chaired by Sir Norman Lindop, into Academic Validation in Public Sector Higher Education (Lindop 1985) substantially influenced subsequent development in quality assurance as did the Report of the Review of the Council for National Academic Awards (Bird and Callaghan 1990). In addition, professional bodies in medicine, engineering, law, accounting, psychology, computing and many other subject areas have a long record of accrediting courses in higher education as a way, for those who complete them successfully, of achieving professional recognition and, frequently, entry to the corresponding profession. But the most far-reaching recent event in the development of quality assurance is the proposals in the White Paper, *Higher Education: a New Framework* (DES 1991).

White Paper proposals

The White Paper states categorically that 'The prime responsibility for maintaining and enhancing the quality of teaching and learning rests with each individual institution,' then immediately shifts attention to the 'need for proper accountability for the substantial public funds invested in higher education,' and continues, 'As part of this, students and employers need improved information about quality if the full benefit of increased competition is to be obtained' (para. 58).

This juxtaposition of important and related but separable issues scarcely makes for clarity, let alone a well integrated set of prescriptions. Indeed, the White Paper nowhere provides a reasoned justification for the adopted policies. The issues of funding of teaching and the legitimate demand for proper accountability are essentially set aside, as are improved information sources for students and employers, except for a brief mention of the latter becoming a responsibility of the 'assessment of quality units' of the Funding Councils. There is also no adequate discussion of competition as it might operate in higher education and, indeed, in so far as the Councils are to be or see themselves as the dominant purchasers of teaching services there cannot be competition on the consumer or client side of the 'market'. It is also noteworthy that the immediate clients, the students, and what might be their role in sustaining effective competition is ignored. But to have considered their possible contribution would, of necessity, have required explicit discussion of their part in paying for their education, which presumably it was felt best to avoid (see para. 14).

Quality audit

The White Paper declares that 'There is a common view throughout higher education on the need for externally provided reassurance that the quality control mechanisms within institutions are adequate' (para. 67). By 'externally provided reassurance' is meant a single body for higher education, 'in which the institutions have the major stake' (para. 68). In an important sense the providers are to judge the merits and effectiveness of their own control mechanisms and quality assurance practices. This form of so-called self-regulation is widely favoured by professional bodies but it may well have the effect of creating a kind of cartel and not be in the best interests of clients. The particular approach proposed is welcomed by both the CVCP and CDP, with the latter emphasizing that 'it will be important to ensure that the unit covers all aspects of quality assurance from inputs through processes to outcomes, and that its methodology [*sic*] fully reflects the range and diversity of provision within the new single sector' (Committee of Directors of Polytechnics 1991: para. 26).

It may be doubted that any single administrative unit can have the breadth of information, knowledge and perspicacity this requires, even with 'industrial and professional as well as academic members' (DES 1991: para. 69). Once more what is going by default – and it is clearly, at least implicitly, accepted by government – is any serious attempt to encourage the growth of a more competitive approach in higher education, which would empower the immediate clients in their exercise of individual choice and in so doing convey a mass of detailed and disaggregated information to providers, who of necessity would have to respond or in the end cease to exist.

The new quality audit unit is also to advise on which institutions might in future be given degree awarding powers. And all validation arrangements entered into by non-degree awarding institutions are to be subject to its approval. The financing of the quality audit unit is not discussed. If the precedent set by the CVCP Academic Audit is followed then all higher education institutions will be required to pay a levy. If there is to be such a unit an alternative would be for it to sell its services to institutions that wish to purchase them on the grounds that its imprimatur would assist in the attraction of students and clients. Further, there would seem to be no good reason why the private sector should be excluded from entering the market for academic audit and similar services.

Quality assessment

Quality assessment is, somewhat artificially, distinguished from quality audit by stressing the role of an 'external review of, and judgements about, the quality of teaching and learning' (DES 1991: para. 60). The emphasis is to be on quantifiable outcomes in the form of 'performance indicators and calculations of value added' and 'through external judgements on the basis of direct observation of what is provided . . . the quality of teaching and learning, its management and organisation, accommodation and equipment' (paras 80 and 81).

It would seem almost inevitable that the roles of the new quality audit unit and the quality assessment unit or units will overlap and in so doing impose additional burdens and costs on higher education; it may be wondered if the benefits will be commensurate. The CDP is also concerned that 'the White Paper places funding and quality assessment in the same hands' and fears 'conflicts of interest if those making quality judgements are part of the funding apparatus' (CDP 1991: para. 27). While this concern is understandable there is clearly a sense in which accountability – or, more basically, rational use of resources – requires that judgements of value received are made implicitly or otherwise, or directly or indirectly by those making outlays. The CDP would obviously prefer it to be indirect. But they take for granted that the dominant source of funding should come through the Funding Councils. Once again, consideration of an alternative approach of allowing clients to exercise their individual choices supported by effective purchasing power has gone by default.

Furthermore, the proposal to make quality assessments by relying mainly on performance indicators and calculations of value added raises serious questions. By definition 'indicators' are imprecise and it is far from clear how one indicator can be related to another. At best, student/staff ratios, for example, are a proxy for student revenue per member of academic staff. What information such ratios convey both within and between institutions is ambiguous and certainly demands most careful interpretation. As for attempts to arrive at 'value added' by relating student entry standards to exit qualifications, this is fraught with difficulties of both calculation and interpretation, making it unclear what policy inferences could be drawn from such a measure. Nor is it clear how the assessment units could possibly have the range of information and knowledge necessary to meet what must be a multitude of varying client requirements in a diverse higher education system. Inexorably, so-called norms and averages are bound to dominate practice and in consequence give rise in a complex system to misallocation of resources.

Conclusions

Higher education is experiencing radical change in the United Kingdom and in many other parts of the world. It is widely seen as a necessary means both to wealth creation, believed to depend critically on the growth and exploitation of so-called knowledge-based industry, and ultimately to achieving status, position and security for individual countries and groups of countries. Electorates are insisting that entry to higher education should be accessible to growing proportions of the traditional age group and be more available generally in flexible and open ways to increasing numbers of persons throughout their lives. The direction of movement is clearly towards a mass higher education system.

This should be a source of excitement for higher education and grasped as a marvellous opportunity to show what it has to offer the individual and the wider world. But this calls for an intellectual and moral confidence – not to be confused with complacency or an arrogant dogmatism – that is not always evident within academe, let alone outside it. Minimally it implies at its best an ethos, an approach to learning, that is open, responsible and disinterested and that demonstrates an acceptance of obligation to the individual, the society and the larger world. No doubt this demands a precarious balancing act, at times hard to recognize or define; but is there a better alternative? In the end the practice of education and learning cannot be value free. Inevitably there is bound to be tension between higher education seen in this way and, particularly, government and other power groups in society.

It would be wrong to infer from this that higher education should be dismissive or patronizing about vocational education or the teaching of skills and development of capabilities in response to individual and social requirements or the pursuit of learning and knowledge that will contribute to the creation of wealth. But this should not be the totality of its responsibilities or commitments. Nor should it be concluded that higher education has some kind of 'right' to financial support from government or elsewhere to allow the former to pursue what it considers to be its most fundamental purposes. It may properly try to persuade government and others to fund it but even then there should be accountability. How this should be exercised is of major importance and is central to quality assurance in the provision of courses.

The University of Ulster, building in part on the practice of others and in common with many other higher education bodies, is taking strenuous measures to ensure high standards of quality in its courses and in the learning and educational experiences it offers students and clients, while at the same time responding to their particular vocational and related preferences. It is generally considered within the university that the measures, which continue to evolve, have worked well but there is little doubt that they can be improved and will need to adapt to new modes of learning and education and not least so-called independent learning.

The reservations expressed earlier about the role of the CVCP Academic Audit Unit or a successor unit 'in which the institutions have the major stake' reflect a concern about those who provide courses largely sitting in judgement on the quality of what they offer. This should be the prerogative of the students and clients, prospective, present and past, if they wish with the assistance of information and advice from independent sources. One way of achieving this would be to try to create a market in which there was no collusion between the providers of courses, and where private bodies could sell information about course quality. It would also be necessary to avoid concentrating purchasing power among a few dominant 'buyers' of courses. But this calls into question the position of the new Funding Councils. Government may talk about competition but it is at best a one-sided competition – more accurately called monopsony; it has given no real sign that it wants a competitive market approach to course provision and course purchase.

It should be conceded immediately that the conditions required for markets to function competitively are stringent and in practice difficult to realize. They can also give rise to important questions of what is equitable. But there are ways of trying to resolve these matters. It is not clear that government made any attempt to explore such alternatives with a view to bringing about a dispersal of power among those who offer and those who purchase courses and so creating a flexible, varied and responsive higher education system. Government remains wedded to a partly administered approach – referred to pejoratively as 'bureaucratic centralism' – which has the effect of concentrating the purchase of course provision, at least indirectly, in the hands of its agencies: the Funding Councils. The case for such an approach has not been made in a cogent and comprehensive way. Certainly it is not to be found in the White Paper.

Acknowledgements

The views expressed in this chapter are not to be attributed to the University of Ulster. I am indebted to the Academic Registrar, Dr Iris Millar, for assistance and helpful comments in the preparation of this chapter; the faults and shortcomings are the responsibility of the author.

References

Bird, R. H. and Callaghan, A. (1990) *Report of the Review of the Council for National Academic Awards.* London: Department of Education and Science.

Committee of Directors of Polytechnics (1991) *Higher Education: A New Framework – Response by the Committee of Directors of Polytechnics.* London: CDP.

DES (1991) *Higher Education: A New Framework.* London: HMSO.

Lindop, Sir Norman (chairman) (1985) *The Report of the Committee of Enquiry into the Academic Validation of Degree Courses in Public Sector Higher Education,* Cmnd 9501. London: HMSO.

6

Assuring Quality through Student Evaluation

Maurice Stringer and Catherine Finlay

Introduction

This chapter describes a scheme for the evaluation of courses by students. It was developed for the Faculty of Social and Health Sciences in the University of Ulster.

A review of the background and purpose of student evaluation schemes is presented, drawing on the considerable North American experience in this area. The validity and reliability of student ratings are examined along with other methodological problems associated with such evaluations. Reactions of staff and students to the introduction of evaluation programmes are explored. An overview is provided of the types of area and questions that students can assess meaningfully with regard to courses. Finally, drawing on this review, the advantages of introducing a course evaluation scheme are outlined with particular reference to the pilot scheme in the University of Ulster.

The background and development of evaluation

Although evaluation is only now becoming an issue in British universities, it has been common practice in the USA and Canada for many decades, particularly in the post-war period. There, evaluation is a typical yearly procedure in all universities and colleges and although it is not mandatory, there appear to be few universities who do not employ a systematic and well-constructed evaluation programme. It is important to distinguish between two types of evaluation: student evaluation of courses and student evaluation of teaching staff (usually called instructor evaluation). In this chapter we will concentrate on the former, although both types of evaluation have received extensive coverage in the literature and are clearly related. In the United States some universities run autonomous, properly staffed education development units, which are given full support by the university administration to handle these evaluations. These units are entirely responsible for the development and maintenance of student course evaluation programmes on a campus-wide basis (e.g. the Centre for Research on Learning and Teaching at the University of Michigan, Ann Arbor, and the Office for Measurement and Evaluation of Teaching at the University of Pittsburgh). These independent faculty development units not only deal with student evaluation packages for courses, but also include a team of professional evaluators who provide pre- and in-service training for academic staff in areas such as course preparation and development, devising new courses, help with interpersonal skills etc. Elton (1984) has suggested the setting up of similar centres in the United Kingdom.

Students' evaluation of teaching has received considerable attention in the literature and has rapidly become a vast area (see Doyle 1975; Dressel 1976; Centra 1979). Indeed, Marsh (1984) claims that 'the study of student evaluations is one of the most frequently emphasised areas in American education research.' Evaluation is thus considered an important area of academic research in its own right, besides being valued for its practical application and assistance in the construction of questions by academics from various other disciplines outside education. Miller (1986) reviewed Faculty evaluation over a ten-year period (1974–84) in the USA and found many positive changes in its implementation. First, there has been a significant increase in the use of evaluation procedures by institutions. Second, a broader database appears to be evident. Third, the survey instruments used are getting better. Miller also points to positive changes that are expected in the next decade, which include the development of a better and more equitable faculty evaluation system that will encompass more sophisticated instruments and ways of using them. Evaluations are becoming more comprehensive and well-defined with more explicit criteria and guidelines. Miller also suggests that evaluation will become more flexible and evaluation decisions will be more individual and department-oriented than in the past.

While the literature concerning the theory and practice of evaluation deals with both student evaluation of courses and instructor evaluation, we will focus, in this chapter, on course appraisal. It would be naive, however, to suggest that course evaluation does not consider input by instructors, since courses are a reflection of these collective inputs. Nevertheless, in the present chapter attention will not be specifically directed towards instructor characteristics such as interpersonal skills, clarity of presentation, voice quality, distracting mannerisms etc., but the evaluation of course characteristics such as organization and workload.

The distinction between course and instructor evaluation also relates to a more fundamental distinction between what has been widely recognized in the literature as two different areas of evaluative research, namely *formative* and *summative* evaluation (Scriven 1967). The terms formative and summative refer to the type of evaluation being carried out and indicate the form that evaluation takes. Formative evaluation is developmental and continuous, and its aim is to encourage course improvement. Those who employ formative evaluation are concerned with the effectiveness of a course and aim to provide detailed diagnostic feedback for course development. Summative evaluation, by comparison, is conclusive and aims less to inform development than to provide an overall judgement of value or quality. Summative evaluation is therefore value-laden and raises the issue of private and public accountability.

Miller (1986) notes that the use of formative evaluative programmes has increased more dramatically in the USA in recent years than summative evaluative procedures, although he questions the actual extent to which universities are using their faculty evaluation systems for developmental purposes. Furthermore, it has been proposed that 'evaluation which is used to improve the course while it is still fluid, contributes more to the improvement of education than evaluation used to appraise a product already placed on the market' (Scriven 1967). It appears that anybody involved in curriculum development is automatically engaged in formative evaluation; thus testing work while it is still being developed and obtaining feedback will produce revisions for change. In fact, Scriven (1967) suggests that 'the greatest service evaluation can perform is to identify aspects of courses where revision is desirable'.

Lomax (1985) introduced the idea of *action research*, which she suggests should incorporate within the evaluation procedure a process or mechanism for action that leads to change. Moreover, she adds, 'good evaluation forms practice – it is no good to have sterile summaries of past events. Evaluation should improve practice and indeed generate new practice.' Lomax reports positive benefits from adopting an action research approach in terms of evaluating for course improvement at Kingston Polytechnic.

Mathias (1984) notes that formative evaluation may not receive the recognition, support or reward by the university for the time and effort involved in the improvement of course and enhancement of quality. If these approaches are not rewarded in a way that is perceived by course teams as fair and just, there will be little motivation for formative evaluation or the improvement it facilitates (Lazovik n.d.). For a further review of formative and summative evaluation see also (Murray 1984; Kogan 1986; Premfors 1986).

The goals of evaluation relate quite closely to the idea of formative and summative evaluation in that the purposes of appraisal lie within two categories: first, improvement and second, decision-making. Doyle (1975) suggests four purposes of evaluation: to provide a basis for administrative decisions on academic rank, tenure and promotion; as a basis for self-improvement; as a criterion for research on teaching; and to advise students on course selection. The first is summative in its aims and objectives, whereas the others relate to formative evaluation for improvement. In addition, Scribbins and Walton (1987) propose that appraisal is introduced to improve learning opportunities for students and to recognize and support effective practice. This can be achieved through identification of areas for development and improvement as well as areas for potential change.

Responses to evaluation

This section details the response to evaluation by British universities and specifically examines the response of university academic staff to such programmes. With the onset of evaluation in the USA and elsewhere, for example, Finland (Jappinen 1987), Australia (Marsh 1984) and Africa (Arubayi 1987), the topic is receiving considerable attention internationally. This focus on evaluation has now arrived in Britain, particularly in response to the Jarratt Report (1985). It appears that the idea of curriculum development has been carried forward from the schools sector, where it originated, to the university level where it is now being implemented (Green 1970). Eraut *et al.* (1980) explain how in the past few years in Britain universities have started to consider the systematic appraisal of their courses and the professional competence of their teaching. In the 1960s, institutions were preoccupied with recruiting appropriately qualified staff and with establishing courses to meet the growing student population. Curriculum innovations were introduced with little time to evaluate their effects or suitability. The goal set for universities now is to develop a system of evaluation that can help to improve the quality of courses and inform development and change.

In general, little published work is available relating to systematic evaluation in United Kingdom higher education institutions. However, Adelman and Alexander (1982) report a large-scale evaluation research programme in two colleges of education in England where it was found that evaluation information was used effectively for the modification and improvement of institutional practices. Furthermore, they found a genuine need to improve the quality of educational and organizational practices as a contribution to institutional growth and development.

How do university staff feel about the introduction of evaluation? Generally, the response by academic staff to the introduction of evaluation is positive. However, student evaluation is clearly a controversial issue, since student ratings constitute a perceived threat to the self-esteem of faculty members (Doyle 1975). Student evaluation can be ego-threatening since course evaluation must to some extent include instruction. Often individuals are anxious that evaluation will not be objective and well-defined, although most concede that some means must be found to achieve improvement. The overriding concern expressed by staff is that evaluation will be used for summative purposes. Ryan and Randhawa (1982) report that although some faculty members felt that evaluation of their courses was an invasion of their professional autonomy, most strongly supported the idea of course evaluation at the university level. Furthermore, Donald (1982) indicates that when course review was introduced in her university there was initial resistance but longer-term attitudes towards the scheme were positive. She explains that the purpose of these review procedures is to act as a planning device that raises consciousness about courses both within them and in relation to other courses in the university (see Chapter 2 for a description of this type of university scheme).

Rutherford (1987) interviewed staff at the University of Birmingham, and found that the majority were in support of evaluation as long as it was administered in a regular and systematic way. Staff proposed that evaluation would be acceptable if they had enthusiastic and positive leadership from senior academics and it was a regular feature as opposed to a one-off cosmetic exercise. They estimated that the passage of time could help to allay fears among staff and inspire confidence in the programme's ability to improve courses.

Some of the problems raised by academic staff are a reflection of their insecurities about the methods used to obtain student evaluations. Many express concern about evaluation, despite feeling the need for such evaluation, because they are uncertain about how this might be effected (Eraut *et al.* 1980). Murray and Newby (1982) found that faculty members were opposed to student evaluation questionnaires that were constructed by course leaders, without consultation, as they felt these would be tailored to fit individual needs. They preferred locally developed terms for the faculty, which could incorporate subsets of items in the same evaluation form for different levels or types of courses, e.g. lecture/seminar. Cave *et al.* (1988) suggest that these objections can be overcome by adopting a two-level evaluation instrument that includes core items used in all departments along with optional items developed by individual departments.

The general response by faculty members to the introduction of evaluation is for the most part positive. Tuckman and Oliver (1968) found that student feedback yields a more positive change than no feedback at all, and that such feedback about courses subsequently engenders behavioural change. As with staff views, there is little information about students' responses to evaluation. The existing evidence, however, suggests that students appear to be in favour of contributing to course appraisal. Lomax (1985) reports how student evaluations of courses at Kingston Polytechnic were perceived by students as particularly useful, since they had limited opportunity to participate in course review procedures. The 1989 summer edition of the *Daily Telegraph* Student Extra included an article concerning student views on teaching and courses. The consensus among students in this survey suggested that their views should be 'taken into account' in such appraisal schemes.

Methodological considerations

This section presents evidence in favour of using student evaluations and examines their reliability, validity and usefulness. Student ratings normally take place at the end of a course and are generally described as informal or formal. Informal or unsolicited student evaluations involve occasional comments to the instructor by a few students in the class. Such opinions may not represent the views of all students and are therefore less useful than more formal systems based on written responses to a set of short-answer questions concerning the course. Using questionnaires to record student judgements of their courses is generally the most favoured method of obtaining opinion (Winter-Hebron 1984). As Mathias and Rutherford (1982) note, the questionnaire is 'the most common form of evaluation technique employed by and recommended by lecturers'.

The task of trying to assess courses is a difficult one. No one method appears to be universally effective or accepted. Moreover, methodologies seem to vary from highly quantified to wildly impressionistic (Fraut *et al.* 1980). However, for the most part student evaluation forms are able to rate the achievement of specific course objectives. For example, a lecturer may ask students to identify any objective that has not been made clear during the course and to explain the reason for this lack of clarity. In format, most rating instruments encourage students to add comments about the course. Open-ended questions, such as 'how do you think the course can be improved?' or 'what did you like least/most about the course?', can be used to elicit student reactions that single response questions fails to tap (Centra 1979). Including an open-ended section on rating forms allows greater flexibility and provides useful insights into areas that may have been overlooked (Heim 1976). Regardless of their purpose, student rating forms should be succinct. It appears that 15–20 minutes should be the maximum time needed to complete a series of questions; anything longer strains student interest and tolerance and diminishes the quality of responses, especially if forms have been completed by the same students for several courses (Centra 1979).

Reliability refers to the consistency or precision of student ratings. To ensure that scores on an evaluation instrument are a true representation of student opinion, those scores must be reproducible upon subsequent testing of the same students rating the same course (Aleamoni and Spencer 1973). Reliability is often determined from studies of inter-rater agreement; that is, agreement among ratings by different students in the same class (Marsh 1984). In general, research indicates that students are honest and reliable raters of course performance (Swanson and Sisson 1971). Furthermore, Lazovik (1972) advances persuasive evidence to suggest that student judgements are consistent. She shows that the diversity of opinion among students becomes a stable measure when the judgements within a class are pooled to obtain a mean.

Centra (1979) claims that the reliability of student evaluations is very good, providing enough students in a class have made ratings. He proposes that average ratings based on as few as eight or ten students provide useful information, but larger numbers are preferable. It has also been found that rating forms given twice to the same students over a short period produce fairly stable results, as do ratings collected a year apart from the same students (Costin 1968). Talbot and Bordage (1986) report similar positive results for course evaluations that were generated directly by students rather than staff. This method, although useful for individual courses, does not allow comparison across courses or subsequent year groups.

The reliability of student ratings may be affected by: extraneous factors, such as computational error; the physical environment, such as lighting and heating; the general motivation for the task; and the task itself, e.g. if the questions are ambiguous or irrelevant. Random errors may also play a role, such as careless reading of items and accidental mismarking of rating scales. Nevertheless, the consensus on student evaluations is that they are reasonably free from random error and are certainly good enough to be used for course improvement purposes (Doyle 1975).

Validity refers to the meaning of student ratings. It is extremely difficult to validate student evaluation of courses because there is no single agreed criterion for effective instruction; that is, what constitutes a good or bad course. Some of the criteria used to validate student ratings include instructor self-evaluations, peer reviews and external evaluators who attend class sessions. Perhaps the most widely accepted criterion for the effectiveness of a good course is student learning. Thus, meaning can be assigned to student evaluations by relating them to measures of student learning. Frey (1973) found that student ratings of their courses were correlated with student learning. Doyle and Whitely (1974) also report moderately high correlations between student evaluations and learning.

A number of factors have been suggested to act as potential biases in student evaluations, e.g. class size, sex of raters, year in university, academic ability, when the evaluation is carried out, reason for taking a course and personality differences. Certain course characteristics may also affect subsequent evaluations, such as the subject matter, course workload and general interest in the course. Research has been carried out into each of these potential biases and the general findings seem to indicate that there is no significant difference in these criteria that would negate the effectiveness of evaluation itself (Costin *et al.* 1971). Centra (1979) reports findings based on over 300 000 students from 16 000 classes in 100 colleges revealing weak or insignificant relationships with course ratings for sex, year in university, academic ability and age. In addition, Feldman (1977) reports few differences between sexes on student ratings. The one area where consistent differences are found relates to class size. It appears that very small classes – those with fewer than 10–15 students – are most highly rated. Those with fewer than 15 students receive high ratings, while classes with 35–100 students receive the lowest ratings (Centra 1979). This is also supported by Marsh (1984), who found that students evaluate small classes more favourably. The timing of the administration of student evaluations may also be important. Crook *et al.* (1982) recommend that evaluations should be carried out shortly before the end of the year, as this provides information to course planners when it can have most impact on a course. It has been suggested that students may be more critical of their courses at the end of the year than at the beginning, although some evaluations may be affected by ratings that are less careful and more *laissez-faire* at the end of a course. It is therefore important to use the same starting and ending times for all groups to avoid confusion with the 'end of term' effect (Tuckman and Oliver 1968).

One final point concerning potential biases is whether or not student evaluations should be anonymous. The consensus appears to be that it is advisable to keep rating forms anonymous, thus ensuring that students cannot be penalized for giving courses low ratings. Some lecturers have argued that signing rating forms motivates students to give more thoughtful responses. However, research has shown that students who sign forms feel obliged to rate their courses more highly than those who do not (Stone *et al.* 1977). Doyle (1975) also points out that students are more willing to participate in evaluation when their anonymity is assured. In summary, research suggests that student ratings are reliable, reasonably valid, relatively uncontaminated by potential biases and seen to be useful by both students and faculty members.

What can students evaluate?

Research on student ratings of courses has identified several common dimensions or groups of items that can be evaluated (see Aleamoni and Yimer 1973; Bradley *et al.* 1983; Renner and Greenwood 1985). For course appraisal, the two most common dimensions for evaluation appearing in the majority of instruments devised are course organization and structure, and course workload and difficulty. Other categories include marking exams and assignments, the learning value of a course, the breadth of coverage, the general impact of the course on students (including 'liking value') and the global or overall effectiveness of the course. Not all rating instruments incorporate all of these evaluative criteria, but the majority include evaluations of organization and workload. Adelman and Alexander (1982) examined the usefulness of workload ratings, finding them to be much more satisfactory than other informal group-based techniques that tend to be affected by group biases. Rather than describe individual categories and questions at length, however, it is simpler to present typical categories and items drawn from an examination of existing questionnaires.

1. Course organization and structure:
   - course well organized;
   - material presented in an orderly manner;

- course objectives stated and pursued;
- class time well spent;
- expectations of student learning made clear;
- student participation lacking/good.

2. Workload/course difficulty:
   - pace of the course too fast/slow;
   - in relation to other courses, this workload was heavy/light;
   - too much/little material was covered;
   - course challenged me intellectually;
   - reading assignments very difficult;
   - too much work assigned out of class.

3. Marking and exams:
   - assignments added to course understanding;
   - exams reflected important aspects of the course;
   - assigned marks were fair and impartial;
   - helpful comments on assignments given;
   - general feedback valuable.

4. Course impact on students:
   - a great deal learned in this course/not much gained;
   - the course held my interest/boring;
   - the course was valuable/waste of time;
   - the course fulfilled my expectations;
   - the course stimulated my interest in this area.

5. Breadth of coverage:
   - course examined applications of research findings;
   - course gave background of ideas/concepts;
   - course gave different points of view;
   - course discussed current developments.

6. Global/overall ratings:
   - overall value of course (excellent to poor);
   - general quality of class time (excellent to poor);
   - classroom sessions worthwhile.

For further reviews of the criteria used in student evaluations the reader should refer to Finkbeiner *et al.* (1973), Renner and Greenwood (1983) and Marsh (1984).

The general format adopted by the majority of current American questionnaires is surprisingly uniform. First, questionnaires consist of a section concerning demographic details of the student, i.e. age, sex, full-time/part-time, year in university, etc. The questionnaires themselves invariably take the form of a rating scale. These scales are often bipolar and students are asked to rate the various aspects of their course on this scale. Doyle (1975) discusses the procedures that should be followed in constructing the questions used in rating scales. He suggests that questions should be phrased objectively and specifically. They should not be a composite of independent traits or qualities; rather each question should refer to a single type of activity. In addition, each question should be based on past or present accomplishments rather than what raters see as future promise. Furthermore, Doyle proposes that questions should be clear and relevant. Short statements that use simple and unambiguous terminology are recommended, as are questions that are precise and to the point.

Open-ended questions are also very popular and are included in most rating scales. These allow a certain amount of flexibility so that students can respond at length to questions such as, 'how much and in what ways do you feel this course has contributed to your education?' Another way to give individual course leaders some flexibility and choice, devised at Purdue University, is known as the 'cafeteria system'. This computer-assisted system allows course leaders to choose from a catalogue of 200 items. Selections can be added to a non-optional set of core questionnaire items. The flexibility inherent in such 'cafeteria' systems, while advantageous, is normally only employed by universities that have independent evaluation centres to support the complexity of this approach. While many American universities employ the cafeteria system (e.g. the University of Illinois at Urbana and the University of Michigan, Ann Arbor) most employ a standard rating instrument. This does not preclude course leaders from including additional items they would like addressed. It is important, however, to ensure that such additional items do not exceed the 15–20 minutes presentation time that is normally allocated to these classroom evaluations.

The evaluation exercise

In 1988, following a proposal to the Executive Committee of the Faculty of Social and Health Sciences of the University of Ulster, funding was provided to develop a student course evaluation programme. This reflected the faculty's commitment to making use of student feedback about courses in a more systematic way. This information, along with other types of evaluation, was recognised as being valuable for course development and course evaluation purposes. Based upon a review of course and unit evaluation questionnaires used in the United States and Canada, a common course evaluation questionnaire was devised for use by all courses within the faculty. Following discussions with the Academic Courses Committee, comprising members of all departments within the faculty, additional items were included in this questionnaire and the procedures for testing all courses in the faculty were agreed. A student evaluation booklet outlining the procedures to be followed was produced and circulated to all senior course tutors and course directors in the faculty, along with sufficient questionnaires to allow all year groups to assess their courses.

Questionnaire and evaluation procedures

The questionnaire was designed to cover a set of central questions concerning courses that had been shown to be areas that students could reliably rate in United States and Canadian questionnaires. The first section, on *attendance* and *course choice*, was included to determine how these two variables affect students' evaluations. The section on *course organization* sought student opinion on the provision and usefulness of course handouts and course assignment schedules. A section on *course workload* was included to assess students' feeling about the demands of their course as well as more general information about the course. Sections on *course content and delivery* were included to provide an insight into students' perceptions of the quality of teaching and the nature and challenge of the material presented to them. Sections on *course assignment/feedback* sought views on the relevance of assignments and the quality of feedback they received from staff. Further sections on *course integration and course impact* examined perceptions of course coherence and impact on students. The final sections of the questionnaire contained questions about the utility of *placement* and the students' *overall evaluation* of their course. Finally, a detachable separate sheet asked students to list two significant strengths and weaknesses in their course. Figure 6.1 shows the evaluation sheet.

Timing and instructions

All courses were administered the questionnaires within the last three weeks of term two. A standardized set of instructions was read out to students to inform them of the reasons for this exercise and the importance of their ratings. All questionnaires were given out and collected by the senior course tutor responsible for the administration of the course. While it is common practice to make student administrators responsible for questionnaire administration, it proved impossible to achieve this for the pilot study. The instructions were:

> The Faculty of Social and Health Sciences is carrying out, for the first time, a systematic student evaluation of all its courses. Student views about courses are being obtained through a common questionnaire. The information gained from this exercise will provide course committees with valuable insights into students' perceptions of their courses. This feedback will help us to improve the quality of courses that we can offer students. We would like you to help us by responding carefully to the questionnaire.

Students were asked to fill in their course code and their year group on the front of their questionnaire but were asked not to put any identifying mark on the form. Completed forms were returned to the senior course tutor, who passed them centrally for checking and onward transmission to the

Course: _____ Year: _____ *N* = _____

KEY: 5 = strongly agree; 4 = agree; 3 = neither agree not disagree;
      2 = disagree; 1 = strongly disagree

Course organization
The course appeared to be well organized   _____
The overall course handout was clear and useful   _____
Course assignment schedules were easy to follow*   _____

Course workload
Students were not given too much material during the course* _____
Units were very similar in terms of their demands   _____
Course material was not too difficult for me*   _____

Course content
Course content was sufficiently challenging   _____
Topics taught were appropriate to this course*   _____
Course content stimulated student interest in the area   _____

Course delivery
Lecturers turned up on time for classes   _____
The quality of teaching was generally high   _____
Course material was well prepared*   _____

Course assignments/feedback
Assignments were relevant to the course*   _____
Feedback on assignments was provided promptly   _____
Feedback on assignments was fair and useful   _____

Course integration
Units on the course fitted together well*   _____
The course helped me to appreciate differing perspectives   _____
As the course progressed links between units emerged   _____

Course impact
I learned a great deal on this course   _____
The course stimulated my interest in this area   _____
The course was useful to me*   _____

Placement
I found the work placement(s) useful*   _____
The placement experience was personally rewarding   _____
Placement helped me appreciate the value of course material _____

Overall course evaluation
In general this course was valuable to me   _____
I would recommend this course to my friends*   _____
The overall quality of the course was good   _____

Please list two strengths and two weaknesses of your course:

Figure 6.1 Faculty of Social and Health Sciences student course evaluation questionnaire.

computer centre. Twenty-five courses within the faculty completed the questionnaire, with over a thousand individual forms being processed.

Scale validity and reliability

Since the selection of sections and items was determined by a review of comparable schemes in the United States and Canada, combined with the fact that most questionnaires cover very similar areas and questions, the validity of the items in the questionnaire will not be addressed here. However, the reliability of the scales used in the current study was assessed using Cronbach's alpha:

Course organization	0.37
Course workload	0.26
Course content	0.44
Course delivery	0.69
Course assignments/feedback	0.56
Course integration	0.58
Course impact	0.80
Placement	0.79
Overall course evaluation	0.70
Overall alpha for all scales	0.85

As can be seen, with the exception of the first three scales the alpha scores are within an acceptable range. The overall alpha score for the evaluation instrument is 0.85. It is perhaps not surprising in retrospect that students should experience difficulty in judging course organization, workload and content. Usually they have little comparative experience of other courses to draw upon when making these ratings.

Analysis and reporting

The data analysis and reporting was of two types. One set of analyses addressed individual courses, while another examined issues across courses. First, a series of standard analyses was carried out for all courses and returned to senior course tutors. This included the individual means of each item on the questionnaire by year group, section means and the overall mean for the group. In addition, the overall faculty means for each item and section were circulated to aid course comparison. This information was discussed at the relevant course committee meeting during the completion of the annual course review forms. Each course committee was asked to return its student ratings, with its course review document, and to include comments in a space provided on the rating form. During the annual courses review meeting the students' ratings and the course committee's responses to them were available for scrutiny by committee members. This allowed panel members both to question senior course tutors about the ratings of their courses, and to note particular strengths and weaknesses in the faculty's overall course provision.

While most of the benefits derived from this type of course evaluation exercise will naturally flow from course development at the level of individual course committees or teams, the data also allow an examination of more general issues that span courses. For example, the single most striking feature of students' ratings across courses in the present exercise was the low rating given to the item concerning prompt feedback from tutors on coursework. This highlighted a deficiency in this respect across the majority of courses in the faculty. The Academic Courses Committee of the faculty, following discussion of this issue with senior course tutors, has revised the faculty guidelines to ensure that course committees and staff members are more clearly aware of this problem and that coursework deadlines are adhered to by tutors. The previous standard of three weeks turn-round to assignments has been replaced with four weeks.

A second noteworthy aspect of the ratings reflected a very positive response by students on professional courses to their placement experiences. With the growing pressure to shorten courses, it was reassuring to faculty members to find that professional placement experiences are so highly valued by students. Ratings for innovative placements in the more traditional academic disciplines, although generally favourable, produced a much more differentiated pattern of response. Closer examination of subjects' responses within these courses revealed that the much greater variety of placement experience being offered in these areas (reflecting the wider employment opportunities that they offer) may cause problems for students in relating coursework to their placement activities. These findings illustrate the importance of including enterprise skills in the undergraduate curriculum (see Chapter 17).

Student attendance and ratings

The database also allows an examination of the relationship between students' ratings on different parts of the questionnaire. To examine the relationship between student attendance and ratings a series of correlations were carried out between attendance and students' scores on individual questions. Table 6.1 summarizes these findings.

While correlation does not imply causation, the findings provide some insight into the relationship between student attendance and ratings of different aspects of courses. The low correlations found between course organization, course workload and course delivery suggest that the demands of the course and the way it is taught do not have any systematic effect on students' attendance! This is surprising since it is often assumed that the workload demands and standard of delivery of courses contribute to students' poor attendance. The results offer no support for this

Table 6.1   Correlations: student attendance and course evaluation

Course organization	0.07
The course appeared to be well organized	0.04
The overall course handout was clear and useful	0.05
Course assignment schedules were easy to follow	0.07
Course workload	0.03
Students were not given too much material during the course	0.03
Units were very similar in terms of their demands	−0.03
Course material was not too difficult for me	0.08
Course content	0.13**
Course content was sufficiently challenging	0.05
Topics taught were appropriate to this course	0.09
Course content stimulated student interest in the area	0.13**
Course delivery	0.02
Lecturers turned up on time for classes	0.01
The quality of teaching was generally high	0.05
Course material was well prepared	−0.01
Course assignments/feedback	0.12**
Assignments were relevant to the course	0.12**
Feedback on assignments was provided promptly	0.10**
Feedback on assignments was fair and useful	0.05
Course integration	0.10**
Units on the course fitted together well	0.06
The course helped me to appreciate differing perspectives	0.09*
As the course progressed links between units emerged	0.08*
Course impact	0.12**
I learned a great deal on this course	0.16**
The course stimulated my interest in this area	0.09*
The course was useful to me	0.08*
Placement	0.12**
I found the work placement(s) useful	0.14**
The placement experience was personally rewarding	0.10
Placement helped me appreciate the value of course material	0.07
Overall course evaluation	0.09**
In general this course was valuable to me	0.10**
I would recommend this course to my friends	0.07*
The overall quality of the course was good	0.07*

* $p < 0.01$; ** $p < 0.001$.

viewpoint. The aspects of courses that appear to influence attendance most
are: whether the course stimulated interest; assignments being appropriate
for the course and the provision of prompt feedback on assignments; the
course being of value to the student; learning during the course and having
a useful placement experience.

The findings suggest that students' attendance could be improved by ensuring that courses:

- stimulate student interest,
- are perceived as valuable and increase learning,
- provide assignments that are perceived as relevant to the course and give prompt feedback on these assignments,
- include placements that students see as being useful to them.

These findings are similar to those reported in American student rating studies, with stimulation of student interest and the provision of constructive feedback being the two most commonly reported factors in students' ratings of courses.

Do students in different year groups rate courses differently?

To determine whether students at various stages of their degree programmes differ in their ratings of courses, ratings by year group were examined using analysis of variance to determine possible differences across the sections of the questionnaire (see Table 6.2).

Table 6.2   Mean ratings (all students) by year group by questionnaire section

Questionnaire section	Year 1	Year 2	Year 3
Course organization	3.6	3.6	3.5
Course workload	3.2	3.3	3.3
Course content	3.8	3.8	3.6*
Course delivery	3.8	3.9	3.7
Course assignment/feedback	3.4	3.5	3.0*
Course integration	3.8	3.9	3.7
Course impact	4.2	4.3	4.3
Placement	4.1	4.0	4.2
Overall evaluation	4.1	4.1	4.0

* $p < 0.01$.

As can be seen from the table, there is considerable consistency in responses across year groups to the different sections of the questionnaire. This suggests that the different year groups are responding to the questionnaire in a similar way, in line with other studies (e.g. Centra 1979). The two significant differences reported involved lower scores by third year students on the course assignment/feedback and course content sections of the questionnaire. It was decided to investigate this further by examining these differences at the item level (see Table 6.3).

Table 6.3   Students' mean scores by item and year group: course content

	Year 1	Year 2	Year 3
Course content was sufficiently challenging	4.0	4.0	3.9
Topics taught were appropriate for this course	3.7	3.8	3.4*
Course content stimulated interest in the area	3.7	3.8	3.7

* $p < 0.01$.

This revealed that third-year students did not feel that the topics covered during their programme were as appropriate for the course as the other two year groups. Since the mean scores for third-year students were quite high anyway, this may simply reflect the greater diversity of topics that are typically taught in the final year of degree courses. As the evaluation exercise is repeated over a number of years a clearer idea of the nature of this difference will undoubtedly emerge. It remains to be seen whether such differences reflect a genuine problem in this area requiring attention to the integrative nature of material in final year courses, or are simply a normal feature of all degree programmes.

In contrast, the differences revealed by examination of individual items across year groups regarding feedback suggested the need for more urgent remedial action. Table 6.4 reveals that feedback from assignments is not perceived by third-year students as being provided promptly and that this is not as fair or as useful as in other years. Clearly this suggests that while there is a general faculty issue concerning the promptness of feedback, it is particularly evident in the final year of courses. The point of these two simple examples is to highlight the developmental and monitoring potential that a course evaluation scheme offers in terms of identifying

Table 6.4   Students' mean scores by item and year group: feedback

	Year 1	Year 2	Year 3
Assignments were relevant to the course	3.9	4.1	3.8
Feedback on assignments was received promptly	2.7	2.8	2.1*
Feedback on assignments was fair and useful	3.5	3.5	3.1*

* $p < 0.01$.

problems in course provision within and across courses. The value of such a scheme is likely to prove more effective over time as more comparative data are built up within the university.

The advantages of a course evaluation scheme

Adoption of a course evaluation approach was found to offer several positive advantages as a preliminary step towards a more comprehensive evaluation scheme. First, since it is distinctly less threatening to individual members of staff than an instructor- or unit-based programme, it allows staff members to appreciate the developmental benefits that can be derived from such evaluations. Second, it provides useful additional information on student views that can be further elaborated upon in staff/student course committee meetings. Third, by running the scheme over several years, a valuable database of student opinion about courses can be built up, providing course teams with a means of assessing the effects of course changes. Fourth, it assures students that their opinions about courses are being considered in a systematic way by those responsible for both their delivery and administration. While student opinion concerning courses is only one of many criteria that can be used to evaluate the quality of course provision, it is worth noting that students' overall impressions of their course are likely to play a major role in the views they express to others about both their course and the institution itself.

Conclusions

The value of obtaining views about how individuals feel about their course experiences is something that, while well accepted in other sectors, such as business and the Civil Service, has been slow to permeate the United Kingdom higher education system. The rationale for the inclusion of evaluation in the university system is encapsulated by Dressel (1976: 338). This is 'to improve the quality of learning and increase the percentage of students who attain the important and agreed goals of learning. All else flows out of and is secondary to that goal.'

Evaluation of courses is necessary for several reasons. First, it is important to evaluate courses directly and not be misled into assuming that good learning in terms of exam achievement necessarily reflects a good course (Fox 1984). Second, the quality of courses must be monitored to ascertain that they are meeting agreed standards and to aid course development by identifying shortfalls and strengths. Evaluation of courses has been shown to produce marked improvements in course effectiveness (Murray 1984).

In the current chapter, the advantage of implementing a course evaluation scheme as an initial step to introduce staff to the positive benefits that can be gained from such programmes was advocated. Ultimately, however, as Adelman and Alexander (1982) note, course evaluation should be something that 'rocks the boat' and institutions should be suspicious of evaluation programmes whose outcomes can be painlessly accommodated. The inclusion of a systematic course evaluation scheme that is supported by the university's course review structures ensures that structured feedback from students is reported both to those who are responsible for delivering and developing courses and to those who administer them. It is important that university administrations afford equal weighting and recognition to the developmental advantages of this information rather than using it solely for judgemental purposes. Over-emphasis of the judgemental aspect of evaluation has been found to remove the developmental advantages that such schemes offer (Rutherford 1987). Newstead (1989) captures this best in suggesting that British universities would be well advised to emulate the openness, thoroughness, democracy and detailed specifications of evaluations in American institutions. Finally, student course evaluation schemes represent an important formal acknowledgement by the university system that student views about their courses are an integral part of both the setting and monitoring of standards in higher education.

References

Adelman, C. and Alexander, R. (1982) *The Self Evaluating Institution*. London: Methuen.

Aleamoni, L. M. and Spencer, R. E. (1973) The Illinois Course Evaluation Questionnaire: a description of its development and a report of some of its results. *Educational and Psychological Measurement*, 33: 669–84.

Aleamoni, L. M. and Yimer, M. (1973) An investigation of the relationship between colleague rating, student rating, research productivity and academic rank in rating instructor effectiveness. *Journal of Educational Psychology*, 64(3): 274–7.

Arubayi, E. (1987) Assessing academic programmes in colleges of education: perceptions of final year students. *Assessment and Evaluation in Higher Education*, 12(2): 105–14.

Bradley, J., Chesson, R. and Silverleaf, J. (1983) *Inside Staff Development*. Windsor: NFER.

Cave, M., Hanney, S., Kogan, M. and Trevett, G. (1988) *The Use of Performance Indicators in Higher Education*. London: Jessica Kingley.

Centra, J. A. (1979) *Determining Faculty Effectiveness*. London: Jossey-Bass.

Costin, F. (1968) A graduate course in the teaching of psychology: description and evaluation. *Journal of Teacher Education*, 19: 425–32.

Costin, F., Greenough, W. T. and Menges, R. J. (1971) Student ratings of college teaching: reliability, validity and usefulness. *Review of Educational Research*, 41(5): 511–35.

Crook, J., Woodward, C. and Feldman, E. (1982) A question of timing: when is the best time to survey graduates to obtain feedback about an education programme. *Assessment and Evaluation in Higher Education*, 7(2): 152–8.

Donald, J. G. (1982) A critical appraisal of the state of evaluation in higher education in Canada. *Assessment and Evaluation in Higher Education*, 7(2): 108–26.

Doyle, K. O. (1975) *Student Evaluation of Instruction*. Lexington, MA: D.C. Heath & Co.

Doyle, K. O. and Whitely, S. E. (1974) Student ratings as criteria for effective teaching. *American Educational Research Journal*, 11(3): 259–74

Dressel, P. (1976) *Handbook of Academic Evaluation*. London: Jossey-Bass.

Elton, L. (1984) Evaluating teaching and assessing teachers in universities. *Assessment and Evaluation in Higher Education*, 9(2): 97–115.

Eraut, M., Connors, B. and Hewton, E. (1980) *Training in Curriculum Development and Educational Technology in Higher Education*. Research into Higher Education Monographs.

Feldman, K. A. (1977) Consistency and variability among college students in rating their teachers and courses: a review and analysis. *Research in Higher Education* 6(3): 223–74.

Finkbeiner, C. T., Lathrop, J. S. and Schverger, J. M. (1973) Course and instructor evaluation: some dimensions of a questionnaire. *Journal of Educational Psychology*, 64(2): 159–63.

Fox, D. (1984) What counts as teaching? *Assessment and Evaluation in Higher Education*, 9(2): 133–43.

Frey, P. W. (1973) Comparative judgement scaling of student course ratings. *American Educational Research Journal*, 10: 149–54.

Green, J. A. (1970) *Introduction to Measurement and Evaluation*. New York: Dodd, Mead & Co.

Heim, A. (1976) *Teaching and Learning in Higher Education*. Slough: NFER.

Jappinen, A. (1987) Current situation regarding the development and use of performance indicators in Finland. *International Journal of Institutional Management in Higher Education*, 11: 2.

Jarratt Report (1985) *Report of Steering Committee for Efficiency Studies in Universities*. London: HMSO.

Kogan, M. (1986) The evaluation of higher education – an introductory review. *International Journal of Institutional Management*, 10(2): 125–39.

Lazovik, G. (n.d.) Evaluation of college teaching – guidelines for summative and formative procedures. *Association of American Colleges*, Occasional Paper.

Lazovik, G. (1972) Course evaluations: what do they mean? *University Times*, 12 October.

Lomax, P. (1985) Evaluating for course improvement: a case study. *Assessment and Evaluation in Higher Education*, 10(3): 254–64.

Marsh, H. W. (1984) Student evaluations of university teaching: dimensionality, reliability, validity, potential biases and utility. *Journal of Educational Psychology*, 76(5): 707–54.

Mathias, H. (1984) The evaluation of university teaching: context, values and innovation. *Assessment and Evaluation in Higher Education*, 9(2): 79–96.

Mathias, H. and Rutherford, D. (1982) Lecturers as evaluators: the Birmingham experience. *Studies in Higher Education*, 7(1): 47–56.

Miller, R. I. (1986) A 10-year perspective on faculty evaluation. *International Journal of Institutional Management*, 10(2): 162–8.

Murray, H. G. (1984) The impact of formative and summative evaluation of teaching in North American universities. *Assessment and Evaluation in Higher Education*, 9(2): 117–32.

Murray, H. G. and Newby, W. G. (1982) Faculty attitudes toward evaluation of teaching at the University of Western Ontario. *Assessment and Evaluation in Higher Education*, 7(2): 144–51.

Newstead, S. (1989) Staff evaluation in American universities. *The Psychologist*, 2(3): 92–5.

Premfors, R. (1986) Evaluation basic units: 7 fundamental questions. *International Journal of Institutional Management*, 10(2): 169–74.

Renner, R. and Greenwood, G. E. (1983) Rating student ratings. *Assessment and Evaluation in Higher Education*, 8(3): 269–73.

Renner, R. and Greenwood, G. E. (1985) Prof. X: how experts rated his student ratings. *Assessment and Evaluation in Higher Education*, 10(3): 203–12.

Rutherford, D. (1987) Indicators of performance: reactions and issues. *Assessment and Evaluation in Higher Education*, 12(2): 94–104.

Ryan, A. and Randhawa, B. (1982) Evaluation at the university level: responsive and responsible. *Assessment and Evaluation in Higher Education*, 7(2): 159–66.

Scribbins, K. and Walton, F. (1987) *Staff Appraisal in Further and Higher Education*. Bristol: Further Education Staff College.

Scriven, M. (1967) *The Methodology of Evaluation*. Social Sciences Education Consortium.

Stone, E. F., Rabinowitz, S. and Spool, M. D. (1977) Effect of anonymity in student evaluations of faculty performance. *Journal of Educational Psychology*, 69(3): 274–80.

Swanson, R. A. and Sisson, D. J. (1971) The development, evaluation and utilisation of a departmental faculty appraisal system. *Journal of Industrial Education*, 9(1): 64–79.

Talbot, R. W. and Bordage, G. (1986) A preliminary assessment of a new method of course evaluation based on directed small group discussions. *International Journal of Institutional Management*, 10(2): 185–93.

Tuckman, B. W. and Oliver, W. F. (1968) Effectiveness of feedback to teachers as a function of source. *Journal of Educational Psychology*, 59(4): 297–301.

Winter-Hebron, C. (1984) An AID for evaluating teaching in HE. *Assessment and Evaluation in Higher Education*, 9(2): 145–63.

7

Institutional Research and Quality Assurance

Roger Woodward

Introduction

Institutional research may be defined as the activity in which the research effort of an academic institution is directed to the solution of its own problems and to the enhancement of its own performance. This dauntingly wide brief is perhaps best characterized by making two distinctions. First, I draw the distinction between institutional research and other research centres. An institutional research unit in a university differs from other research centres that the university might establish in that the role of the latter is to harness the research resources of the university to the solution of the problems of external clients, whereas for institutional research it is the university itself that is the 'client', and the problems addressed by institutional research are those that arise within the university in the execution of its primary functions of teaching and research. A second helpful distinction to make is that between institutional research and the more familiar area of research in higher education. For research in higher education, findings are of interest in their potential to characterize general features of institutions, their students and the staff who work in them. For institutional research, however, this question of generalizability of findings is not so central, since it is the sponsoring institution that is the essential focus.

It follows from this that the aims of institutional research cannot be established as an autonomous set of professional precepts, developed in concert with like-minded scholars and in isolation from specific institutional needs. Instead, they are largely determined by a requirement to be responsive to needs as they arise in a particular institution. Generalization is more likely to apply to methods and approaches than to findings.

The need for universities to concern themselves with assuring quality in their teaching provision has been keenly felt in recent years. As argued in Chapter 1 and elsewhere in this book, there are many reasons that can be adduced for this, at many different levels of analysis. Perhaps at the most general level is the feeling that grew throughout the 1980s that individual recipients of the services of large institutions had the right to expect good service from those institutions. The obvious power of the large bureaucracy, relative to that of the individuals they served, could not be used to evade their responsibilities to their clients. The interest in questions of quality assurance in the commercial world has been discussed in Chapter 2. At a more specific level, there are dangers in the current situation in the UK. Although the literature on teaching appraisal in higher education is extensive (e.g. Elton 1984; Marsh 1984), there is little evidence for its widespread and systematic use within the university sector. Since the publication of the Jarratt Report in 1985 in UGC/UFC has moved rapidly and, at least initially, with minimal consultation to establish appraisal of the research performance of universities.

Whatever the merits of the current system of research appraisal and of arguments concerning teaching appraisal, the present state of affairs leaves universities dangerously exposed to a position in which teaching is allowed to suffer. This remark is not intended to be pejorative in the sense of being critical of the commitment of those who work in universities, but it is consonant with common sense and, no less importantly, with theoretical predictions from accepted models of human and animal behaviour. Behaviour analysts have, for many years, known of the concept of behavioural contrast (e.g. Fantino and Logan 1979). When an animal is required to perform a task with two components, each of which has independent but similar schedules of consequences, it will distribute its effort about equally. If the schedule is then changed so that the reward for performance on one of the components is increased then, not surprisingly, effort directed to that component increases but effort directed to the unchanged component does not remain unchanged; it decreases to the same extent that effort to the first component increases. This effect is known as behavioural contrast. It occurs in a range of experiments and is an important consideration in the implementation of clinical therapies.

The situation in which university teaching staff are required to work on two tasks, teaching and research, and where the reward structure for the latter is increased, leads to the prediction that effort directed to teaching will, in the absence of any change in reward or recognition for that task, decrease. This prediction is difficult to put to empirical test since the required measurements have not been taken, and if they were the very act of measurement would probably affect the behaviour in question.

The task I now turn to address is that of moving beyond quality as an aspiration for university teaching and examining some steps for its practical implementation. In particular, I will focus on the role of institutional research in meeting some of the provisions required by BS 5750.

Some contributions of institutional research in meeting the requirements of BS 5750

Roger Ellis, in Chapter 2, has considered at length the requirements that a university might be expected to meet if it were considered adequate to BS 5750 in its teaching function. My aim in this section is not to go over that material in detail but to identify some key features in which institutional research may have a key role.

There is a danger in over-inclusiveness. The nature of institutional research, as outlined above, and the encompassing nature of the provisions of BS 5750 could lead to an identification of the function with the requirement, with the institutional researcher crying, 'I can play that part,' like Bottom in Shakespeare's *A Midsummer Night's Dream*, to each role that arises. Describing a role for institutional research in this area is easier than delimiting that role. My aim here is to consider some specific aspects of BS 5750 where the functions of institutional research are particularly useful.

Record keeping

BS 5750 lays particular stress on the requirement for record keeping. Section 4.6 reads: 'The supplier shall develop and maintain records that demonstrate achievement of the required quality and effective operation of the quality system.' The records that are required for monitoring university teaching would need extensive consideration. They would certainly include objective measures of student performance, data sometimes known as 'performance indicators'. They would also include measures of student views on the quality of aspects of university provision. I will discuss this latter point more extensively in a later section, but first I will outline the particular role of institutional research in the maintenance of records of objective data.

Records are, of course, properly kept by the administrative departments of a university, who have the responsibility to make returns to statutory national bodies. Information returned to such bodies is used to provide valuable publications of the nationwide statistics. In the United Kingdom these would include the CVCP/UFC 'Management Statistics and Performance Indicators' and the USR series 'University Statistics'. The records which, I would argue, an Institutional Research office should keep are subsets of these or, indeed, need not be physically distinct. They would be functionally arranged in such a way as to permit the analysis of data for the solution of likely problems. The information required for quality monitoring is mostly present in administrative records, but work needs to be done to make this information apparent and usable. In many cases there is, in common parlance, the problem of not being able to see the wood for the trees.

An example of this would be the computation of a common index of student intake quality. In the UK this would normally be the 'A' level points score. While the central administrative record would properly keep a record of the grades of each 'A' level held by individual students, there needs to be a downloading of these data to permit the calculation of the consequent points score. Were this calculation a straightforward matter it could easily be effected within the central record, but the calculation is not straightforward. There are, at the time of writing, three different methods of counting the 'A' level score in operation by the national bodies in the UK: the UCCA, the USR and the CVCP/UFC Committee on Performance Indicators. All prescribe that only the best three held by any individual candidate shall count, but they differ in the points awarded for the different attainment grades and in the definitions of students over whom the averaging should be conducted. For quality monitoring purposes calculations will have to be undertaken with specific reference to any particular national comparison that may be required. There may also be circumstances in which a new calculation may be desired for use in an institution. We may, for example, wish to drop the restriction that only the three best examination results may count. A particularly valuable use of these records for quality monitoring purposes is that of estimating likely effects on the measures of proposed changes in institutional policy. For example, if it were proposed to increase the minimum entry requirement to a university, we would wish to estimate its likely effect on recruitment, on 'A' level points score and on final degree attainment.

A further problem with records kept for administrative purposes is that the level of analysis required for returns to national bodies may be inadequate for the quality monitoring purposes envisaged here. The subject category 'business and management', for example, may contain many courses in any one university. To record data on, say, withdrawal rates in this area may demonstrate a problem in comparison with nationally available data, but it is only by examination of the data from individual courses that the institution can find where the problem lies and consequently determine appropriate remedial action. This problem may, indeed, be exacerbated as universities increasingly move to a unit- or module-based system, rather than a course-based system.

Before we leave the topic of data records it is worth commenting that, while they are a necessary component for the assurance of quality, they have quality concerns of their own. Gose (1989) has discussed problems in assuring the accuracy of data of this sort, and there are many standard approaches to checking for errors in data files. However, the approaches used are almost always checks internal to the system, such as tests for values in acceptable ranges. Checks are seldom made by referring the data record to some external source of evidence. For example, we may keep a record of applicants who were offered a place at the university but who declined the offer. Do we ever check the data by writing to a sample of those individuals to enquire if the record squares with their perception of events?

In some cases the issue of quality of records extends beyond the concept of accuracy. Properly applied, 'accuracy' is a question that can only be asked of situations where there is some external definitive referent with which it is, at least in principle, possible to compare the data. If the data agree with the referent we call them accurate, and if not we call them inaccurate. Often such an external referent is lacking, either for want of proper definition or because the arbitrariness of a specified definition is not fully appreciated. In cases like this questions of accuracy may only obfuscate questions of quality, perhaps because they divert attention from questions about the appropriateness of the definitions with which we work. An example of this is the issue of data concerning student voluntary withdrawals. A student may be recorded as having withdrawn from the university when he in fact transferred to another course. We may safely call this an error: the record should have shown a transfer code instead of a withdrawal code. Suppose, however, that the student really did withdraw, in the sense that he signed a form to that effect, and then the next week enrolled on another course in the same institution, perhaps because he was unaware of correct procedures or perhaps because a new option was presented. The student will not regard himself as having withdrawn from the institution, but it is misleading to regard the data as inaccurate in this: the issue is one of definition. A further complication arises if a student fails examinations badly but, rather than having his studies terminated, is offered a stringent programme of resits and perhaps a requirement to repeat a year. This may prove too daunting a prospect and the student leaves. The records may, without error, show him as having voluntarily withdrawn; but this will probably be far from the student's perception of events.

Records for the assurance of quality must contain results of subjective ratings as well as the objective data discussed above. Most immediately we think of student questionnaires but, as discussed in Chapter 2, the 'clients' for higher education can be construed as categories of individual other than the student. In particular, they can include employers. Questionnaire preparation and analysis are central issues for institutional research. It is important to consider this under the heading of 'record keeping' because of the value of gathering data from questionnaire studies over a period of time. The record of these results can allow results from a class in a given year to be set in the context of corresponding data from other years. Employers' perceptions, where these can be continuously monitored, can also provide valuable year by year comparison.

There is an important continuation of my quotation from section 4.6 of BS 5750 given above: 'The record shall be retained and made available for evaluation by the purchaser's representative.' It goes without saying that the confidentiality of any individual student's data or opinions would not be breached, but the implication of Section 4.6 is that students and, perhaps, employers should be given the fullest access to results of student feedback on courses.

All of this assumes, of course, that measurement instruments are in place. The continuous measurement needed to generate the records required by BS 5750 places particular burdens on the measurement instruments. It appears that they need to be kept the same from year to year or there is no sense in which longitudinal comparisons can be made on the record. At most, revisions would have to be minimal. The requirement for good measurement instruments may exceed our present capabilities, and this introduces another relevant provision of BS 5750.

The development of measurement instruments

Section 4.4 of BS 5750, on planning, reads: 'The supplier shall establish a procedure for ... the identification of any measurement involving measurement capacity that exceeds the known state of the art or any new measurement capability needed to inspect the product.' Saranne Magennis, in Chapter 14, contrasts the rich young man in the Bible, who asked what he should do to inherit eternal life, with the enquirer who seeks what he must do to enhance the quality of university teaching. The former was told to give up everything that he had but the latter should try everything that he has. Magennis argues for a range of approaches and for the importance of having the professionals concerned closely identifying with and, indeed, assuming the ownership of appraisal systems for university teaching.

Research into measurement instruments for student views on teaching has been undertaken for many years and good measurement instruments are available (see Marsh 1984, for example). However, as can be seen in Chapter 6, much of the research is done in an American context and its applicability to other cultures of university education in Europe may be questioned. Diversity is an important source of the richness of European university education and this diversity extends to individual institutions within countries. There is an important function, therefore, in developing or adapting measurement instruments to meet the particular circumstances of individual institutions. However, if comparisons between units, courses or departments within institutions are to be possible then there must be commonality of measurement instruments within the university. The need, therefore, is for research and development of measurement instruments for the individual institution. This, as described in this chapter's introduction, is the specific function of institutional research.

Research is clearly needed into an area of measurement for the recognition of teaching quality: that is, what do we mean by good or effective university teaching? We can, and do, ask students to judge whether the teaching they had experienced was good or bad; but there is little articulated characterization on what is meant by good or bad teaching in this context. Institutional research has been heavily involved in a project aimed directly at this problem, and this is discussed more fully by my colleagues Saunders and Saunders in Chapter 11. In this project we attempt such a characterization through a process of reflective dialogue among expert teachers. Research into what students perceive as good teaching is at a more elementary stage. A repertory grid approach is being employed and is yielding some useful initial material.

Student views on teaching

I now turn to consider the more specific topic of student views on teaching. In this section I consider some general issues and in the next I present a short case study.

The definition of quality offered by Roger Ellis as 'that which gives complete customer satisfaction' raises immediate questions of whom we mean by the client (following Lewis Elton's point, in Chapter 8, that 'client' is a better word than 'customer' for the recipient of a professional service) and how we measure satisfaction. Roger Ellis has discussed possible interpretations of the word client. For present purposes I take the student as client. This is not to reduce the validity of other nominations, but the case seems strong for three reasons. First, it is the students who make their investment of time and experience in the teaching service that the university offers. This is an important investment since, for the majority of students, it is made only once in a lifetime. Second, it is the student who is the most direct recipient of the service. Third, it is the student who makes the selection among alternative suppliers of the service, i.e. the different universities to which admission might be sought. This choice is not unconstrained, of course, since any university may decide to admit or to refuse any particular student.

In considering the measurement of student satisfaction with teaching we should immediately address what is perhaps the most fundamental question: why should we be concerned with student satisfaction? Funding of universities does not depend on it in a manner similar to that in which the funding of UK universities depends partly on the quality of their research. Students, as noted above, for the most part have only one experience of full-time university education and so the test of satisfaction important to the motor industry – 'Would you buy the same car again?' – has no analogue. The choice that young people make of universities is not informed by an authoritative publication on students' satisfaction with the services of the alternative suppliers.

The unambiguous answer to this question is the moral one. The very fact that we invite young people to entrust us with their once-in-a-lifetime opportunity for higher education behoves us to do all in our power to ensure the quality of the experience. If this sounds too sententious we should consider Lewis Elton's point that the moral imperative to excellence, irrespective of extrinsic sanction, is an important characteristic of a profession.

A more pragmatic reason for attending to student satisfaction with teaching is that students, although they cannot themselves remake their decision in the light of experience, can tell others. The potential for such personal recommendation to affect applicants' choice of university will depend on the extent to which the university takes its students from a localized geographical area, where it will be more likely that applicants will be personally aquainted with current and former students of the university. The University of Ulster is such a case: 76 per cent of its undergraduate students come from Northern Ireland. In 1987 the Institutional Research Unit asked all incoming students to complete a questionnaire concerning sources of influence in their choice of university. Respondents were offered six categories of people who could be expected to have significant influence on their choice: school principals, school careers officers, other school teachers, university staff, parents and former students. They were asked to tick those who had influenced them in favour of attending the University of Ulster. Former students were by far the largest category of positive influence, ticked by 65 per cent of respondents. It thus appears that there are gains in application to the university as a consequence of the satisfactory experience of former students. We cannot, however, be sure that it was satisfaction with teaching that these former students had in mind when making their recommendations.

We now turn to a specific case study in the measurement of student satisfaction conducted in the University of Ulster in 1989.

A case study investigating student views on teaching

There are at least three approaches to gathering data on which to base the appraisal of teaching. We may consider an expert systems approach in which characterization of successful teaching is developed by systematically examining the practices and the views of those recognized to be experienced and successful in this field. A second approach, which this study is concerned with, is to secure students' views on the teaching performance of their tutors. This is common in the USA but only recently becoming established in the UK. A third approach is that of taking objective measurement, such as examination success, perhaps corrected for students' entry level to produce what is sometimes referred to as an index of 'value added', to determine what students have gained from their education at an institution (see PCFC/CNAA 1990, for a review of approaches to such measurement).

A fourth approach would be the systematic and critical appraisal of the behavioural interactions of which commonly occurring teaching situations are comprised. Such an analysis has the potential to go beyond discovering *that* teaching has been successful to discovering *how* it has been successful. Examples would be the identification of behaviours likely to maintain student concentration or to identify appropriate checks for student comprehension.

It is not clear how we should judge the relative status of results produced by these four approaches. There is some evidence that student and staff ratings tend to agree, but both bear little relation to objective criteria; this is a variety of what de Winter Hebron (1984a) described as a 'collusion of expectation' in which students and staff mutually reinforce untested expectations. Consideration of this issue would, no doubt, be informed by data but it would be wise to consider in advance what judgements might be appropriate in the event of conflicting results. Perhaps the soundest judgement at this stage is that each source of data is necessary but not sufficient in forming a judgement about successful teaching. Data from experts are insufficient because of the danger of cultures of expertise becoming divorced from community requirements, a danger well encapsulated it the familiar jibe against medical expertise: 'the operation was a success but the patient died'. Data in the form of student feedback are insufficient because of the danger of operationalizing good teaching as popular teaching. There is sometimes said to be a danger in higher education of lecturers courting popularity by avoiding the most difficult issues in their curriculum. It might appear that objective data are sufficient, or at least have a more fundamental status than the others. We must, however, consider it possible that a student attains his or her success in spite of, rather than because of, the institution's provision. Students may have a very poor opinion of the standard of teaching and, recognizing the need to pass their examinations, seek help from other sources. Objective descriptions of effective teaching behaviours are also necessary in order to determine the steps that might be taken to enhance teaching performance.

The Institutional Research Unit has projects on hand to obtain data from three of these sources. Securing expert teachers' perceptions of good teaching is the subject of Chapter 11 by Christine Saunders and Eric Saunders. The present study is concerned with students' views.

There is an extensive literature on appraisal of teaching but, as is discussed by Saranne Magennis in Chapter 14, little derives from experience in the British Isles. Among the most emphasized points are:

1. The distinction between formative and summative appraisal; that is, appraisal for development and appraisal for evaluation and judgement, with the former, of course, being preferred by participants. Although very attractive, this distinction is hard to sustain for it is difficult to imagine a developmental appraisal that is not, in some sense, judgemental, and it is also difficult to imagine a judgemental appraisal which is not also potentially developmental.
2. The distinction between appraisal of courses and of teaching on those courses is frequently made, but it is hard to imagine that students could be expected to distinguish between a good course badly taught, and vice versa.

3. An important distinction is that the appraisal of teaching is not to be identified with the appraisal of teachers. The latter must take many more factors into account, including the context in which teaching is delivered as well as other aspects of the teacher's work. This would encompass research, consultancy and community service but, more importantly for the present problem, activities such as curriculum development and course leadership and administration.

The present study

In the present study, which is described in full by White *et al.* (1990), it was considered best to attempt to be exhaustive in the sense that all finishing students of the university should have the opportunity to express their views, and so a questionnaire was the only feasible option for data collection. de Winter Hebron (1984b) concluded that using questionnaires to record judgements is the most favoured method of obtaining student opinion. Although anonymity is often considered best in studies of this sort we wished to relate the data collected to objective data on student performance and so a confidential rather than an anonymous approach was employed.

Two qualities that must be attained by any measurement instrument are validity (the instrument measures what it purports to measure) and reliability (it does so consistently). Validity is a hard concept to deal with for we have no definitive source of student opinion with which to compare results from our questionnaire. Face validity (do the questions appear to address the issues under consideration?) can be established as well as relationship with less formal sources of information. Reliability can be examined in terms of internal consistency by examining the relationship among answers. Lazovik (1972) advocated the use of rating scales from which a derived class mean gave a reliable measure.

The present questionnaire used Likert-type rating scales and also a range of open-ended questions to which respondents could give answers unconstrained by alternatives presented by the investigators. Questionnaires should aim to have a completion time of not more than 15–20 minutes (Centra 1979). We aimed for a completion time of 12 minutes.

The questionnaire was constructed and submitted for panel evaluation seven times before the investigators were satisfied with content, wording and layout. It was then submitted for piloting to classes who would not form part of the final investigation. The objective of the pilot was to identify any questions that needed clarification and to check on required response times. In the event, few changes were required as a result of the pilot. The final version of the questionnaire is given in Appendix 7.1.

Administration

The questionnaire was to be administered to all completing students in the university in 1989, a total of nearly 3200. Administration by post would be costly and suffer from the usual difficulties of low response rate from postal enquiries. Administration during classes would be very costly in terms of staff time and also difficult to arrange at a time when classes were coming to an end as students prepared for their final examination. The solution arrived at was to administer the questionnaire at the graduation ceremony. Discussions with administrative staff organizing the ceremonies confirmed that this would be feasible provided the time taken was short. Questionnaires were placed on individual seats before the ceremony and the Registry Official in charge gave instructions for its completion along with other instructions for the graduands. They were collected immediately on completion by institutional research staff. Those not attending the ceremonies were sent questionnaires by post with prepaid reply envelopes.

There were deep concerns about this arrangement. Would the graduands take the exercise seriously? Would the instant judgements required be spurious because respondents had little time to consider their answers? The first concern was difficult to evaluate; experience alone would provide the answer. The second concern was countered by two arguments. First, it seemed implausible that individuals who had daily experience as students in the university for up to four years would not have already considered in some depth the questions we were asking. Second, the question of whether instantaneous answers would differ significantly from answers which respondents could consider at their leisure could be put to empirical test by comparing answers from the postal enquiry, recognizing, of course, that there could be respects in which the two groups differ.

Results

In the event the administration of the questionnaire went very smoothly. It was well received by respondents, with very few hostile or flippant responses. In total, 2718 completed questionnaires were received, an overall response rate of 85.1 per cent. Response rate by course varied from 79 to 100 per cent for questionnaires administered at graduation and from 35 to 50 per cent for questionnaires administered by post. The question of whether answers would differ between the postal and face-to-face administration was examined. There were only two questions that evoked a difference in answers, and these differences were slight.

Another reservation concerned the possibility that evaluations of teaching gathered at the point of graduation would merely be a reflection of student success: those who did well might give positive responses while those who did less well might give poor responses. This was tested by comparing ratings between honours graduates of award categories from

Table 7.1 Mean ratings on questions concerned with lectures, seminars and practicals and overall yearly mean ratings analysed by award category of graduates (standard deviations in parentheses)

	Award category				
	I	*IIi*	*IIii*	*III*	*All*
Lectures	3.8 (0.7)	3.9 (0.8)	3.7 (0.8)	3.6 (1.0)	3.8 (0.8)
Seminars	3.5 (1.0)	3.6 (1.0)	3.3 (1.0)	3.4 (1.1)	3.5 (1.0)
Practicals	3.6 (1.0)	3.7 (1.0)	3.4 (1.0)	3.3 (1.1)	3.6 (1.0)
Year 1	3.6 (0.8)	3.7 (0.9)	3.6 (0.9)	3.7 (1.0)	3.7 (0.9)
Year 2	3.7 (0.9)	3.7 (0.8)	3.6 (0.9)	3.3 (1.1)	3.7 (0.9)
Year 3	3.9 (0.9)	3.9 (1.0)	3.7 (1.0)	3.3 (1.1)	3.8 (1.0)
Year 4	3.9 (1.0)	4.1 (0.8)	3.7 (0.9)	3.5 (1.1)	3.8 (0.9)

first to third class honours. Results are presented in Table 7.1, which shows some evidence of a limited tendency for lower evaluations among those who did less well. Lower second and third class honours graduates gave slightly lower than average ratings.

Reliability may be assessed by the low variance of ratings within classes, the primary unit of analysis. The internal consistency of answers may be assessed by relating answers on numerical ratings with verbal answers to open questions. This showed good agreement; some examples of comments from respondents who gave low ratings are shown in Table 7.2. Although Table 7.2 presents only three examples, it illustrates a widespread tendency for verbal comment to reflect numerical ratings.

If quality is identified with student satisfaction then it is important to ask what degree of satisfaction the respondent must express before we can properly say that satisfaction has been attained. We can, if it is felt appropriate, use the upper two points on the five-point Likert-type scale, where these have been identified as 'good' and 'very good'. In that case the percentage of respondents giving these ratings, rather than the mean rating, would be the usable measure. A low level would always give cause

Table 7.2 Examples of responses to an open question concerning the greatest difficulty for respondents who gave low ratings on numerical questions

Numerical answer	*Verbal answer – greatest difficulty*
Q. 14: lecturers available = 2	'access to lecturers'
Q. 3: availability of library books = 2	'access to books'
Q. 16: feedback = 1	'inability of lecturers to accept feedback'

for concern and it is gratifying to note that ratings were generally good in this study. It is always more fruitful, however, to base conclusions on comparisons rather than on absolute values. These comparisons can be longitudinal (are this year's students less satisfied than last year's students?) or across courses (are students from Course A less satisfied than those from Course B?). The former requires data to be collected using the same instrument over a period of years: a desirable state of affairs, as discussed above, but universities want usable data soon after an investigation, rather than having to wait for the annual data to accumulate. In the case of comparisons across courses we need to know the fair basis for comparison. A tutor for a subdegree course where ratings compared unfavourably with those of a degree course might justifiably object that the differences in ratings were not to be associated with comparative deficiencies in teaching quality but with differences in level of course: subdegree students could be supposed generally to give less favourable ratings than do degree students. Institution-wide enquiries, such as the present study, can provide the evidence on this issue. A measurement model can be established that allows the extraction of variance associated with any significant factors, such as mode and level of study or age and gender composition of the class.

Dissemination of results

It is important in an exercise such as this to stress the positive results, as well as to attempt to understand the less pleasing results. It is thus good to notify faculties of the courses that receive the highest rating from students. The course is the only natural unit of analysis. Averaging results over the university or even over faculties has little meaning except to provide a baseline against which course results may be judged.

Means of ratings are the usual form in which data are reported, but the variance must be low for this to be meaningful. In some cases students on a particular course may give widely differing assessments. This is uncommon, but where it does happen it appears to be that an innovative teaching style appeals strongly to some students but is disliked by others. In these instances the data must be examined in categorical form before reporting.

Summary

In this chapter I have described some of the functions of institutional research and related them to specific requirements of BS 5750. Record keeping and the development of measurement instruments were discussed. The particular advantage of institutional research in the role of quality assurance is that it is institution-wide, yet sees institution specificity as no disadvantage. The measurement of student satisfaction was particularly important since it is close to the essence of the concept of quality as encapsulated by the Standard. This area illustrates the advantages of the institution-wide concerns of institutional research.

References

Centra, J. A. (1979) *Determining Faculty Effectiveness.* London: Jossey Bass.

de Winter Hebron, C. (1984a) Some problems and pleasures of teaching part-time management students. *Studies in Higher Education*, 9(2): 169–81.

de Winter Hebron, C. (1984b) An aid for evaluating teaching in higher education. *Assessment and Evaluation in Higher Education*, 9(2): 145–63.

Elton, L. (1984) Evaluating teaching and assessing teachers in universities. *Assessment and Evaluation in Higher Education*, 9(6): 97–115.

Fantino, E. and Logan, C. (1979) *The Experimental Analysis of Behavior.* San Francisco: W. H. Freeman and Company.

Gose, F. J. (1989) Data integrity: why aren't the data accurate? *AIR Professional File*, 33.

Lazovik, G. (1972) Course evaluations: what do they mean? *University Times*, October.

Marsh, H. W. (1984) Student evaluations of university teaching: dimensionality, reliability, validity, potential biases and utility. *Journal of Educational Psychology*, 76(5): 707–54.

PCFC/CNAA (1990) *The Measurement of Value Added in Higher Education.* London: CNAA Publications Unit.

White, O. M., Curry, N. and Woodward, R. J. (1990) Student views on teaching and other aspects of provision in the University of Ulster. Mimeo, University of Ulster.

Appendix 7.1

(A2)

STUDENT SURVEY
ALL DATA COLLECTED ON THIS QUESTIONNAIRE WILL BE PROCESSED ON COMPUTER IN ACCORDANCE WITH THE UNIVERSITY OF ULSTER'S REGISTRATION UNDER THE DATA PROTECTION ACT (1984).

LABEL (positioned for window envelope)

/5 – 11   /12 – 15   /16

I would be most grateful if you would complete and return this questionnaire in order to assist the University with its Course Review and Academic Planning procedures. Your responses will be confidential. Thank you for your co-operation.

Dr. O. M. White

PLEASE READ ALL INSTRUCTIONS AND QUESTIONS CAREFULLY.

PLEASE RETURN THE COMPLETED QUESTIONNAIRE TO THE *RIGHT-HAND END* OF YOUR ROW AS SOON AS YOU CAN.

ANSWER ONLY THOSE QUESTIONS APPLICABLE TO YOU AND YOUR COURSE.
IF A QUESTION DOES NOT APPLY PLEASE LEAVE THE ANSWER COLUMN UNMARKED.

<u>BEGIN HERE:</u>

PLEASE CIRCLE (eg. M /Ⓕ) to indicate your gender: M / F   —/17

1. Which statement best describes your situation?
   (please tick one)

   I am seeking employment   ——

   I have secured Permanent employment   ——   —/18

   I have secured Temporary employment   ——

   I will be pursuing further Full-Time study   ——

                                     Other   ——   —/19

   _____
   (Please specify)

PLEASE CIRCLE THE APPROPRIATE CHARACTER TO INDICATE YOUR ANSWERS TO THE FOLLOWING QUESTIONS: 5 – VERY GOOD; 4 – GOOD; 3 – AVERAGE; 2 – POOR; 1 – VERY POOR. IF ANY OF THESE DO NOT APPLY TO YOU OR YOUR COURSE, PLEASE DO NOT MARK THE ANSWER COLUMN.

2. If you have secured a job, please indicate to what extent it makes use of your education at the University of Ulster:

	Very Good				Very Poor	
	5	4	3	2	1	—/20

3. How would you rate the availability of the resources you may have needed for your course?

	Very Good				Very Poor	
Library books	5	4	3	2	1	—/21
Lab/Workshop Facilities	5	4	3	2	1	—/22
Micro Computer Facilities	5	4	3	2	1	—/23
Mainframe Computer Facilities	5	4	3	2	1	—/24
Sports Facilities	5	4	3	2	1	—/25
Other (Please specify) _____	5	4	3	2	1	—/26

IF YOUR COURSE DID NOT INCLUDE PLACEMENT OR SANDWICH ELEMENTS PLEASE GO STRAIGHT TO QUESTION 8.

4. If your course included Placement periods, how would you rate these with regard to the following?

	Very Good				Very Poor	
Work Experience	5	4	3	2	1	—/27
Future Employability	5	4	3	2	1	—/28
Relevance to Course	5	4	3	2	1	—/29

5. How would you describe the supervision of your Placement(s) by the University?

	Very Good				Very Poor	
	5	4	3	2	1	—/30

6. How would you rate the University's contribution to your preparedness for your Placement?

	Very Good				Very Poor	
	5	4	3	2	1	—/31

7. How many visits did your supervisor pay you per Placement?   —/32

8. Please assess the standard of teaching in your:

	Always				Never	
Lectures	5	4	3	2	—	—/33
Seminars	5	4	3	2	1	—/34
Practicals	5	4	3	2	1	—/35

9. How would you rate the coordination of subject matter between Lectures, Seminars and Practicals which formed your course?

  5   4   3   2   1   —/36

10. How would you describe lecturers' attitudes to any problems you may have brought them?

  5   4   3   2   1   —/37

QUESTIONS 11, 12, 13 AND 14: 5 – ALWAYS; 4 – USUALLY; 3 – SOMETIMES; 2 – RARELY; 1 – NEVER.

	Always				Never	
11. In your opinion was class content generally relevant to your assignments, etc?	5	4	3	2	1	—/38

12. Did your lecturers make use of the following teaching aids?

Handouts	5	4	3	2	1	—/39
Overhead Projector	5	4	3	2	1	—/40
Slide Projector	5	4	3	2	1	—/41
TV/Video	5	4	3	2	1	—/42

13. Do you feel teaching aids were constructively used?

  5   4   3   2   1   —/43

14. Were your lecturers available outside class when you wanted to see them?

  5   4   3   2   1   —/44

QUESTION 15: 5 – FAR TOO MANY; 4 – TOO MANY; 3 – ABOUT RIGHT; 2 – TOO FEW; 1 – FAR TOO FEW.

15. Were there suitable numbers of Lectures, Seminars, Practicals and Assignments for your requirements on the course?

	Far Too Many				Far Too Few	
Lectures	5	4	3	2	1	—/45
Seminars	5	4	3	2	1	—/46
Practicals	5	4	3	2	1	—/47
Assignments	5	4	3	2	1	—/48

16. How would you rate the marking of your assignments, etc, with regard to:

	Very Good				Very Poor	
Fairness	5	4	3	2	1	—/49
Providing Feedback	5	4	3	2	1	—/50

17. Please place these assessment methods in your order of preference (6 = most pref.; 1 = least):

Exams	—	—/51
Assignments	—	—/52
Practicals	—	—/53
Project	—	—/54
Continuous	—	—/55
Other	—	—/56

Please specify: _____ —/57

18. Please indicate your overall view of the Teaching Quality of your course in each year of study:

	Very Good				Very Poor	
1st Year	5	4	3	2	1	—/58
2nd Year	5	4	3	2	1	—/59
3rd Year	5	4	3	2	1	—/60
4th Year	5	4	3	2	1	—/61

Other (Please specify) _____ —/62

19. Which subject on your course do you regard as having been the best taught in each year of study?

1st Year _____ —/63–64

2nd Year _____ —/65–66

3rd/4th _____ —/67–68

20. Which subject do you regard as having been the least well taught in each year of study?

1st Year _____ —/69–70

2nd Year _____ —/71–72

3rd/4th _____ —/73–74

21. For each year of study, please list any subject you regard as having been irrelevant to your course:

1st Year _____ —/75–76

2nd Year _____ —/77–78

3rd/4th _____ —/79–80

22. Please state below two main sources of difficulty you encountered in pursuing your studies:

RECORD 2

_____ —–/1–2

_____ —–/3–4

23. If you would like to make any further comments or suggestions please use the space below:

_____ —–/5–6

8

University Teaching: a Professional Model for Quality

Lewis Elton

Introduction

It is becoming increasingly accepted in the commercial world that the quality of a product or service cannot be maintained either externally from outside an organization or internally from the top of the organization. What is required – and this concept is a principal tenet of total quality management (TQM) – is a total commitment to quality by all members of the organization, although there will always be a need for some external pressure to ensure the continuation of this commitment. In some ways such a commitment may seem a familiar concept to those who carry out a profession, since it is an important feature of any professional work for those who engage in it to accept full responsibility for their work. In practice, in university teaching – and I shall use the term 'universities' throughout this article to stand for all types of higher education institutions – this has frequently fallen short of what is required, for three quite separate reasons. First, quality criteria have not been adequately identified and it is indeed neither simple nor uncontroversial to do this. Second, academics have in the past seen their responsibility as pertaining largely to themselves and to their professional associations rather than to their clients and to the organization in which they worked. Finally, we shall see that there must be considerable doubt as to whether those engaged in university teaching can in any real sense be described as professionals.

In universities, we are concerned with two central activities, teaching and research. Academic attitudes and practices are quite different in these two activities and, within the current academic culture, it is much easier to identify quality and professionalism in research than in teaching (Elton and Partington 1991). One difficulty in connection with university teaching, as with any public service, is that, in the case of service industries, health care and education, the product and the production line – taking over these words from manufacturing industry – are based largely on the actions of qualified professionals. Yet the behaviour, whether effective or not, of professionals is largely hidden from objective scrutiny (as pointed out in Chapter 2).

This is demonstrably true of university teaching, which its practitioners often consider to be an activity conducted in private between not always consenting adults. To make professionals publicly accountable for their work and to do so without affecting the work negatively is a crucial issue faced by all the professions, for it is perfectly possible for public accountability to lead to a deterioration of quality (Elton 1991a).

This chapter will, within the context of university teaching, first discuss the concepts of quality and quality assurance and then turn to the question of professionalism. Only then will it be possible to put forward a model for quality assurance in university teaching and to tackle the difficult question of how to provide public accountability and at the same time to maintain or even increase quality.

Quality and quality assurance in university teaching

The word 'quality' is used at present most confusingly in two very different senses. In the first sense it carries with it connotations of excellence (Pirsig 1974). For this I shall use the word 'standard'. The word 'quality' I shall confine to its technical meaning, as defined by the British Standards Institution (BS 5750, 1987 and 1990), i.e. 'the totality of features or characteristics of a product or service that bear on its ability to satisfy a stated or implied need,' and I have already used it in this sense in the introduction. I prefer this definition to the similar one of Ellis (1988: 7) as that 'which gives complete customer satisfaction', since the British Standards definition explicitly recognizes that the 'stated or implied need' may in a professional service be in part defined by the professional who supplies the service. Ellis (Chapter 2), in explaining his definition, says that 'for much professional activity the producer plays the role of the consumer in judging the quality of his actions'; hence there is no real difference between the two definitions. Incidentally, the professionals perform a dual role, not only do they have an expert understanding of the needs of their customers, they also have needs of their own, related to the maintenance of their professionalism.

Who is the 'customer' in higher education? Is the word even appropriate for a professional relationship or would 'client' be more appropriate? Words carry possibly inappropriate concepts and meanings with them as they are metaphorically transferred to other contexts, and although identifying such contradictions is part of the stock-in-trade of academic discourse, academics have sadly failed to recognize it in the pseudo-business discourse of the past decade. With this reservation in mind, let us analyse the concept of 'customer' in higher education.

It is common at the moment to say that students are the customers because they pay for the service in fees, but – using the same kind of language – in another sense they are the 'product' for which employers, government, professional associations and society are the customers. In many European countries the very idea of students as customers, let alone as products of higher education, would be totally rejected; they are partners with academics in the pursuit of knowledge. In any case, most of the fees and the other costs of university teaching are borne by the government via the funding councils. So is it the latter who are the customers? What is clear is that there is a multiplicity of customers, not all of whom can be completely satisfied simultaneously.

So on to quality assurance. In the commercial market, the external pressure, which I postulated as needed to fulfil the requirements of TQM, is provided by the customers, who may have a choice between different producers who supply goods or services, and who also have means of redress if they are not satisfied. To provide informed choice, even for such a simple object as a refrigerator, it is necessary to have consumer reports that provide appropriate performance indicators, something that has proved exceedingly difficult, highly contentious and probably very unreliable for, say, a degree course (Johnes and Taylor 1991). To provide redress is even more difficult, since dissatisfied students have lost more than money: they have lost perhaps three years of their lives. For all these reasons, it has in the past been largely the professionals who have been the guardians of quality in a professional service, not the customers. But they should not be the sole arbiters in this matter; they may become negligent or they may be wrong or they may use their power unethically. Following earlier remarks about TQM, I suggest that they should have the prime responsibility for controlling the quality of their work, but that the external pressure that is always necessary should come through public accountability for their work. Other possibilities, which include external measures of quality, offend against the basic tenet of TQM, stated earlier, that the maintenance of quality cannot be imposed from the outside.

Any scheme for quality control requires three steps:

1. Agreement on the needs that have to be satisfied.
2. Identification of the activities which have to be assessed for their quality.
3. Establishment of procedures that ensures that this quality is maintained.

The documentation of these three steps constitutes a 'quality assurance system' and the availability for public scrutiny of that documentation then provides what is called 'quality assurance'.

Agreement on needs should come out of a negotiated accommodation between the needs of all the relevant 'customers' and of the professionals who provide the service. It relates to the objectives which the service aims to achieve and to the standards of the processes by which they are achieved. In practice, not all concerned have equal access to the resulting negotiations.

Thus the objectives of a university degree in, say, engineering, are negotiated between engineering teachers and their professional association, possibly with an input from government, regarding the numbers and kinds of engineers that the course is to produce. The standards at which these objectives are to be achieved are likely to involve the same groups with the addition of an external examiner in the discipline of the degree and colleagues in the university in other disciplines. Neither objectives nor product standards are directly influenced by the students: those who consider taking the course exert an influence through the choice that they can exercise between different courses open to them, while those on the course may have influenced it through their evaluation of it. In the main this influence is often restricted to its process standards – what in the here forsworn sense of the word quality is often referred to as the 'quality of the learning experience' – but this need not be so. Society has even less direct influence, although it has not been unknown for its influence to make itself felt through the press. In less directly vocational courses, say in history, students may have a great influence, but the main direct influence on objectives and product standards is likely to come from the teachers of the subject and the external examiner, who between them also represent the interests of their discipline.

The specification of needs separately in terms of objectives, product and process standards is quite essential. An illustration from the hotel trade may make this clearer: the objectives and often the process standards of a hotel are given in its brochure; its product standards are provided by the AA star rating; quality assurance is provided by an assessment of the effectiveness of the control processes that ensure the quality of the service, by, say, the *Good Hotel Guide*. It would appear that the assessment in this case is wholly external, but in practice this is not so – for the best hotels in the *Guide* it is clear that the assessment essentially consists of a verification of the internal quality control processes, i.e. the quality assurance system, together with a sampling that these processes actually provide quality control. Similarly, in a university, one objective might be to produce a degree course in engineering, with its product an honours degree, while the process standards would relate to the total experience of students on the course.

The idea that the effectiveness of a quality assurance system can be verified selectively in terms of what one or more particular control processes reveal is common in financial audits and is called an 'audit trail'. It was introduced into university quality assurance by Professor Stewart Sutherland, Chair of the sub-committee of the Committee of Vice-Chancellors and Principals (CVCP 1990) that set up the Academic Audit Unit, experience of which in part provides a basis for a practical scheme for quality assurance in university teaching, to be described below. However, before one can formulate such a scheme, it is necessary to ask how far university teachers can in fact claim to be professionals in the sense that this term has been used so far.

University teaching as a profession

What might be the criteria of a profession? The list below has been gathered mainly from Ellis (1988) with some ideas of my own, but it is similar to those provided by others, e.g. Lewis and Maude (1952: 55) and Larson (1977: 208). It is in no sense authoritative and others may add to or subtract from it. I suggest that a list of criteria for a profession ought to include all or most of the following:

- an underlying discipline or cognitive base;
- a body of practitioners;
- a disciplinary organization;
- induction, training and licensing of members;
- communication channels between members;
- rewards and sanctions for members;
- self-reflection, leading to improvement;
- corporate evaluation and feedback;
- a code of ethics and accountability to the profession;
- corporate accountability to society;
- quality assurance of the profession.

The professions of law and medicine would probably satisfy all the above criteria and critics might, not unjustifiably, add another:

- the ability to ensure high standards of remuneration.

This is not, however, a criterion that would apply to the engineering profession, which otherwise also satisfies all the criteria, or to academics as researchers, who otherwise satisfy many of the criteria. Their underlying discipline is not of course 'research', but the discipline in which they research, such as physics or history. However, their claim that they are members of a profession of, say, physicists or historians is not strong, since they cannot apply sanctions to members and do not have a corporate accountability to society. It is also doubtful whether peer review provides quality assurance, although the process of peer reviewed publications assists in the maintenance of standards.

The situation is much worse, when it comes to teaching, as was recognized many years ago by Ashby (1969: 5), who noticed 'a curious gap in the attitude of the profession to that part of its duty which concerns teaching.' In principle, there is an underlying discipline, and the Germans even have a word for it, *Hochschuldidaktik*, i.e. the pedagogy of university teaching, but few academics are aware of it. There is also a body of practitioners, namely the body of university teachers, but there is no disciplinary organization, induction and training are barely minimal, few know of the journals that should be their communication channels, and neither rewards nor sanctions exist to any significant extent. There is now evaluation and feedback, through appraisal of individuals and increasingly through self-validation corporately, and there is quality assurance through such bodies as the Council for National Academic Awards and the Academic Audit Unit. There is essentially no formal accountability to either the profession or society.

It is apparent that university teachers at present do not constitute a profession. One major obstacle, which could be removed fairly easily, is their lack of training. If this were removed, many of the other criteria for a profession would in due course be fulfilled. No other profession would consider that those who had not been trained and induced into the profession would be able to maintain quality criteria or even enunciate such criteria. In fact, in the past few years many of our academic leaders have publicly declared that they did not know how to judge quality in university teaching, thereby demonstrating that, as academic teachers, they were less than professional. In contrast, a small band of quite unimportant people who have actually made university pedagogy their discipline have for over a decade published papers (e.g. Elton and Partington 1991) and written books (e.g. Brown and Atkins 1988) that clearly showed that there was no particular difficulty in establishing criteria for quality in university teaching in general, and quite recently (Tysome 1991) the Further Education Unit of the Department of Education and Science has made an attempt to formulate these in terms of competencies. Once proper training has been established, academics may also be expected to engage in the important activity of self-reflection (Schön 1983).

There is a second and more serious difficulty, which stems from a conflict between multiple loyalties. As teachers, academics ought to have a double loyalty, to their discipline, which represents *what* they teach, and to university pedagogy, which represents *whom* they teach. The first loyalty, which coincides with their principal research loyalty, is therefore to their discipline association, and this is generally their strongest and often only loyalty. The locus of their second loyalty is more in dispute. It could be the appropriate disciplinary association, i.e. the Society for Research into Higher Education, but for many it is more likely to be their university, for that is where the students are whom they teach. It could be both. Academics as teachers thus potentially have three legitimate and separate loyalties, not an easy position to be in. It is, however, inevitable and has to be allowed for in the professionalization of university teaching. This conflict of loyalties is not actually confined to teaching; there is – or at least ought to be – a similar conflict in research, where 'individual academics and leaders of research entities have a much more direct and active interest in maximising their operations in a project market of their speciality than in the prosperity of their university' (Ziman 1991). This latter conflict is sometimes avoided by a neglect of the institutional loyalty, but this is neither desirable nor even possible in teaching.

Once academics are professional as teachers, they will have to be aware of one feature of professionalism that was enunciated most brutally by Shaw (1908), namely that a profession is 'a conspiracy to hide its own shortcomings'.

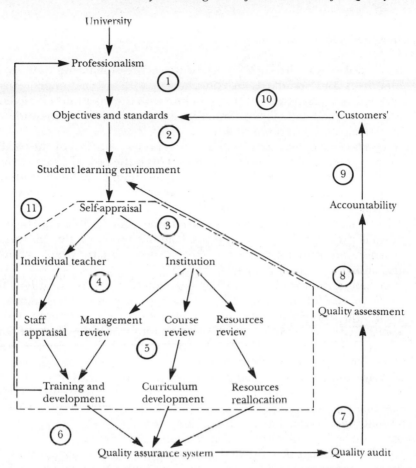

Figure 8.1 A model for quality assurance in university teaching.

A model for quality assurance in university teaching

We now face a difficulty. In discussing quality assurance for university teaching, we postulated that in line with the tenets of TQM, quality assurance had to arise out of the professionalism of the providers, but we then found that university teachers did not constitute a profession. At the same time, all the evidence of the past decade points to the fact that the strongest pressure for a greater professionalism arises from the public demand for quality assurance. This is a dialectical situation, in which, at any one time, demands for better quality assurance lead to greater professionalism, which in turn leads to better quality assurance. Our proposed model includes a feedback process that allows for this. It is described in Figure 8.1.

The stages of the model, with examples of how they might work out in practice, are as follows:

1. The university, through its growing professionalism, defines its objectives and standards in consultation with its customers. (Institutional and departmental plans, in line with the institutional mission, are established in collaboration with representatives from students, employers and the community.)
2. These objectives and standards are interpreted in terms of the totality of the student learning environment. (This is the task of course teams, which, in addition to academics, again might include students, employers and members of the community, as well as those from the central services of the university.)
3. The learning environment is monitored and evaluated through formal procedures of self-appraisal at the levels of the individual teacher and of the institution. (These procedures are preparatory to the similar procedures under 4 below.)
4. The self-appraisal of the teacher is followed by staff appraisal; the self-appraisal of the institution by the appraisal of courses, management and resources. (The current procedures for staff appraisal in some of the universities and those for appraising departments and institutions, which derive in the polytechnics from their CNAA experience, provides examples.)
5. Where appropriate, the outcomes of the appraisals lead to staff training and development, course development and resource reallocations. (Some examples of good practice are beginning to become available across the higher education system.)
6. Procedures 3–5 constitute the quality assurance system.
7. Quality assurance is in the first instance provided through scrutiny by an external quality audit or similar process. (The Academic Audit Unit is developing good procedures, but it at present lacks externality.)
8. A direct quality assessment of the learning environment is provided by regular external peer review and the work of external examiners, which are monitored by the audit process. (At present, such practices exist, but they are mostly inadequate.)
9. Accountability to 'customers' is provided through both audit and assessment, both publicly available. (The Academic Audit Unit issues reports to audited universities, which the Unit expects them to publish. Peer reviews and external examiners' reports are not published at present.)
10. In the light of evidence emerging from the quality assurance process, the university redefines its objectives and standards in consultation with its customers.
11. As a result of training and development, the staff of the university increase their professionalism. Much of this is likely to be in course teams, in connection with curriculum development.

The model follows the general approach to quality assurance in this book:

(a) Setting standards for a good service (1, 2, 10).
(b) Monitoring performance against standards (3, 4).
(c) Remedying shortfalls (5, 11).
(d) Involving consumers in setting and monitoring standards (1, 9, 10).
(e) Managing and evaluating the system for the above (6, 7, 8).

An important feature of the model is that it is developmental. It will fail if the quality assessment is either too weak initially, so that the university does not feel itself under pressure to become more professional, or remains in place too long, so that the university remains inappropriately under tutelage.

The present position, since the abolition of the binary line that divided universities from polytechnics, is that all Higher Education Institutions (HEIs) will be audited by an agency corporately responsible to them, similar to the current Academic Audit Unit. This agency is therefore not independent of the HEIs as a body. The White Paper (DFS 1991) and the resulting Further and Higher Education Act of 1992 incorporated such an audit, but added to it an external quality assessment, generated by and directly responsible to the new Funding Councils. After a pilot assessment exercise in both England and Scotland, which was based largely on the traditions and experience of HMI, who conduct assessments wholly externally, Scotland has abandoned this approach and is instead proposing that the assessment should consist of an evaluation of an institution's own quality assessment by assessors recruited for this task by the Funding Council. These assessors would be experts recruited largely from HEIs; what is not clear is whether these would include not only subject experts, but also, as they ought to, educational experts. The use of external experts parallels my proposal of external peer review (see point 8 in Figure 8.1); however, the Scottish proposal is more external to the HEIs than my suggestion, which is that not only the assessment process but also the outcomes should be audited and the results be made publicly available. The English Funding Council has proposed a second pilot exercise, so that its final decisions are not likely to be available for some time. Whatever form the assessment process will eventually take, in both England and Scotland, it is quite definite that it will influence funding decisions. This direct coupling of quality assessment to funding decisions has serious dangers, in that it removes any real ownership of the assessment from the HEIs. Past experience has shown that this can result in quality actually decreasing; whether the Scottish approach, which at least starts from self assessment can avoid this danger remains to be seen; any approach that is even more external – such as the one that was tried out in the pilot exercises – is most unlikely to avoid it.

Cost-effectiveness through appropriate resourcing mechanisms

Having cast doubt on the wisdom of placing the Quality Assessment Unit with the Funding Councils, I want to draw attention to a way that this placing could be turned to advantage. It is well known that 'throwing money at problems' is rarely a good way to solve them; what is perhaps less well known is that quite small sums, judiciously targeted, can have an effect out of all proportion to their size. An Assessment Unit within the Funding Councils might be well placed to give appropriate financial advice.

The argument depends essentially on the premise that institutions as well as individuals classify their needs in general in a hierarchy originally put forward by Maslow, which is such that a need at a particular level is not perceived as important until those on the levels below are satisfied. The hierarchy has five levels:

5. Self-actualization.
4. Self-esteem.
3. Love and belonging.
2. Safety.
1. Physiological.

There are of course individuals whose personal hierarchies to some extent reorder these levels – one only has to think of the proverbial artist starving in a garret who considers self-actualization more important than the physiological needs for food and shelter – but an institution, whose behaviour is governed by the behaviour of its many individual members, is unlikely to allow such reordering.

While crumbling buildings may in due course reduce universities as institutions to the physiological level, this has not yet happened. On the other hand, in the present financial climate, where bankruptcy looms, many have clearly found themselves working at the safety level. The result has been what I have called elsewhere (Elton 1989) the Micawber effect in higher education, namely that the difference between being just in the black and just in the red has an effect on institutional attitudes out of all proportion to its size. When resources just exceed basic needs, universities can work at least at level 3, i.e. they tend to cooperate with each other, even if it may be unreasonable to expect that they love each other. If such cooperation is reciprocated, they may move on to develop their own individualities in accordance with their value systems, traditions etc. Broadly speaking, that was the experience of the universities during the expansion of the 1960s and even of the less expansionist 1970s. In the hard 1980s, when resources just failed to match basic needs, universities were reduced to level 2 and started to compete with each other for scarce funds to an extent that is harming the system. A telling example, and by no means the only one, is the effect that the competition for overseas students has had on the standing of British universities abroad. The deleterious effects of competition in a climate of scarcity have been recognized by Sir Graham Hills, the very hard-headed former Principal of Strathclyde University, who has given it as his opinion (Wojtas 1991) that 'cuts must be applied evenly, otherwise you destroy a sense of collegiality, but rewards can be as selective as you like.'

Bearing in mind that 'there is no mechanical relationship between a relative quality judgement and a funding decision, or there shouldn't be' (Ball 1991), what might be funding mechanisms that would ensure both effectiveness and efficiency in line with the principles enunciated above? The UFC policy towards research has been to achieve this competitively through selectivity and hence through concentration of effort in a comparatively small number of universities. Such an approach is clearly inappropriate for teaching, where it is necessary to achieve both effectiveness and efficiency in all universities in an expanding system. Teaching also benefits from cooperation rather than competition, as has been amply demonstrated within the Enterprise in Higher Education (EHE) Initiative (Elton 1991b). The EHE practice of bids for funding, followed by five-year contracts, the achievement of which is assessed annually through institutional visits during the year and an audit of self-assessment at the end of the year, could provide an appropriate funding model. Another possible model is the American model (HMI 1991), in which funding is dependent on accreditation and the adequate quality required for it. The model proposed below uses both the EHE and the US model. In it, the total funding T consists of two parts, $T=ST+JT$, as follows.

ST   This part is adapted from the US model and is much the larger part of the total T. Funding is based on an institutional plan, negotiated between the university and the Funding Council, with funds being essentially allocated on the basis of agreed student numbers in different cost centres. Universities receive their money on the basis of adequate quality, as verified by quality assurance and assessment. If a university falls below that quality, it is given a period in which to improve, during which it might even get increased funds in order to help it to improve, but warned that it risks cutbacks of agreed student numbers if there is no improvement. A financial inducement could come through the Funding Council giving larger numbers of fully funded students to those universities whose missions, plans and curricular objectives are explicitly in line with national needs. This will increase the proportion of students that are fully funded compared to those funded for fees only and thus increase the average funding per student.

JT   This part is adapted from the EHE model, regarding funding on the one hand and quality audit and assessment on the other. It selectively supports proposals by universities for teaching excellence through improvements, backed by staff and curriculum development, designed to lead to better teaching at greater efficiency without loss of quality. An important feature of *JT* would be to encourage developments that are carried out cooperatively in several universities and/or that lead to dissemination of teaching improvements throughout the higher education system. At the same time, the criteria for success would be norm-referenced between universities, thus introducing an element of competition. In contrast to research selectivity, where the reward is for past excellence, the *JT* factor rewards the promise of future excellence.

Resourcing levels, professionalism and quality

A similar approach, on the basis of the Maslow levels, can be taken to allocating resources within a university. Institutional rewards to academic staff and due recognition of their work are related to 'love and belonging', i.e. level 3, and once universities are at that level they must realize that by differentially 'loving' different contributions from their members, they can strongly influence the latter's behaviour. At present, they are rewarding research far more than teaching, through differences in the recognition and resourcing of these two activities and in the extrinsic rewards to individuals available for them (Elton and Partington 1991). However, quite a small shift in resources towards teaching, combined with a genuine recognition of the value of the work, can have a most significant effect on the quantity and quality of effort put by academic staff into teaching, as the current Enterprise in Higher Education Initiative is demonstrating (Elton 1991b). What has been shown there is that if, in their attitude to teaching, institutions reach Maslow level 3, the effect of rewards and recognition on individual staff is respectively at Maslow levels 3 and 4. Such extrinsic motivational factors are the prerequisite for the all-important intrinsic motivation associated with level 5, which in turn leads to institutional effects at levels 4 and 5. The initiative has also given support to the hypothesis that cooperation is superior to competition in improving the cost-effectiveness of teaching.

The collegiality, which Hills wishes to reinforce, and the shift of resources towards teaching are both positive aspects of a recognition of the increasing professionalism of university teaching. It has to be recognized however, that there is a negative side to this. A university that rewards all its staff for good work and wants to make them feel members of a collegial society may find that some of these members are content to stay at the safety level and do little to contribute to the common weal. Universities have always had a few such people, who took advantage of the system, and they have considered this a small price to pay, since it appeared to be more than balanced by the work and enthusiasm of the majority. However, if in the past dangers of inefficiency may have arisen from academics being too little controlled, the danger now is the opposite. Recent experience has shown that, when universities and their staff are reduced to the level of safety, then they all, or nearly all, play the system. And then both quality and effort deteriorate to the point where, even without any quantified cost–benefit analysis, the results are obviously inferior.

Conclusion

The last remark reinforces earlier conclusions that quality cannot be enforced from outside the university; neither, it may be added, can it be enforced from inside by top management (Pollitt 1990). It can only be achieved through the joint commitment and effort of all those inside it. What this requires over the next few years is:

- a rapid increase towards the professionalization of university teaching;
- the establishment of TQM practices at all levels of each university;
- increasing recognition and resourcing of teaching and rewards for excellence in it.

The achievement of these three objectives amounts to a radical change in culture, ethos and values of universities, which will be resisted by many inside them. Hence external pressures from, say, an independent assessment unit will be needed to 'unfreeze' the present system, in the telling phrase of Kurt Lewin, and to encourage change. But it is equally important that this pressure is removed, once the change has been institutionalized. If this does not happen, the system will eventually change to one that is even worse than the present one, for permanent tutelage leads first to decline and dependence, and then to revolt. This is one lesson that the West can learn from recent events in Eastern Europe.

References

Ashby, E. (1969) *The Academic Profession*. London: Oxford University Press.
Ball, C. (1991) Quality and qualities: an overview. In Schuller, T. (ed.) *The Future of Higher Education*. Milton Keynes: SRHE/Open University Press.
Brown, G and Atkins, M. (1988) *Effective Teaching in Higher Education*. London: Methuen.
BS 5750 (1987 and 1990) *Quality Systems, Parts 0 to 4*. London: British Standards Institution.
Committee of Vice-Chancellors and Principals (1990) Letter to Vice-Chancellors and Principals, N/90/108, 15 May. London: CVCP.
DES (1991) *Higher Education: a New Framework*, Cmnd 1541. London: HMSO.
Ellis, R. (ed.) (1988) *Professional Competence and Quality Assurance in the Caring Professions*. London: Croom Helm.
Elton, L. (1989) Higher education in Britain: future uncertain. *Zeitschrift für Hochschuldidaktik*, 13: 122–36.
Elton, L. (1991a) Teaching excellence and quality assurance. *Zeitschrift für Hochschuldidaktik*, 15: 102–15.
Elton, L. (1991b) Enterprise in higher education: work in progress. *Education and Training*, 33: 5–9.

Elton, L. and Partington, P. (1991) *Teaching Standards and Excellence in Higher Education: Developing a Culture for Quality.* London: CVCP.

HMI (1991) *Aspects of Education in the USA: Quality and Its Assurance in Higher Education.* London: HMSO.

Johnes, J and Taylor, J. (1991) *Performance Indicators in Higher Education.* Milton Keynes: SRHE/Open University Press.

Larson, M. S. (1977) *Rise of Professionalism: a Sociological Analysis.* Berkeley: University of California Press.

Lewis, R. and Maude, A. (1952) *Professional People.* London: Phoenix House.

Pirsig, R. M. (1974) *Zen and the Art of Motorcycle Maintenance.* London: Bodley Head.

Pollitt, C. (1990) Doing business in the temple? Managers and quality assurance in the public service. *Public Administration,* 68: 435–52.

Schön, D. A. (1983) *The Reflective Practitioner.* London: Temple Smith.

Shaw, G. B. (1908) *The Doctor's Dilemma.* Reprinted 1946 at Harmondsworth: Penguin.

Tysome, T. (1991) Staff face snakes and ladder review. *The Higher,* 15 November.

Wojtas, O. (1991) Following the gospel according to Groucho. *The Higher,* 20 September.

Ziman, J. (1991) Academic science as a system of markets. *Higher Education Quarterly,* 45: 41–61.

Part 2

Identifying Quality

9

Teaching Styles of Award-winning Professors

Jerry M. Lewis

Introduction

This chapter looks at the teaching styles of award-winning professors. (Professor is used in this chapter in the American style of occupation, not the British style of rank: it is equivalent to teacher.) The data are primarily drawn from in-depth interviews with such professors at Kent State University in Kent, Ohio, USA. The analysis is supported by popular writings about successful teachers as well as the limited literature on the subject. The chapter concludes with policy discussions in areas including the value of teaching awards, student evaluations, peer evaluations and the hiring of staff.

John Henry Newman (1912) wrote that a professor displays 'science in its most complete and winning form, pouring it forth with the zeal of enthusiasm, and lighting up his own love of it in the breast of his hearers.' There are many ways this 'lighting up' can be achieved in the educational enterprise. It is the perspective of this chapter that award-winning professors represent a rich fount of resources of knowledge and expertise in lighting up undergraduates. Both the neophyte teacher and the experienced professional can learn from outstanding teachers. However, it is difficult to get at the knowledge and expertise of these teachers in a systematic way.

The quest for knowledge about award-winning teachers is often complicated by stereotypes that shape perceptions of outstanding teaching. When one tries to study teaching, even excellent teaching, one is confronted with two problems. First, there is the 'bad day' stereotype. The argument is that most university professors are, because of training and intellect, good teachers but are prone to off or bad days on occasion. Hence, when studying teaching, the researcher must be careful in assuring that he or she has not caught the teacher being studied on a 'bad day'. Second, there is the 'pornography' problem. Paraphrasing a well-known American Supreme Court Judge (Potter Stewart) who said, 'I can't define pornography but I know it when I see it,' this stereotype says that it is difficult to define (and study) outstanding teaching, but easy to recognize it.

My solution to these stereotypes was to study award-winning professors. First, these teachers were clearly not having 'bad days' when I studied them – at least in terms of teaching. Second, they had been defined by both students and peers as distinguished in their profession. Many of these had been so recognized on a number of occasions.

Kent State University

Before I discuss the results of my research, it seems appropriate to look at the cultural context and environment of these excellent teachers. That is the city of Kent and Kent State University. The University was founded in 1910 as a college and became a university in 1935 when it expanded beyond its original teacher-training goals. It is located in north-eastern Ohio. It is roughly 470 miles (about 760 kilometres) west of New York City and about 40 miles south-east of Cleveland, Ohio. Kent State University (KSU) consists of the main campus plus eight regional campuses. The main campus in Kent is a large, wooded site on about 1200 acres of slightly rolling land with 100 buildings and a golf course and airport nearby that are affiliated with KSU. The library has over a million volumes in its open stacks.

The university is so large that it operates a bus system, which is also available to residents of the city of Kent ('Tree City') as its main routes reach various points in Kent. The city has a population of 30 000, and that rises to around 54 000 when the students are attending KSU. The university employs 1000 faculty members and 3000 other employees. The dormitories house 7000 students, mostly freshmen. Many students commute each day or evening and also work. The city of Kent has numerous houses and apartments that are rented to students.

The Kent campus offers baccalaureate, masters and doctoral study programmes, while the regional campuses offer associate (two-year) degrees as well as basic courses for the foundation of finishing a degree at the main campus. There are about 170 major career fields. For undergraduates, students may work toward a variety of BA degrees (four-year programmes that working students often finish in about five or six years or more). The following colleges cover the major programmes: Arts and Sciences, Business Administration, Education, Finance and Professional Arts, Architecture, Journalism, Music, Nursing, Physical Education. The Graduate College, the Graduate School of Management and the Graduate School of Education have 13 degrees in 32 programmes at the master's level. There are two doctoral degrees in 18 major areas.

Kent has many fine programmes, graduates over 3800 each year, and has an international reputation in such fields as liquid crystals, architecture and psychology, to name the main ones.

The Distinguished Teaching Award (DTA)

The DTA is given every autumn to three teachers at Kent State University. About 60 to 80 teachers are nominated. The award carries a prize of $1000. Professors are nominated using ballots that are distributed to students, staff and alumni (see Appendix 9.1). Early in the autumn of each year, the Alumni Association appoints a committee of students, staff and alumni to choose the award winners. Generally ten professors are selected as finalists. They will receive the Outstanding Teaching Award (OTA). Then the committee picks three staff members as Distinguished Teachers. The awards are presented on homecoming weekend, with both the DTA and OTA winners receiving considerable public recognition. In general, both DTA and OTA winners treat the award as a significant item for their curricula vitae.

Each autumn the ten outstanding teacher awards (OTA) are announced. From these ten, the Distinguished Teacher Award (DTA) winners are selected. The ten are acknowledged at a banquet and given plaques, and the three that receive the $1000 prizes are announced at that time. All are given a write-up in the local newspaper. There is also a wall with photographs of each year's DTAs just outside a special dining room open to the public and the university community in the student centre. This constitutes a hall of fame.

There are three assumptions about the award process. First, because each committee begins *de novo* every autumn, they generally work out procedures following the guidelines of the Alumni Association for standards of teaching excellence. Second, no particular subject is inherently more teachable. Thus, from the point of view of *subject matter*, every professor has a chance to be nominated for the award. Third, every professor has a chance of being nominated for the award in terms of student exposure. If a professor is a strong teacher, this will become known and consequently he or she will be nominated by a colleague, a student or a former student for the award competition.

Teaching styles of Distinguished Teaching Award winners

I begin by discussing the research procedure and then turn to the examination of types of teaching styles.

Research procedure

I tape-recorded in-depth interviews with the winners of the Alumni Association's Distinguished Teaching Award (DTA). I completed interviews with 50 of the 65 eligible candidates. The interviews were transcribed, and I did a qualitative analysis for this chapter. The interviewing focused on several aspects of undergraduate teaching. First, the professor's social and academic background was described. Second, various aspects of the teaching enterprise were explored, including: philosophies of teaching and learning; styles of lecturing; lecturing support materials, such as handouts, overhead projections or films; and outside-the-classroom projects. Third, techniques of testing and grading used by the professor were investigated. Fourth, the perceptions that the award-winning professor had of the joys (and sorrows) of undergraduate teaching were examined. These interviews generated a wealth of material about the craft of teaching represented in the three divisions of the university (sciences, social sciences and humanities) as well as many of its departments.

Styles of teaching

I was able to identify five styles of teaching used by the professors interviewed. They are presented in order of importance and are labelled goal-setting, preparation, enthusiasm, humour and (last but not least) performance.

Goal setting

Award-winning professors clearly have goals in mind when they organize and present their undergraduate courses. These goals are a mixture of the philosophical and pragmatic. They want to communicate the excitement of their discipline as well as the core knowledge of the subject, particularly in its most up-to-date form. To illustrate, I draw on the comments of three teachers, from English, Geology and Psychology.

> [My goals] are to teach a sense of order . . . within the enjoyment of what one is reading and the questions that one asks there is an inner order. In addition I want to communicate why I am an English major.
> (English professor)

> I try to make the student feel that what I was teaching them at that moment was the most important possible thing that they could learn in their entire four years of undergraduate studies.
> (Geology professor)

> One major goal that I think of myself trying to accomplish is to challenge everyday misconceptions . . . I view that as perhaps one function of the course and maybe one function of liberal arts.
> (Psychology professor)

In their comparative study of award and non-award winning professors, Tollefson and Tracy (1983) found this to be the second most important variable for both groups. That is, goal setting was second ranked by them. (The first ranked characteristic was enthusiasm, which is discussed here separately.)

Preparation

Award-winning teachers spend considerable effort and time on preparation. Tollefson and Tracy (1983) report this to be the third most important variable. Indeed, during my interviews, I became concerned about my own preparation when I learned through the research how much time professors spend getting ready for lectures.

> [Preparing a lecture on a Shakespeare play] I'll go over it three or four times and I will write. Then, I'll look at the notes from the critics and see how they fit into my own ideas.
>
> (English professor)

> The day before I was going to lecture on a particular subject, I would go through my file of overhead projection displays . . . So, I would go through my mental gymnastic of my lecture the second time. In a sense, I went through my lecture three times before I gave it to the class.
>
> (Geology professor)

Another professor in the sample, a sociologist, said he prepared three times as well: at the start of the semester, at the beginning of the week of the particular class and on the day of the lecture.

Enthusiasm

This is probably the best known variable associated with good teaching. Both of the groups in the Tollefson and Tracy study ranked it as the most important factor in outstanding teaching. However, my interviews indicate that enthusiasm is not as one-dimensional as it might seem. I found a difference between enthusiasm for the subject and enthusiasm for students be they quick to learn or less than quick. Students, in some instances, can get in the way of the professor. I had expected the kindly 'Mr Chips'. That was clearly not the case.

> I want to share my enthusiasm. So I take off a mile a minute in the classroom and feel free to digress.
>
> (English professor)

> I try to make the student aware of the fact that . . . regardless of what they are going to do in subsequent life, geology is going to impact on them.
>
> (Geology professor)

		Class situation	
		Planned	Spontaneous
Context	Subject	I	II
	Non-subject	III	IV

Figure 9.1 Uses of humour by award-winning teachers.

Humour

The factor of humour was important to the teachers. I found that they used it in a variety of ways, which can be summarized in the following typology. One dimension concerns the extent to which the humour is spontaneous or planned, the other the degree to which the humour relates to the subject matter of the course (see Figure 9.1). These two dimensions interact to produce four prototypes:

   type I, planned related;
   type II, spontaneous related;
   type III, planned unrelated;
   type IV, spontaneous unrelated.

Thus the situational variable ranges from planned to spontaneous humour. A planned act of humour is one that the teacher anticipates using at a specific time in the course. It can range from a cartoon on an overhead projection to a long joke. In contrast, a spontaneous act of humour occurs at any time in the class and can range from a witty remark based on a student comment to a messed-up experiment in chemistry class.

The contextual variable relates to the subject of the course. The acts of humour are directly related to the subject of the class or not directly related. For example, a professor might want to illustrate a point in the lecture with a joke or cartoon. Many American textbooks also do this in both the social and natural sciences. In contact, some professors like to use humour that is not necessarily related to the topic of the course.

The vast majority of humour falls into type I, although instances of types II and III were reported in my interviews with the outstanding teachers. Here are examples of type I.

I will pun. That's the limit of my intellectual ability to create humour is the pun. And they are usually very terrible. I will frequently lighten a situation.

(English professor)

I think the most humorous thing I did was tell stories, often on myself,

about a geological situation. [I slipped] off the edge of the cliff and fell
40 feet.

(Geology professor)

The psychology professor is often a type III in his use of humour: 'One
liners. I guess if I could be Johnny Carson sometimes. I would like to be one
of those stand up comedians.' Another professor, a sociologist, begins
almost every lecture with a joke that may be type I, but often is not related to
the course subject matter (type III).

Performance

Many award-winning professors enjoy the performance aspect of teaching.
Some actually report some sort of a high from the lecturing experience.
When one hears 'I would really miss teaching,' I think this refers to the
entertaining aspects to a large extent. An administrator from another
university said it bluntly: 'All good teachers are hams.'

When I presented this variable at the University of Ulster, it caused a
reaction – most of it negative. One member of the audience went so far as to
ask if teachers should join the Royal Shakespeare Company. While I do not
want professors to go that far, I think they should be sensitive to the
performance dimensions of effective lecturing.

In my own teaching, I have been influenced by the analytical theory of
Erving Goffman as developed in his book, *The Presentation of Self in Everyday
Life* (1959). His theory of social interaction, called dramaturgy, uses
theatrical images to explain impression management. Impression management is exactly what professors do in the classroom. They affect students in
more ways than simple words. The entire performance counts. Goffman
notes that in any social situation there is a 'front' region where social acts are
carried out and a 'back' region where these acts are prepared. Further,
social action in front regions is generally contradicted in the back region.
For Goffman, both these regions are socially determined. For example, a
professor can struggle with a point in the back region of his or her office.
Further, he or she can express this struggle on the face or through body
language. However, when the professor enters the stage (front region) of
the classroom, this struggle must disappear, and an aura of confidence in
one's ideas should be presented. In other words, walking into a classroom is
much more than just 'walking into a classroom'. *The teacher is going on stage.*

Walter Dyer reported the teaching of Charles Edward Garman, a famous
philosopher at Amherst College in Massachusetts. When he illustrated a
point, it was theatre. Dyer wrote (Peterson 1946):

Garman's illustrations were famous and wide in scope. He drew from
sociology, economics, business, politics, literature, domestic relations,
and law, as well as from religion and philosophy. In making his
academic points he dealt with living issues. He displayed a positive
genius for apt illustration and example. A large part of the value of the

course was the imparting of general knowledge as well as the stimulation of thinking.

One of Garman's illustrative anecdotes was so characteristic and succinct that some of us learned it verbatim and were accustomed to recite it in unison on frivolous occasions. It was first presented, I believe, in connection with a discussion of the doctrine of the atonement or vicarious punishment. It ran as follows:

'In a shire town in England a man was sentenced for stealing sheep, and the judge said, "I convict you not for stealing sheep but that sheep may not be stolen in the future." Then the culprit arose in open court and said, "What is that to me?" And sure enough,' concluded Garman, leaning over his desk and fixing us with his piercing gaze, 'what was it to him?'

It is impossible to describe the impressive manner in which Garman presented his illustrations, or their effectiveness in driving home his point. It was largely in the way he did it. I shall never forget the day he recited Tennyson's *Flower in the Crannied Wall*. It was like listening to the voice of an oracle.

Clearly Garmon saw the value in performance.

The humour and performance variables were not found by Tollefson and Tracy (1983) to be important by the faculty in their samples, although earlier research by others did report that presentation skills were important. However, the prevalence of these two factors in my interviews justifies more research into the questions raised by these variables.

In summary, my interviews with award-winning teachers identified five factors that shaped these outstanding teachers' perceptions of the teaching enterprise. They were: goal-setting, preparation, enthusiasm, humour and performance. I do not wish to claim that all professors have to use the approaches I have identified in this sample of successful teachers. But I do suggest we can learn from them.

I think there are several things that both the beginning teacher and the veteran would gain from examining the reflections of award-winning professors. First, at the lowest level, new techniques can be learned. Second, and more importantly, the teacher adds to insight of his or her own joys and tribulations about teaching by learning of the experiences of award-winning professors. They do learn that they are not alone. Finally, and most importantly, these teachers generate a sense of pride in their craft. There are many good men and women who continually struggle with questions about what is good undergraduate teaching and learning. In concluding my chapter I want to raise some policy questions that stem from my research.

Policy issues

There are three policy issues relevant to my research. They are: the value of teaching awards, student evaluations and the hiring of staff.

Teaching awards

As the reader can clearly see, I am in favour of teaching awards for university lecturers. Indeed, at my own university it is possible to win an award at the departmental, collegiate and university levels as well as from professional societies and associations. Perhaps we Americans overdo awards, but they do have value. The psychological value of positive rewards, such as awards and public recognition, is well documented, as is the basic value of compliments and encouragement. What are the basic values for teaching awards?

First, *awards recognize the teaching accomplishments of men and women who have put considerable thought into their craft.* I found that the money and honour of the awards were deeply appreciated by the teachers I interviewed.

Second, it created a cadre of people who are *willing to share their teaching expertise* with others. For my research, only one professor refused to be interviewed and he, ironically, was from the College of Education. It is possible that this cadre can, as role models, become a source of innovation for the teaching process – although it would be 'Pollyannish' or overly optimistic of me to claim that this happened at Kent State.

Third, teaching awards *squarely commit universities to the proposition that teaching is important.* (Knowledge alone does not mean one can communicate it to others automatically.) This commitment to the importance of teaching often waxes and wanes with academic fashion or administrative leadership. However, a 'baseline' teaching award does serve as a friendly reminder to the university leadership that the staff and students value teaching.

The giving of teaching awards may carry with it some social costs. As Tollefson and Tracy (1983) note, 'non-award winning faculties frequently argue that teaching awards are won capriciously.' In a 1975 study that I replicated in 1990, I looked at one aspect of the fairness question to see if the OTA and DTA winners reflected the demographic of the faculty. The data for 1975 are reported in Table 9.1. For data sources, I have used current faculty records, general catalogues, graduate catalogues, Kent State University archives and a few interviews with nominating committee members.

It would be expected that the distribution of staff in the two award categories would parallel that of the general faculty. That is, if we assume that good teaching is possible in any subject and nomination and election procedures are fair, then the award categories should reflect the demographic characteristics of the general faculty population.

In evaluating the evidence in this report, I treated any percentage difference of 10 per cent or more as a real difference. Thus, with regard to sex, the data show the DTA and OTA award winners reflecting the sex ratio of the 1974–5 faculty distribution, while the DTA category is over-represented by holders of the doctorate. Academic rank in the OTA is

Table 9.1 Selected demographic characteristics of distinguished and outstanding teaching award winners

Demographic characteristic	DTA (n = 23)		OTA (n = 39)		1974–5 faculty (n = 836)	
	f	%	f	%	f	%
Sex						
Male	18	78	33	85	644	77
Female	5	22	6	15	192	23
Highest degree						
Doctorate	16	70	25	64	492	59
Masters	6	26	8	20	289	35
Bachelors	1	4	1	3	45	5
Other	0	0	5	13	10	1
Academic rank						
Professor	6	26	12	31	252	30
Associate prof.	10	44	13	33	241	29
Assistant prof.	4	17	12	31	263	31
Instructor	1	4	1	2.5	80	10
Unknown	2	9	1	2.5	0	0
College/school						
Arts and Sciences	16	69	20	51	322	39
Business Admin.	2	9	3	8	72	9
Education	1	4	4	10	157	19
Fine and Prof. Art	2	9	6	15	186	22
HPE and R	2	9	5	13	46	5
Library Science	0	0	0	0	8	1
Nursing	0	0	1	3	45	5
Time at KSU (mean years)	12.8		9.1		9.1	

close to the general faculty distribution, but the associate professor rank is over-represented in the DTA category because of the three-year rule (see below). The variables of college award winners and time at KSU seem to be clearly out of phase with the 1974–5 staff distribution. The latter variable, time, is easy to understand since the rules of the award programme specify that a professor must have been at KSU for at least three years before he is eligible to be nominated. (I found only two cases where the three-year rule was not followed.) However, the college of the winners is a puzzle. Arts and sciences are greatly over-represented in both DTA and OTA categories, although more so in the DTA group.

The data suggest two things. First, the OTA category is more representative than the DTA category. This fact, combined with an examination of the total distribution of award winners compared to the faculty of 1974–5, suggests that the top twelve really reflects quality teaching. On the other hand, there are some biases in the selection of the DTA, most notably in the area of the college of the winner, with an over-representation of arts and sciences staff. I replicated this study in 1990 and found a slight decline in the percentage of arts and science teachers who had won the award. There was a corresponding increase in the percentage of professors from other disciplines.

In summary, every effort should be made to ensure that the reality and the perception of reality are very close to each other. Every effort needs to be made to guarantee that all staff have a fair chance of winning the awards.

Student evaluations

The United States probably does more student and peer evaluations than Britain or Europe. Nevertheless, the accountability trends will probably increase as the student consumer movement in academia increases.

The teachers in my sample generally approved of student evaluations and used them to study their own teaching. This was particularly true of any qualitative material. What they objected to was the use of teaching evaluations for tenure and promotion, particularly when administrators gave much attention to small quantitative differences.

My interviews indicate that the questions on teaching evaluation forms are too narrow in focusing primarily on student–teacher interaction and levels of learning. While these variables are certainly important, my interviews indicate that evaluation should be broader, looking at issues of goals as well as the presentation aspects of college teaching.

Hiring of staff

In the United States, it is estimated that there will be at least a 50 per cent turnover in staff in the 1990s. Consequently, considerable numbers of staff will have to be hired for replacements. I think this fact has two major implications for hiring. My research indicates that newly minted PhDs should be evaluated in broader terms than just knowledge of subject and research abilities. Good teaching is a fairly complicated process, and we must decide if new staff are going to make the commitment to quality. In the interview process for selecting new staff, some schools do include a requirement of a presentation by a prospective teacher to get some idea of the quality of the ability to teach – to communicate to a class and with a class.

Second, and clearly related to the first point, is the notion of teacher training. Those of us in the business of training PhDs must ensure that our students are willing and prepared to think about the complexities of quality teaching. We must think of our PhDs as more than researchers and ask them to be, even in training, total faculty members. This suggestion may call for considerable reorganization in the way PhDs are trained in the United Kingdom and Europe. There are various ways some graduate programmes meet this need for exposure to the ideas of excellent teaching, including some credit given for a short course (with lots of individual practice time and evaluation) in teaching, seminars, schedules of guest lectures by graduate students with peer and faculty evaluation and constructive discussion of the presentations before and after any additional class-leading time by the advanced graduate student.

Conclusions

This chapter has described Kent State University's Distinguished Teaching Award and the sociological context in which it has developed. It has presented results of in-depth interviews with winners of the award. Five teaching factors were identified as used by these professors. The chapter concluded with some policy suggestions derived from the research.

Appendix 9.1   The Kent Alumni Association's 1990 Distinguished Teaching Awards

You are invited to submit your nomination for the 1990 Distinguished Teaching Awards, Kent State University's most prestigious faculty honors.

Sponsored by the Kent Alumni Association and funded through the KSU Foundation, the Distinguished Teaching Awards competition is in its 24th year. To date, cash grants amounting to $68,000 have been presented to 65 top faculty members. This indicates the importance which the Alumni Association places on superior classroom teaching.

On Homecoming Weekend, October 5 and 6, 1990, a minimum of three KSU faculty members will be honored with cash awards of $1,000 each for their outstanding achievements in collegiate teaching. But first they MUST BE NOMINATED, and that is up to you.

All Kent students, alumni, faculty, and staff members are eligible to submit nominations for the awards. We ask that before completing a nomination form, you *review completely the eligibility requirements* listed in this brochure. There are a great many ideas concerning what constitutes effective teaching which, in part, may arise from variations in subject matter, grade level of the students, and class size. It is hoped that the general criteria will aid you in making an effective nomination.

Make your nomination *as complete as possible*. Of necessity, the judging must be somewhat subjective and the committee which selects the finalists and winners generally tends to place emphasis on the *quality* rather than the quantity of nominations. A new selection committee is named each year and is composed of nine students, six faculty members, a representative of the office of the Vice President for Academic and Student Affairs, and three alumni.

Return your ballot in person or by mail to the Kent Alumni Association, Alumni Center. All nominations must contain your signature and the contents will be available only to the selection committee and to members of the Kent Alumni Association's Awards Committee. Deadline for nominations is July 2, 1990.

Eligibility

1. A faculty member, to be nominated, must have been on a full-time teaching contract at the Kent or any regional campus of the University for a minimum of *five years*, including the current academic year.
2. A faculty member must have taught at least one course in *two* of the *three semesters* during each of those *five academic years*. (For purpose of these awards, Summer Sessions are considered one semester and the academic year extends from the beginning of Fall Semester through Summer Sessions of the following calendar year.)
3. Those receiving the awards must be on a current University contract during the semester in which the awards are presented.
4. Those who have won a Distinguished Teaching Award in previous years are no longer eligible. A complete list of previous winners is printed here.

Honored

Photos of all winners, engraved in metal, are enshrined in the DTA Hall of Fame across from the Schwebel Garden Room on the third floor of the Kent Student Center.

Winners

These previous winners are no longer eligible for Distinguished Teaching Awards:

Rudy Bachna
Joseph Baird
Kathleen Bayless
Normand Bernier
Carol Bersani
George Betts
Mary Kay Biagini
Fay Biles
Richard Brown

Lawrence Kaplan
Marvin Koller
Bebe Lavin
Jerry Lewis
Sanford Marovitz
John Mattingly
John Mitchell
Vernon Neff
Gerald Newman

Ottavio Casale
Stanley Christensen
Robert Clawson
Barbara Cline
Richard B. Craig
Kenneth Cummins
Thomas Davis
Norman Duffy
Donald Dykes
Halim El-Dabh
Keith Ewing
Raymond Fort
Glenn Frank
Doris Franklin
Alfred Friedl

Nenos Georgopoulos
Raymond Gesinski
Hugh Glauser
George Harrison
Virginia Harvey
William Hildebrand
Herbert Hochhauser
Emily Hoover
John Hubbell

Lowell Orr
John Parks
Vivian Pemberton
Paul Pfeiffer
L. Brian Price
Thomas Pynadath
Thomas Reuschling
Jeanette Reuter
David Riccio
James Rinier
Michael Rogers
Carl Rosen

Gwen Scott
Paul Sites
Mel Someroski
Nathan Spielberg
Robert Stadulis
Robert Tener
Martha Walker
Evert Wallenfeldt
Kathleen Whitmer
Harold Williams
Donald Wonderly

Official Nomination Form
Distinguished Teaching Awards

Please check your status: ☐ student; ☐ alumnus/a; ☐ faculty/staff.

Name of nominee _____

Nominee's department _____

Your full name _____

Your address and phone (students – Kent address; faculty/staff –

department) _____

_____

For Students – Your college, year, major _____

For Alumni – Kent degree(s), date(s) granted _____

List courses taken under nominee (number or title) ——————————

——————————————————————————————————

Approximate date(s) course(s) taken ——————————————

Caution: *This is not a popularity contest. Simply submitting a faculty member's name is not enough. Only those nominations which include complete information are forwarded to the selection committee.*

Rate your nominee on a scale of 1 to 5 (top score is 5) in each of the following categories and use space provided to explain the teacher's performance in each area. Give examples.

Ability to communicate subject matter effectively. ——————————

——————————————————————————————————

——————————————————————————————————

——————————————————————————————————

——————————————————————————————————

——————————————————————————————————

Demonstrates a comprehensive knowledge of subject matter. ——————

——————————————————————————————————

——————————————————————————————————

——————————————————————————————————

——————————————————————————————————

Communicates an enthusiastic interest in the field of study. ——————

——————————————————————————————————

——————————————————————————————————

——————————————————————————————————

——————————————————————————————————

Stimulates thinking and develops understanding. The student's intellect is challenged. ——————————————————————

——————————————————————————————————

——————————————————————————————————

——————————————————————————————————

——————————————————————————————————

Methods of evaluation genuinely reflect the student's understanding of relevant course material. _____

_____

_____

_____

_____

_____

Take a personal interest in students and is willing help. _____

_____

_____

_____

_____

(LIMIT COMMENTS TO ADDITIONAL SHEET PROVIDED ON REVERSE SIDE.)

References

Goffman, E. (1959) *The Presentation of Self in Everyday Life*. New York: Doubleday.
Newman, J. H. (Cardinal) (1912) *The Idea of a University*. Notre Dame, IN: University of Notre Dame Press.
Peterson, H. (ed.) (1946) *Great Teachers*. New York: Vintage Books.
Tollefson, N. and Tracy, D. B. (1983) Comparison of self-reported teaching behavior of award-winning and non-award winning university faculty. *Perceptual and Motor Behavior*, 56: 39–44.

10

The First Distinguished Teaching Award in the United Kingdom

Elaine Thomas

So far as we know the University of Ulster (UU) is the only university in the UK to have a distinguished teaching award scheme. In the USA, on the other hand, such schemes are relatively commonplace. How has this North American practice transplanted to the UK? The major aim of this chapter is to describe the first year of implementation of a distinguished teaching award at the University of Ulster. First, however, it is necessary to give a brief outline of the context and history of the scheme.

The idea of an award for distinguished teaching first surfaced at a senior staff conference held for heads of departments, deans and pro-vice-chancellors. At that time research was the major topic: research selectivity, research achievements and the promotion of research were all being discussed. In this context many senior staff felt that the importance of teaching needed a continuing or even extra emphasis. The idea of a distinguished teaching award was welcomed as part of a package of measures that would address teaching and learning. Every encouragement was given to the proposers of the scheme to promote its introduction in the university.

Enthusiasts for the scheme included two deans of faculty who had encountered established schemes in the USA. Roger Ellis had visited Kent State University, Ohio, where he was impressed by their distinguished teaching award scheme. A task group was established under his chairmanship to undertake a feasibility study and make a formal proposal to the university. Jerry M. Lewis of Kent State University (KSU) was invited to act as a consultant to the group. He produced comprehensive details of the Kent State scheme. The task group used the KSU distinguished teaching award as a model and considered how it might be applied at UU. The KSU scheme is described in Professor Lewis's chapter. While the UU scheme is modelled on this there were several significant differences between the universities. KSU has a large proportion of staff on teaching-only contracts. Student evaluation of their teachers is an established procedure and evidence is available on file about all staff. Their Alumni Association is well developed and indeed it operates the distinguished teaching award scheme from its own offices, thus maintaining an appropriate distance from the university and its disciplinary and promotional procedures. In contrast the staff of UU are on conventional teaching and research contracts; there is no university-wide system of student evaluation of teaching; and the Alumni Association is in its infancy. The scheme would have to be run by the university and it was essential to keep it separate from appraisal and managerial decisions.

The KSU nomination form employed seven criteria, which were discussed and, modestly, adapted. Six of the criteria were seen as easily applicable and required no change. One criterion – 'demonstrates comprehensive knowledge of subject matter' – was not included as it was felt that it would be reflected through other criteria. A new criterion – 'provides regular and useful feedback on students' course work' – was included as reflecting an important aspect of lecturers' work that appeared to be of importance to students.

The well established KSU scheme had introduced an intermediate stage of Outstanding Teacher. Those who received this formed the population from whom the distinguished teachers were selected. This was felt to be over-elaborate for a new scheme. The award was construed as being an award of the university on the recommendation of Senate and hence properly bestowed at an annual congregation. The award at KSU was, of course, from the Alumni Association. The financial reward at KSU was matched by £500 at UU.

While there was widespread support for the scheme in the university, particularly perhaps from those who felt that teaching was being undervalued in relation to research, there were nevertheless several objections that had to be addressed. First, there was an anxiety that a scheme devised for an American university might not successfully transplant to the UK. Distinguished teaching awards were thought of as characteristic of the American university approach, which differed significantly from that of the UK. It had to be recognized that there were significant differences between the cultures of American universities and those in the UK. However, teaching was now being given a much higher profile in the UK system and many innovations, for example modularization, credit accumulation and transfer and possible teaching-only contracts, were being modelled on the USA system.

Concern was expressed that the award might be primarily for those of long experience and this might not recognize excellence in an innovative young high flyer. It was confirmed that the scheme was based on achievement and not length of service.

The expression 'willing to help' in one criterion was thought to confuse teaching with professional counselling. The scheme was confirmed as applying to teaching. However, the effective teacher would have to take into account personal problems that affect learning, and might, for example, direct the student to Student Services for professional help.

The constitution of the panel could not be based exactly on that of KSU, which balanced peers, present students and alumni. The UU panel was based on peers and present students but with the hope that in due course the Alumni Association would play a more prominent role. The selection of students for the panel was a matter for the Students' Union, who would have to take into account subjects, modes of study, campus location, gender and any other relevant factors.

It was thought that nomination and indeed award would be no more than popularity contests. There is, however, strong evidence, admittedly from the USA, that distinguished teaching awards are not mere popularity contests. Rather it is the case that students prove to be remarkably discriminating consumers whose views usually coincide with those of informed faculty members.

It was thought that awards might be a cause of dissension. Experience in the USA is that they are more likely to be a matter of pride, not only to the individual but also to his or her department and faculty.

There was concern that this distinguished teaching award might become embroiled with promotion, discretionary points and accelerated increments. It was made clear from the start that the distinguished teaching award would be completely separate from such procedures. It would be an award made at Congregation on the recommendation of Senate, the senior academic body, whereas promotion in the university is the responsibility of the Staffing Committee of Council acting on the recommendations of the Academic Staff Progress Committee. No doubt individuals being considered for promotion would wish to adduce similar evidence with regard to their teaching as might have been relevant to a distinguished teaching award, and in this sense there might be some conjunction. However, promotion is based on a number of variables, of which teaching is only one.

Concern was expressed on the capability of the panel to make judgements on what was essentially second-hand evidence. It was pointed out that the Senate would be receiving recommendations from a panel on whose judgement in relation to agreed criteria it would have to rely. Obviously much would depend on the good sense with which the Committee went about its work. This is true of virtually every other aspect of university business. It was asked whether external assessors might be involved in the work of the selection panel. While this was not envisaged in the first instance it might be considered desirable in future.

A final hiccup in the approval of the scheme occurred when union representatives at Council argued that they had not been consulted formally. Fortunately the AUT supported the scheme in principle since it coincided with their commitment to the development and recognition of excellence in teaching. The situation was retrieved through a further stage of discussion where several helpful modifications were made to the format. Nominees who wished their application to be considered were to be invited rather than required to put forward evidence beyond a mere curriculum vitae. Furthermore, they were able to nominate a person to support their case who might be but would not have to be their head of department.

The scheme follows an annual cycle beginning with nominations in the autumn term and culminating with awards at the July Congregations. All staff and students of the university are informed through posters, items in appropriate house newspapers and circular memoranda of the introduction of the scheme and the opportunity to nominate individually or collectively. Nomination requires the completion of a printed form with assessment of nominees against the seven agreed criteria. Self-nomination is not permitted nor should nominees be informed at the initial stage of nomination.

A selection panel then considers nominations received and determines whether a *prima facie* case has been established. Where this is so nominees are informed and asked if they wish their nomination to proceed. If they do they are invited to provide a supporting statement and curriculum vitae highlighting their teaching experience and achievements and the name of a colleague familiar with their teaching who would be able to warrant to its standard; this colleague might be their head of department. Further consideration is given to this material by the selection panel, who finally recommend to Senate up to three persons for the distinguished teaching award. The award consists of a framed certificate which is presented at Congregation together with a financial award of £500. The names of award winners are recorded on a role of honour mounted on each campus.

The scheme worked its way through all the appropriate committees of the university and was generally welcomed as part of a new strategy to enhance the perceived value of teaching and to improve quality in it. Other components of the strategy included the introduction of a teacher training course (described in Chapter 16); a research project to identify salient features of good teaching as perceived by experts (see Chapter 11); and a commitment to good teaching being a criterion for promotion and discretionary points.

Appendix 10.1 sets out the scheme as approved. Once approved it was handed over to the selection panel chaired by the author.

Implementation of the scheme

Implementation of the university's Distinguished Teaching Award Scheme commenced in the autumn term of 1990 (having gained the approval of Senate). All full-time staff of the University of Ulster, with a minimum of three years of service, are eligible for the awards and invitations for nominations were made in December 1990 to current and former students of the university and academic staff members, through posters circulated and displayed throughout the four Campuses and by advertisement in *UU News*, the university's bi-monthly publication. Guidelines accompanying nomination forms indicated that self-nomination was not permitted, and that nominees should not be informed at the initial stage of nomination.

Membership of the selection panel, which automatically prohibits eligibility for the award or acting as nominator, included five representatives of Senate plus the chairperson, four student representatives nominated by the Students' Union and two members nominated by the Convocation.

Nominations for Distinguished Teaching Awards were submitted on a nomination form, and allowed nomination by one or a combination of students, former students and academic staff. The nomination form required that the nominator, if a student, indicate name, address and course details, and, if a member of staff, the department and campus. The form also required that courses or units taught by the nominee, and dates involved, be provided. Once this basic information was provided, the nominator was asked to score from 1 to 5 various categories representing criteria and to comment upon the performance in each category, giving examples. These criteria, which underpin the whole exercise, consisted of the following seven statements:

1. Communicates subject matter effectively.
2. Provides regular and useful feedback on students' course work.
3. Communicates an enthusiastic interest in the field of study.
4. Stimulates thinking and develops understanding.
5. Challenges the student's intellect.
6. Uses methods of assessment that reflect the student's understanding of relevant course material.
7. Takes a personal interest in students and is willing to help.

At the close of nomination, in mid-January 1991, 46 completed nominations were received. The selection panel met in late January to consider these nominations. It is worth noting that, at this first meeting, as well as at following meetings, the panel was reminded of the purpose of the Distinguished Teaching Award and members involved themselves in continuous debate about the issues involved in correctly and fairly implementing the scheme. Publicity for the scheme indicated the following:

> The Senate of the University has given approval for the establishment of a Distinguished Teaching Awards Scheme. The awards will mark, in tangible form, the importance which the University attaches to high quality teaching and excellence amongst its staff.

All members of the panel attending the meeting had looked in depth at the nominations submitted. Several nominees had been nominated by more than one person, and the actual number of individuals nominated was less than 46. The purpose of this first meeting was to determine whether a *prima facie* case was established in the case of nominations, before moving to the next stage of the scheme.

As with any innovation of this kind, the scheme is being both implemented and refined at the same time. It soon became clear to the panel that further criteria would need to be applied in order to discriminate between nominations. We had to organize and respond to the information in a way that would help us to place nominations in some kind of order, and to compare nominees' suitability for further consideration. Important observations emerged in our discussions. For example, a range of evidence from different types of nominator helped to make a case convincing. More and more, as we looked through nominations, it became clear that the comments of current or former students were particularly helpful in the first stage of the selection process. It was noted that some of the questions on the nomination form were detected as being less relevant than others. For example, concerning question 6, inviting nominators to score and comment upon the degree to which the nominee 'uses methods of assessment that reflect the student's understanding of relevant course material', some nominators queried the meaning of the word 'reflect', and expressed uncertainty in their responses. One nominator wrote above the space provided 'not a good question' and suggested that the word 'probe' replace 'reflect'.

As well as the categories set out on the nomination form, discussion took place about further criteria that were needed to help in the assessment of each nomination. These were finally agreed as follows:

1. Diversity of nominators.
2. High scores in each category, irrespective of the number of nominators.
3. Range of comments.
4. Quality of perceptiveness of comments.
5. Sustained evidence.

Using the agreed criteria, we were able to select a number of nominees for whom *prima facie* cases existed, and who were suitable for further consideration. These nominees were then written to by the chairperson, asked if they wished their nominations to proceed to the next stage, and invited to provide a supporting statement and curriculum vitae highlighting their teaching experience and achievements. They were also invited to suggest a colleague familiar with their teaching, who might be their head of department, with whom their nomination might be discussed. They were informed at this stage of the name(s) of nominators, so that they might, if they wished, nominate a further colleague rather than duplicate information.

The panel next met in March 1991 to consider the supporting statements and curricula vitae received from nominees in conjunction with the original nominations. Further criteria were discussed and devised to aid us in our work. These were as follows:

1. Own insight into teaching experience.
2. Evidence of innovatory teaching techniques.

3. Evidence of further objective comment, through peer recognition, student comment or external examiners' remarks.
4. Breadth of teaching-linked experience, evidence of willingness to broaden own approach.

At this stage, the panel was able to select further from the nominations using these criteria, and agreed to progress several nominees by contacting the colleagues suggested by the nominees and asking for specific information to aid the discussions. Evidence of outstanding teaching ability was requested, and, where there was no evidence of student comment, the panel requested evidence of student corroboration of the nomination. The panel met next in April 1991 to consider the selected nominations in the light of all available information. At this meeting the panel was able unanimously to recommend to Senate three members of staff for the Distinguished Teaching Awards.

The outline given of the implementation of the Distinguished Teaching Awards scheme in its first year clearly indicates that, as deliberations continued, it became desirable to modify the scheme in various ways. The Committee made a detailed report of proposed amendments to the Academic Policy Committee of Senate, which, in turn, reported to Senate its recommendation for approval of the changes. The modifications concerned changes to the content of the nomination form, measures to prevent canvassing and recommendations covering the most appropriate term of office for each of the categories of panel membership, bearing in mind the need to balance experience and new blood.

It was also recommended that, in future, staff nominations should be corroborated or seconded by one or more students. This recommendation highlights the value placed by the panel upon student comment and was also seen as a way of ensuring, from the outset, a diversity of nominators. It was also proposed that a 1–10 scoring system should be introduced for the nomination form, in the hope that this might invite a wider range of potential scores from nominators.

The criteria the panel had devised during its discussions were also presented for approval. Thus, mechanisms were agreed that would help to organize and evaluate the information presented at the various stages of the scheme.

Evaluation of the scheme

The description of the work of the panel, application and adoption of criteria and proposed modifications has been presented, quite deliberately, as a *series of decisions made*. The panel undertook its work with both diligence and thoroughness, aware of the importance of its task. A factual account has been presented which shows the *results* of the deliberations rather than dealing with the underlying issues which are implicit. These issues require

172   *Elaine Thomas*

attention, and it is perhaps best to dwell upon them separately from the account of the panel's work.

It is important that any distinguished teaching award scheme is seen to be valid and credible. The role of the selection panel, its thoroughness and its credibility are crucial, as no contenders for an award which says they are outstanding teachers must feel that the award is easily given. Nor must their peers feel that it has been awarded lightly or, more importantly, *inappropriately*. The message that the award conveys is important to both the recipient and the institution, in that it places real value upon good teaching practice. As well as conveying the message that the University of Ulster values good teaching, it is also important that those who are successful are seen by others as role models, and feel a real sense of achievement.

Thus, the *credibility* of the scheme is fundamental, matched equally by the *reliability* of the scheme. In order to elicit information that is comprehensive, useful, accurate and meaningful an onus is placed upon the original nomination form used at an initial stage of the selection, and, in the case of successful nominees, referred to throughout the following stages. If one is satisfied that the form is designed in the most suitable fashion, then it must be acknowledged that the scheme is also testing the nominators. While nominators are proposing and evaluating their teachers or their peers, their own efforts to express their views are being judged and used. This was evident, when, at the first stage of the panel's work, we devised the criterion 'quality or perceptiveness of comments' to help organize and prioritize the information presented on the form. The grading scheme of 1–5 was less useful as most nominators, having decided to put nominees forward, would tend to score them consistently highly anyway. A scoring system would be more varied if those completing were 'scoring' a range of teachers and making comparisons, rather than presenting a case on behalf of someone they already strongly supported.

Considering the inclination or motivation to nominate inevitably makes one reflect upon initial publicity for the scheme, and encouragement or promotion by interested parties and individuals. Departments or faculties have, to date, varied in their response to the scheme. One would expect heads of departments, for example, to promote the scheme for at least two reasons. First, it would be good policy to promote the department and its achievements. Second, one would wish to promote the concept of good teaching among its staff and students. The first year of the scheme presented a relatively small range of nominees from such a large institution. This is likley to be related to a modest start in terms of dissemination of information. Already, the second year has yielded far more nominations. Graduating students were informed individually of the scheme in July 1991 and this has perhaps led to a stronger and broader response. It was also anticipated that presentation of the actual award at graduation ceremonies would have an encouraging effect.

The University of Ulster is distinctive in the breadth and range of subjects and courses it offers. The university consists of seven faculties –

Education, Science and Technology, Social and Health Sciences, Art and Design, Humanities, Business and Management and Informatics – plus a Department of Adult and Continuing Education. Each faculty offers its own extensive and diverse subject expertise, embracing a wide range of levels of courses and appropriate teaching methods. In considering outstanding teaching, one is aware of the differing styles, ethos and traditions surrounding practice, and that the role of the teacher varies from subject to subject. Professor Jerry Lewis of Kent State University, in his observations about teaching quality, places great emphasis upon actual performance, relying implicitly upon a lecture format. Rewarding or acknowledging good teaching requires analysis of a far wider range of teaching modes. The nomination form used in the Distinguished Teaching Awards Scheme is designed in a way that should cater for varying modes, but it has yet to be tested fully. A broader response should yield interesting results and test the scheme and the panel further.

The seven criteria on the nomination form are oriented towards students' responses or peers' observations of those responses. Most of the criteria would be applicable in any level of study. For example, one expects, or hopes for, effective communication (1) and enthusiasm for subject (3) from all teachers. However, the ability to challenge the student's intellect might be exercised more fully in a PhD supervisor than in teachers on more basic or introductory courses. One may argue that, in a university, we should challenge the intellect of all students all the time, but this is not realistic. Diagnosis of the appropriate level of expectation and the ability to help students to reach that level would be a skill worth detecting in an outstanding teacher. Comments made on the nomination forms in 1991 showed that students understood the need for an outstanding teacher to gauge the appropriate level of expectation, and to challenge the students' intellect to a degree that was relevant to the level and field of study.

At the second stage of the selection procedure, where successful nominees were invited to provide supporting statements, the panel was presented with information of a different kind. Here we were suddenly considering the *nominees'* views of *themselves*, which understandably required a different approach. The facts presented in a curriculum vitae, showing history, background and experience, were matched by statements displaying variously pride, a sense of achievement, great modesty, cautious restraint and thoughtful reflection. At this stage we found ourselves debating, very thoroughly, what was meant by 'outstanding teaching'. The nomination form provided information based upon a student-centred approach to the issue, but the evidence with which we were now presented indicated that criteria incorporating self-evaluation, peer assessment and understanding of the higher educational context would be required. Nominees' own insights into their teaching experience were considered invaluable. Nominees at this stage had been given no detailed outline of what their supporting statement might cover. This was entirely for them to decide and varied considerably in length and style. Some nominees confirmed, in their statements, the accuracy of information presented by students via the nomination form, and showed their own perceptiveness concerning the importance of the criteria. However, while it was helpful that the student-centred information was enhanced, the panel sought out further means of discriminating between nominees. Some, for example, showed a clear grasp of the relationship between research and teaching, and were able to sustain a substantial research output that informed their teaching and helped to maintain their role as 'exemplars'. Others revealed their own perceptions of their development as teachers, and were able to look back at their careers and specify improvements made to areas of weakness. The ability to place oneself in a context, to reflect upon and analyse one's practice, was evident in some statements and, at times, revealed the attitude of the individual to teaching, displaying commitment and describing an actual philosophy.

The supporting statements were used by some to highlight achievements, and, studied in conjunction with accompanying curricula vitae, presented information not previously considered. Another important criterion then became clear. When comparing nominees, the breadth of teaching-linked experience was noticeable in some cases. This was often matched with an evident willingness to broaden the approach to teaching. For example, some nominees had attended conferences, seminars or courses about subjects related to education or the teaching of their subject. Others had considerable experience as examiners of their subject, often at secondary as well as tertiary levels, which would obviously broaden their understanding of their own subject within the educational continuum. Evidence of innovatory teaching techniques was provided by some nominees and seen as an indicator of commitment to development and improvement of teaching methods. Some nominees chose to submit, with their statements, examples of external examiners' reports as evidence of further objective comment. Peer recognition at this stage was a useful criterion, and the panel was able to use all the information presented to look for acknowledgements from peers, such as election to or membership of recognized and prestigious societies or groups.

At the final stage of selection, contact was made with the colleagues suggested by the nominees in order to clarify issues and to request any further information to provide maximum balance. Evidence of student views was requested where it was lacking, and this gives an indication of the clear view emerging from the panel, that student corroboration was an essential factor. At the final meeting, all evidence relating to the remaining nominees was studied again, criteria were re-examined and applied and decisions made based on accumulative and thorough investigation.

In order to examine the lessons learned from the exercise and future application of the scheme, it is worth separating out three issues: first, the *criteria* used to determine the suitability of nominees for the recommendation for a Distinguished Teaching Award must be questioned; second, the *process* used to arrive at the recommendations requires consideration, finally, the *message* to be conveyed by the whole exercise should be addressed.

The criteria

The task group that evolved and presented the initial scheme for use by the University of Ulster considered that the majority of the criteria used to elicit nominators' comments in the Kent State scheme were applicable to teachers at the University of Ulster. This overall agreement was reached relatively easily, and, bearing in mind that the three members of the task group represented three diverse faculties (Education, Social and Health Sciences, and Humanities), this agreement represents an important and significant view. The proposal to use six out of seven of the criteria used by Kent State suggests that 'universal' agreement about important qualities in good teachers at a certain level of generality may not be too difficult to determine. Admittedly one UK university and one USA university do not represent all higher education institutions, and Western ideology and influence will inevitably be dominant. However, given the possible difference in style, emphasis and perceptions, agreement about these criteria is very encouraging. The addition, by UU, of the criterion covering the provision of regular and useful feedback to students, replacing the US criterion requiring comments about demonstration of 'a comprehensive knowledge of subject matter' is interesting and represents an important emphasis in the Ulster scheme. It is difficult to ascertain the way in which the issue of feedback to students is addressed in the US scheme, as the student evaluation scheme of teachers, which may include such a response, is referred to by Professor Lewis in Chapter 9 but is not mentioned in the documentation concerning Kent State's actual DTA scheme.

The most noticeable difference that has emerged after one year of implementation is to be seen in the University of Ulster's panel's need to devise further criteria at the second stage of the selection procedure. The first criteria were devised to organize and prioritize presented information on nomination forms. The second set of newly proposed criteria was devised to use the information requested from the nominees.

It is at this point, perhaps, that comparison between the two schemes should cease. It is important that the University of Ulster evolves a scheme suitable to its own practice and, while comparison with the Kent State scheme has provided an extremely useful starting point, it is important that any DTA scheme employed by the University of Ulster should be designed bearing in mind the university's requirements, relating to qualities considered relevant in good teaching as perceived by academics here. It is hoped that the exercise may be of benefit as a model for UK universities, wherein one may expect to find similar characteristics, aspirations and principles. Therefore, perhaps the four criteria devised by the panel at the second stage of the selection process provide clues to qualities that might 'distinguish' a UK university teacher today. Emphasis upon insight, innovatory techniques and breadth in both approach and relevant experience, plus evidence of further objective comment, would seem appropriate indicators, but would it then represent a distinctively 'British' approach? These criteria do represent a peer-based view rather than a student-centred view, and perhaps give an indication of a resistance to overt emphasis upon customer satisfaction, and an assertion of the need for respect from peers and understanding of contemporary educational context.

The process

Reviewing the process used to implement the DTA scheme in its first year in UU, it is clear that a modest beginning covering publicity for nominations affected the scale and range of response. There is little doubt that future implementation of the scheme will yield more nominations. Actual membership of the panel will change each year as award-holders replace teaching staff appointed by Senate and, eventually, alumni replace members nominated by Convocation. The selection procedure should continue to be reviewed by the panel while implementing the scheme. The amendments made in light of the experience of the first year should lead to an effective system, but there should still be room for suggested improvements. It was agreed by Academic Policy Committee and Senate that, in the event that the number of nominations received was so large as to cause difficulties, the chairperson could be authorized to form a sub-group to give preliminary consideration to all nominations received. It was confirmed that the chairperson should serve for three years in order to facilitate consistent decision-making.

Looking beyond the medium term, it is worth considering further the role of the Alumni Association in the procedure. While the association is in an embryonic form at present, once established it may help with the organization, funding and profile of the scheme. The Kent State University scheme stresses the importance of involving alumni in the nomination and selection of distinguished teachers. Nominations from this source are likely to be more mature and thoughtful, as past students may perceive a teacher's strengths more clearly in retrospect and provide a reflective analysis incorporating their own experience since graduation.

The message

In setting up a scheme of this kind, the university was aiming to give an important signal to staff and to students. The award clearly signifies the value placed upon teaching of real quality and asserts this message at a time

when many staff are coming to terms with the relationship between research and teaching.

The initial reception to the scheme during its first year of implementation at the University of Ulster was tentative, if judged by numbers of
nominations. As indicated previously, dissemination of information was
modest and calls for nominations elicited uneven responses across a large
institution. However, responses to the scheme in principle, as indicated by
senior staff comment, were all positive, and once the scheme yielded actual
results in the form of recommendation of awards to Senate, all responses
were supportive and encouraging.

All nominees invited to provide supporting information responded seriously and with evidence of some pride in having been selected. There have
been, to date, no negative comments received concerning the purpose and
importance of the scheme. In fact, there has been widespread support for
the implementation of a scheme that is emblematic of the university's
commitment to recognizing and promoting excellence in teaching. While
the Kent State University runs a well established system that clearly embraces the same message, it is worth reflecting upon differences in style and
context. In the United States, 'teaching-only' contracts are available for
academic staff, and teaching as an activity has a high status. There is a
serious commitment to teaching, which may be accompanied by a style and
approach to teaching that is different from that found in the United
Kingdom. Stereotypical British characteristics do not embrace the earnest
approach that some associate with a US style. Traditionally the British are
reticent about success and cautious about appearing to be immodest. Promotion of one's strengths is not common and it would not be considered
appropriate to boast about success. Equally, there is a resistance to any
'show business' hyperbole about the activity, and a scepticism about popularity stakes. When Professor Lewis gave his lecture on 'Teaching styles of
award-winning professors' (May 1989) he was taken to task by University of
Ulster staff about his promotion of the concept of 'performance', with
accusations of too much stress upon theatricality.

While we wish to convey to staff the importance of the scheme, it is
important that it is respected and taken seriously. An interesting and
symbolic way of illustrating the difference between US style and UK style
in this matter is shown in the way the two schemes record, present and
acknowledge successful award-holders. When Professor Ellis visited Kent
State University he was shown a room set aside in which were engraved
portraits of each of the award-holders, each with a spotlight. This is
referred to as the 'Hall of Fame'. In Ulster, the equivalent means is served
by erecting a hand-carved, wooden plaque on each campus, to be
carefully painted with additions to the roll of honour when an award is
given. These two means of expression show an underlying difference in
attitude that is quite reassuring. A Distinguished Teaching Award scheme
at the University of Ulster will build upon its own strengths and traditions
quite naturally, as the people responsible for its introduction and

implementation, while aware of practice elsewhere and willing to learn from it, are also champions of an institution that embraces both tradition and innovation.

11

Expert Teachers' Perceptions of University Teaching: the Identification of Teaching Skills

Christine Saunders and Eric Saunders

The context of the study

Government policy, in the 1987 White Paper, *Higher Education: Meeting the Challenge* (Cmnd 114), specified 'the quality of teaching' among the factors by which quality in higher education as a whole could be judged, and affirmed that the maintenance of high standards in teaching could be assisted by systematic arrangements for staff training and development. This affirmation of the importance of teaching had not escaped the attention of authors of previous official reports including the University Grants Committee's *A Strategy for Higher Education into the 1990s* (1984), the Jarratt Report in 1985 and the Lindop Report in the same year. However, studies documented around the same time noted that there was little agreement over the description of quality and warned there was no reliable way of assessing 'good teaching' because of the subjective nature of judgements about quality (Williams and Blackstone 1983; Moodie 1986; Andreson and Powell 1987). Elton (1987), on the other hand, was more optimistic in his review of the complexities of describing and assessing teachers and teaching, and asserted that the technical difficulties of assessment could be overcome.

The government's overt focus on quality and its heightened interest in the value to the nation of money spent on higher education led to the demand for a system of institutional and individual staff appraisal that gave weight to the assessment of teaching performance in the allocation of funding and as an aid to the evaluation of teaching staff. Earlier reports by the UGC (1984) and Jarratt (1985) outlined the virtues of appraisal and its benefits to the universities and to their staff, while polytechnics and colleges, because of their involvement with CNAA, had already built into their procedures a form of staff appraisal in the planning and review of programmes of study.

The establishment of a new academic standards unit at King's College, London, underlined the Committee of Vice-Chancellors' resolve to raise teaching standards in universities. This principle was endorsed by the Vice-Chancellor of the University of Ulster in 1989 in his response to the UGC's proposed research selectivity exercise, in which he outlined the university's strong commitment to both research and the continuing maintenance and enhancement of teaching. The evaluation procedures of the university already included research, consultancy and staff development in its monitoring and evaluation of programmes of study, and external examiners' reports were key elements in the annual review of courses. However, it was recognized that, while research could be assessed through peer judgement, and administration and course development activities were open to public scrutiny, there were few indicators of teaching performance that would enable the university to arrive at a more objective assessment of teaching quality. The system of staff appraisal, therefore, which took account of faculty and departmental development plans and included a review of administration, research and teaching, was frustrated by a lack of agreement over the criteria against which teaching quality could be assessed. In turn, judgements about the ways in which academics conducted their teaching as a basis for staff development or promotion could not be advanced in the absence of some form of positive staff appraisal based upon an agreed means of quality assessment. From the management point of view of quality assurance and control, the university would benefit from a system that could identify the development needs of staff and seek to devise means by which teaching effectiveness could be enhanced.

No one underestimated the complex task of evaluating teaching and of setting up appropriate management and organizational structures to support effective teaching. All courses in the university were subject to carefully devised procedures for the review of course quality through periodic course reviews and annual course appraisal reports. This included the evaluation of course aims and objectives, teaching and learning strategies, resources and assessment procedures. It was clearly understood that the effectiveness of teaching and learning could only be assessed with some degree of confidence if all other factors were carefully planned and monitored. While cognizance was taken of the knowledge, skills and abilities students achieved through their programme of study, in other words 'what' is taught, the processes and methods used to achieve the realization of the course aims and objectives were still comparatively underdeveloped. 'How' courses were taught and how decisions about teaching quality were arrived at had spawned more heat than light and little advance had been made in attempting to arrive at widely agreed criteria of quality in teaching and learning processes.

The University of Ulster, therefore, had a tangible and long-standing commitment to an ethos that placed teaching and learning in the forefront of its quality control system and actively encouraged projects aimed at arriving at more objective judgements about teaching that could be used in practice. The university had also built teaching and learning into its formal appraisal of staff performance, and maintained that in principle teaching performance could be given equal weight with research and administrative performances in the evaluation of staff for promotion. The appraisal system, therefore, aimed to maintain and improve performance (formative) and to judge its effectiveness (summative).

The challenge to find more systematic means of arriving at decisions about teachers was timely. It coincided with the results obtained from a major research project into the identification of key communication skills for speech therapists (Saunders and Caves 1986), which, in turn, had its source in earlier work into the development of means of assessing student teachers' practical teaching skills (Saunders and Saunders 1980). As a result of discussion between the two principal researchers who had carried out the previous research, and senior management, a research project was designed to identify, analyse and evaluate the effectiveness of a range of teaching skills and techniques, which could be used in a proposed staff teaching appraisal guide. The project, located in the University Institutional Research Unit, was funded for a period of two years from January 1990. The research team comprised one full-time research officer, the two authors of this report and the Director of the Unit. The proposal, therefore, grew naturally from the earlier work of the researchers' analyses of professional skills. In spite of the warning from authors of earlier studies that there were no widely agreed criteria of quality, the principal researchers were not deterred from continuing with this complex task since they were aware that the main responsibility for achieving and maintaining high quality and standards lay with the university itself, and a wider level of agreement was not a condition of the successful completion of the study.

Design of the study

A fundamental premise of this study, which had emerged from our previous investigations, was that a consultative mode of enquiry was a key element in eliciting and clarifying perception of effective professional practice. A similar conclusion was reached by Elton (1987), who claimed that teachers can arrive at characterization of good teaching through group discussion and analysis. It was also maintained that the adoption of an eclectic research strategy would be equal to the task. There were a number of reasons for arriving at this decision.

First, the resources for this project were limited and in the time available there was considerable doubt about the feasibility of classical research designs in which variables such as sample sizes, pilot studies and techniques of analyses were specified in advance. Second, it was considered that research into the identification of professional skills was in its infancy and there was no theoretical rationale for the selection of particular skills. One major factor inhibiting work in this field was the implicit nature of professional know-how or tacit knowledge. Attempts to describe professional action had proved resistant to explicit definition (Eraut 1985) and techniques used in our previous studies in uncovering and eliciting information expert teachers already 'know' but may not be able to articulate demanded a flexible research strategy. Third, work with experienced school teachers and speech therapists had established the validity of drawing upon the expertise of experienced professionals to arrive at practice-created knowledge of teaching through collaborative modes of enquiry. By design this required 'expert' teachers in collaboration with researchers pooling their knowledge and expertise through critical and reflective self-evaluation and peer group analyses of teaching as an ongoing process. Consequently, the progressive identification and analysis of skills was always problematic and required reviews of strategy as the research unfolded. Finally, the involvement of expert teachers in the generation of a portfolio of teaching skills that could be identified in practice would sharpen their perceptions and enhance their ability to analyse teaching. In turn, these teachers could prove invaluable in staff development programmes in the future.

In essence, therefore, an eclectic strategy was adopted, which allowed procedures to be revised and new ones devised in the light of experience. This enabled the research team to keep the study within manageable limits, to offset unanticipated problems, to prepare reports that were intelligible to teachers and to give adequate time for the ongoing challenges of integrating, distilling and interpreting data. It was also important at the early stages to realize that different teaching modes, lectures, seminars, practicals, tutorials and so on would generate different types of skills. We should try to capitalize on the expertise of teachers in a range of teaching modes and enable them to identify skills that represent meaningful differences in a variety of teaching situations. Given the duration of the project, staffing, resources and the time involvement of members of staff in a number of group discussion sessions, it was decided to restrict the research to the three most common modes of teaching identified through a review of course documents in the university. These were class teaching, seminar teaching and practicals.

The consultative approach

It was proposed that consultation between teachers should take place in separate meetings to encourage specific discussion of the skills associated with distinctive modes of teaching. Sessions followed a similar format and results were recorded separately. In each session participants were given specific tasks to complete, the results were analysed between sessions and provided the basis for the elaboration of further tasks in succeeding meetings. The fact that these sessions were seldom longer than three hours and each was task specific did wonders to concentrate the mind and ensured that an individual's contribution was relevant and vigorously argued. Of course differences of opinion did occur and there were problems of reconciling conflicting views of teaching. The fact that members were willing to try to understand each other's perspectives and modify their own views accordingly was a feature of each group's professionalism. Without this form of cooperation the project would have come to nothing.

At the outset, therefore, we were aware that a collaborative mode of enquiry brings with it some major problems and challenges. Attention to personal and interpersonal relationships of teachers from different subject areas and research staff was a critical factor in maintaining commitment and interest and reducing tensions in each group session. It was necessary to create a climate in which illuminative, constructive and intelligent criticism was encouraged as the project developed. Throughout the investigation it was important to utilize techniques to gather and interpret information that did not distort the views of the participating groups. This entailed different forms of recording group sessions and the production of reports that were the basis of further discussion in the next session, to ensure that the researcher's interpretation of each session was an accurate representation of the group's understanding of the previous session's deliberations. Because we were wholly dependent upon the group's version of the realities of teaching, the authenticity of these reports was open to further revision as a result of ongoing discussion, analysis and interpretation.

Another major concern was to ensure that skills should be grounded in observable behaviour. The research team, apart from setting the task and keeping to the timescale, played a largely reactive role, clarifying and resolving issues when approached, final decisions resting entirely with the group itself. Videotapes were also used to record and later to test the accuracy of descriptions of skills derived from earlier workshop sessions.

Finally, where individual members of a group could not attend a particular session, special arrangements were made to afford them the opportunity to comment on changes made by the group in their absence. This ensured the continuing commitment of each member and a collective response to tasks which depended upon the full participation of all staff in each session. This was often time-consuming but was an essential feature of the research.

What follows is a detailed review of this consultative approach in action. Emphasis is placed on the methodology and techniques employed, rather than the substantive results. The intention is to give some guidance on the procedural decisions required at different stages of this consultative study. The study was divided into four stages. They were:

Stage I: identification of expert teachers in different modes of teaching.
Stage II: development of schedules of teaching skills.
Stage III: refinement of the schedules.
Stage IV: validation of the schedules.

Stage I: identification of expert teachers in different modes of teaching

In the absence of any clear-cut information regarding the size of each group, it was decided that no group should contain more than 12 members, making 36 staff in total. This arrangement would make it possible for members to be open and reflective in discussion without the attending intimidations and anxieties that could accrue in larger groups. (Francis 1989).

It was also decided to select staff who reflected the size and make-up of each of the seven faculties within the University of Ulster and the Centre for Continuing Education. Thus, for example, Social and Health Sciences, one of the larger faculties, were asked to put forward six members of staff while Art and Design, one of the smaller faculties, was asked to submit names of three staff members. Account was also taken of the range of disciplines, location of teaching staff across the four campuses and gender, to ensure an equitable representation.

In the selection of 'expert' teachers, deans were approached to enlist their support in nominating and freeing staff to join the research team. A meeting was held with each dean, preceded by a letter outlining: the rationale for this university-wide initiative; the work participants would undertake; the date of commencement of the project, April 1990; the number of sessions, eight in total; and the time commitment of around three hours per session. The meeting was invaluable in describing in some detail the purpose of the project and its value to the staff development plans of each faculty, and in answering queries that inevitably arise when projects of this type are being undertaken. Deans were then asked to complete a proforma giving the name, designation, department, campus location and teaching group of members of staff selected to participate. As a result, 37 staff members (26 males and 11 females) were approached and agreed to take part in the project. The research team was reasonably well satisfied that the ratio of male to female staff, the range of teaching subject areas and each campus were fairly represented. The decision to combine teachers from different faculties was based upon previous research findings, which indicated that what makes an effective teacher is roughly the same regardless of academic discipline (Pohlmann 1976; Erdle and Murray 1986).

Stage II: development of schedules of teaching skills

The initial session

Following the identification of 37 expert teachers, Dr George Brown, recently retired Reader at the University of Nottingham and now employed by the Training Agency, launched the project. As National Coordinator of Academic Staff Training for the Committee of Vice-Chancellors and Principals for the previous five years, Dr Brown was in an ideal position to articulate the unique aspects of this innovative study and the key role to be played by all the participants. To sensitize the teachers to the arbitrary and idiosyncratic nature of teaching, Dr Brown involved his audience in a series of exercises aimed at identifying the problematic nature and outcomes of different styles and modes of teaching. The positive response from the teachers and their willingness to enter into open discussion on controversial issues in a most realistic and informed manner was very encouraging and promised well for further workshop sessions.

The second part of this session described in broad detail the purpose of the project, the basis on which each member of staff was selected and invited to participate, the length and location of each session and the tasks ahead. Care was taken to emphasize their key role as experienced teachers and the value of the pooling of practice-created knowledge through collaborative enquiry. Careful steps were taken to convince the groups that we, the research team, were approaching them as experts and that our main role was to enable them to communicate their expertise through free-ranging discussion.

This led to the third part of the session, which warrants a more detailed explanation. It was important at this stage to involve teachers individually in the analyses of their own subject in the context of the group's teaching mode. While there are many approaches to obtaining data about teaching, including participant observation, interaction analyses, inventories, self-reports, interviews or questionnaires, the technique that seemed most appropriate in identifying classroom behaviour and had been used in our previous studies was the 'critical incident' technique (Flanagan 1954). This technique consists of a set of procedures for collecting information about behaviour in specific teaching settings from those in the best position to make observations and evaluations. It aims to provide descriptors of behaviour that can actually be observed and it should seek to produce accurate, objective and unbiased accounts of specific acts. By using this technique a record of critical behaviour can be obtained from teachers' first-hand knowledge and experience in face-to-face situations.

The purposes of the next exercise were to involve teachers individually in assessing their own discipline-based experiences in the three modes of teaching and to provide the research team with data, through a modified form of the 'critical incident' technique, for comparison. However, it was recognized that skills of teaching are context-bound and any skilled resolution of a problem in the classroom or workshop demands a detailed knowledge and understanding of the particular setting in which teaching takes place. Consequently, the first task was to identify contextual factors that influence decisions about teaching strategies in planning, preparing, presenting and evaluating teaching. While it was acknowledged that the procedure would lead to a plethora of information, previous research had confirmed that individually described incidents or factors in this case were not independent of each other; that these possessed some generality and could be classified into a limited number of categories, each made up of related behaviour. The task set was: 'Identify 12–20 contextual factors that influence the kind of decisions you make in terms of planning, preparing, presenting and evaluating your teaching.'

Individual responses were recorded in teachers' private time and returned to the research officer for collation and loose classification. Results, which were stored on computer, produced 214, 261 and 235 statements from class teaching, seminar teaching and practical teaching situations respectively. These were recorded and classified in separate reports, which provided the focus for the next session. For example, the classification adopted for seminar teaching was gender of students, characteristics of students, student knowledge and ability, timetabling, teaching space, resources, health and safety, subject content, goal-setting, organization, feedback and review, student participation, student response and assessment. Individual items were grouped under these headings.

Sessions 2 and 3

In session 2 each group member was given a copy of this report, which provided the frame of reference for the session, and was asked to consider the appropriateness of the loosely classified system and amend it if necessary, adding, removing or reclassifying any items he or she thought fit. As a result some items overlapped and were combined, some were removed, new ones emerged and the classification systems were amended. Group discussion was an essential device in refining, clarifying and identifying skilled behaviour as a result of constructive and critical appraisal of typical teaching situations. From the involvement of teachers, collaboratively refining and interpreting their descriptions of contextual factors influencing teaching behaviour, a common language was beginning to emerge, based upon a shared interpretation of events and a common understanding of the relationship between the meaning of terms and an individual's perception of the realities of teaching. Clearly the validity of any schedule depends upon the ability of the observer to perceive patterns of behaviour accurately, which, in turn, assumes a common understanding and operational agreement about the features of the behaviour under observation.

At this stage we were satisfied that the 'unscripted' and 'intuitive' nature of professional action was being revealed by this joint mode of enquiry. Yet we had anticipated that this could become a largely 'theoretical' exercise where the search for common meanings and shared interpretations, however important, was not sufficiently rooted in practice. In line with the consultative approach, it was still necessary to ensure that the teachers' observations were grounded in their knowledge of the complexities of their own teaching encounters with students. This is a prerequisite of the identification of skills used to resolve the day-to-day problems of class, seminar or practical teaching.

While we were satisfied that, within the bounds of time, teachers were now in a position to make a more detailed examination of skilled teaching behaviour, we were concerned that their views should be reflected in contexts that confronted them in their everyday routine work with students. From our earlier research we know that it was critical to ensure that teachers had the opportunity to test their observations against the realities of specific subject-bound teaching contexts. The fact that the first two sessions had alerted them to a range of contextual factors that influenced decisions about teaching was no guarantee that these factors existed wholly or partly in all situations. We needed further evidence of more specific contextual factors that teachers take into account when teaching their subject. In our previous research in secondary schools, teaching contexts were pre-specified by the research team as a result of first-hand knowledge of the subject areas under examination. In the present research, which embraced a range of subject specialists, it was decided that each member of each group should be asked to consider the original list of contextual factors and use it to describe one particular problematic lecture, seminar or practical encountered in the immediate past, and record it in a brief transcript. The purpose of this third session, therefore, was to create a range of problematic teaching situations, each different in context from the others. Transcripts were constructed and details exchanged with other group members, and where there was too much overlap of one with another, teachers were asked to re-think and identify another problematic situation not covered by anyone else in the group. This was a time-consuming task, which took anything from four to eight hours to complete. It produced 37 descriptions of teaching situations or teaching scenarios that had recently been encountered. For instance, problematic key features cited in one practical session set in a psychology of skilled performance laboratory workshop referred to:

> a class of 33 first year undergraduate students working in groups of six per computer because of lack of resources. They are lively, outgoing and usually work well in groups, although the individual range of competence in computing is variable. Attendance at this Friday afternoon session has been poor although the group is enthusiastic about laboratory work. The group has had two 2-hour theoretical lectures previously. There is no technical support and computing equipment is limited.

We were now in a position to probe further the range of skills adopted by each teacher when faced with a distinctive problematic situation of this type. The next task, therefore, was to ask teachers to complete a pro-forma in their own private time in which they were asked to 'list 12–20 statements you would offer as advice to an inexperienced colleague faced with the

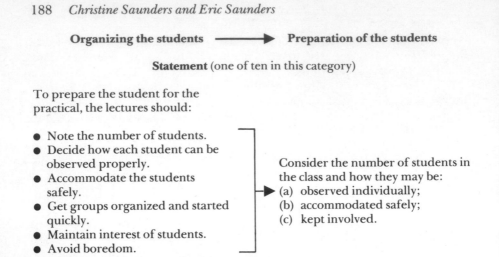

Figure 11.1 Practical teaching group category.

situations described in your scenario.' This exercise resulted in a range of responses in the 37 teaching contexts that were returned to the research officer, who again compiled them into a loosely classified system in a paper circulated at the next session.

Sessions 4 and 5

As a result of this experience, approximately two hundred statements were generated by each group and loosely classified by the research officer into broad categories of teaching for ease of handling at these sessions. From these data it was anticipated that through further discussion, analyses and interpretation the number of statements would be reduced to a more manageable level. An assumption underlying this exercise is that teaching behaviours are not independent of each other, that they possess some generality and can be classified into a limited number of teaching skills, and that each skill is analysable in terms of related, observable behaviour. It is also assumed that these skills can be classified into broadly based categories of teaching, such as planning, preparing, presenting and evaluating any lesson.

The major task of these workshops was threefold. Group members were asked to consider the meaning of each statement and its relationship to others, and then review its membership to a particular teaching category. This led to some changes in the category system and the refinement and reduction of the number of statements attached to each category. Figure 11.1 may help to illuminate the process. The results of these two workshops provided three provisional schedules of teaching skills: class teaching contained 88 items in seven categories; seminar teaching contained 66 ileⅢs ⅢⅢe categories; practical teaching contained 70 items in nine categories.

Stage III: refinement of the schedules

At the end of Stage II we had produced three lists of teaching skills over a period of six months through five group consultative sessions. At this point in the research we were reasonably satisfied that the schedules reflected expert teachers' perceptions of effective practice. Nevertheless, to maximize the validity of the exercise, which was centred in the university, it was felt that all full-time teaching staff should have the opportunity to reflect and comment on the component skills and their relevance to current practice. This is based on the premise that while experienced practitioners have identified the skills, more convincing evidence can be obtained by asking individual teachers for their responses. This entailed contacting over eight hundred teachers in the university. As we had no detailed information on any one individual's modes of teaching (although we assumed everyone would use class and seminar means of conveying information) we decided on a strategy which, on the face of it, would result in responses that would enable us to refine each schedule further. The total cohort of teaching staff was divided arbitrarily into three groups, each group being given two of the three schedules, and invited to complete one of the two schedules closest to its preferred mode of teaching.

The schedules were designed as a questionnaire in which the teacher was asked to assign the importance of each skill on a scale of 1–5 or to indicate if the skill was not applicable. A response rate of over 50 per cent, which included an almost equal response rate for each mode of teaching, was statistically analysed and a number of items were deleted using the following two criteria. First, if 10 per cent or more of the respondents indicated that a skill item did not apply it was deleted. Second, in class teaching if any skill item had a mean of less than 4.0 and a standard deviation of more than 1.0 it was also deleted. Similarly, any skill item with a mean of less than 3.5 and a standard deviation of more than 1.0 in seminar and practical teaching was removed.

Figure 11.1 showed the item and its descriptor remained unchanged, whereas in other categories some statements and their descriptors were reviewed. Another example from the same teaching mode illustrates the procedure:

Category: Preparation of materials and examples – unchanged.
Statements:
- Prepare a clear, printed handout – retained.
- Prepare a series of overhead transparencies – deleted.
- Decide on the appropriate timing of the distribution of any handout – retained.

● Provide a range of materials or equipment to permit student choice where this can be accommodated in the objectives of the practical – deleted.

This exercise led to no changes in the category system but a reduction in the number of skill items in class teaching, seminar teaching and practicals to 45, 41 and 56 respectively, and provided the frameworks for the final phase of the research.

Stage IV: validation of the schedules

At this stage of the project it became necessary to validate the further refinements in the schedule of skills provided by the large-scale exercise against each group member's interpretation of its validity in practice. Group discussion had been a useful device to refine, clarify and identify skills as a result of constructive, critical appraisal of teaching. The university full-time staff involved in reviewing the schedules sought some further evidence of the appropriateness of the skills and gave some assurance of their support for the process. However, the validity of any schedule of skills rests upon the degree of fit between an individual's interpretation of each descriptor and its relationship with student behaviour in the classroom seminar setting or practical workshop.

The next step, therefore, was to discuss whether the derived teaching skills could be observed in lessons taught in the university; to state by what means a particular skill in the schedule could be observed and recorded; to give actual instances of the skill being used in a lesson, and to examine the consistency of these instances. Clearly the success of direct observation of teaching behaviour depended upon the ability of the observer to perceive patterns of behaviour accurately, which in turn assumed a common understanding and operational agreement about the features of the behaviour under observation.

Since it would have been impractical and, indeed, inappropriate to test the schedules against ongoing teaching situations in the university, video recordings of selected classroom and workshop activities were made. To ensure a range of activities in a variety of teaching settings each of the 37 members of the project team was asked to identify one lesson that could be used as a videotaped exemplar. The research team, in consultation with the teachers, then selected nine lessons representing distinctly different activities in each of the three teaching modes, each lesson consisting of the written plan of the lesson, a videotape of the teaching situation and the teacher's evaluation of the lesson. The purpose of this exercise was explained to students, who, without exception, agreed to take part. We also assured staff that the films were their property and that they would not be used as a personal evaluation of their own teaching. Consequently, on viewing the videotape each member of staff had the right to withdraw the tape or be refilmed. One teacher exercised this option and a further lesson was filmed. The recorded session used for analysis covered the following subject areas:

Large group teaching
- Art and Design
- Consumer Studies
- Nursing

Seminar group teaching
- Law
- Peace Studies
- Women's Studies

Practical Group Teaching
- Biology
- Hotel and Catering Management
- Physiotherapy

The most practical means of eliciting teachers' views was a self completion questionnaire, which was completed immediately following an analysis of the written plan, the videotape and the written evaluation. From our previous research we were aware that observations improve when observers are asked to focus on a limited number of dimensions at one time, the optimum being around 18. To achieve this a review of the lesson was divided into four sections that coincided with the broad phases of teaching contained in each schedule. Part 1 contained the beginning of the lesson, parts 2 and 3 the lesson development, and part 4 the conclusion of the lesson. Each phase was analysed separately. For example, group members viewed the early part of the film for around 10–15 minutes, and completed the relevant section of the questionnaire. This was followed by a group discussion to verify consistencies or differences in their interpretations of each skill item. At this point no attempt was made to modify, add to or discard any item. Each group then viewed a second film adopting similar procedures but with the added task of refining the schedule. This has been completed and a preliminary analysis of one of the schedules leads us to conclude that the process of refinement will result in a list of skills in each teaching mode of around 25–30 component skills.

Concluding comments

The work to date describes the efforts of one institution to come to terms with some of the problems of arriving at agreement on the key skills of teaching in the classroom in seminars and in practical sessions. The study confirms that, by drawing upon the expertise of experienced teachers through collaborative modes of enquiry, one can tap practice-created knowledge and achieve a clearer identification of a range of teaching skills. However, is there any reason to believe that the emergent 'schedules' of teaching skills are in any sense valid? Clearly there are difficulties in specifying skills of professional effectiveness since there are no widely agreed criteria of quality in higher education teaching. Consultative methods ensured that the skills identified had high face validity; that is, they seemed to be the most relevant skill to current teachers in the university. Perhaps our work will encourage more studies of this type by independent researchers so that the most valid skills of teaching will emerge from further consensus-convergent validity approaches.

Further work has still to be completed on the reliability and practical usefulness of each compendium of teaching skills. In the context of this consultative study the most important form of reliability is inter-observer reliability, the level of agreement of observers over the identification or occurrence of a skill. The limitations of time and resources will provide only one opportunity for each group member to test the reliability of the component skills in another teaching mode. We realize that a more stringent form would be to teach it to another new group of professionals who could use it for the analysis of classroom practice.

Finally, this project was narrowly focused upon the identification of teaching skills and in this sense the project was highly specific and short-term. Nevertheless, we are aware that teaching quality, however defined, can only in the end be judged against student learning outcomes. A further step in assessing the validity of the schedule will be to test it against students' perception of the key skills of teaching. The degree to which students and teachers agree on skills that characterize effective teaching will be important in the clarification of the complex relationship between teaching and learning.

References

Andreson, L. W. and Powell, J. P. (1987) Competent teaching and its appraisal. *Assessment and Evaluation in Higher Education*, 12(1): 66–72.
Elton, L. (1987) *Teaching in Higher Education: Appraisal and Training*. London: Kogan Page.
Eraut, M. (1985) Knowledge creation and knowledge use in professional contexts. *Studies in Higher Education*, 10(2): 117–33.
Erdle, S. and Murray, H. G. (1986) Interfaculty differences in classroom teaching behaviours and their relationship to student instructional ratings. *Research in Higher Education*, 24(2): 115–27.
Flanagan, J. C. (1954) The critical incident technique. *Psychological Bulletin*, 51(4): 327–59.
Francis, E. (1989) Discussion and imagery: an experiential learning program for teachers. *Small Group Behaviour*, 20(3): 344–56.
Jarratt, A. (Chairman) (1985) *Report of the Steering Committee for Efficiency Studies in Universities*. London: CVCP.
Lindop, Sir N. (Chairman) (1985) *Academic Validation in Public Sector Higher Education: the Report of the Committee of Enquiry into the Academic Validation of Degree Courses in Public Sector Higher Education*, Cmnd 9501. London: HMSO.

Moodie, G. G. (ed.) (1986) *Standards and Criteria in Higher Education*. Guilford: SRHE and NFER/Nelson.

Pohlmann, J. T. (1976) A description of effective college teaching in five disciplines as measured by student ratings. *Research in Higher Education*, 4: 335–46.

Saunders, C. and Caves, R. (1986) An empirical approach to the identification of communication skills with reference to speech therapy. *Journal of Further and Higher Education*, 10(2): 29–44.

Saunders, E. and Saunders, C. (1980) The assessment of teaching practice – a study. Mimeo, Ulster Polytechnic.

University Grants Committee (1984) *A Strategy for Higher Education into the 1990s*. London: HMSO.

Williams, G. and Blackstone, T. (1983) *Response to Adversity: Higher Education in a Harsh Climate*. Guilford: SRHE.

12

Teaching Standards from Quality Circles

Jennifer Boore

Introduction

Institutions of higher education have two sets of customers for their courses and teaching, the students and those who employ the graduates. Both groups can reasonably have an expectation that at the end of a programme of study the student will have acquired knowledge and skills that make him or her fit for employment in whatever sphere is appropriate.

In order to reach this end, both the *content* and the *presentation* of the programme undertaken have to be of a quality that will achieve the desired result. An increasing emphasis is now being placed on the provision of a high quality of education, as demonstrated by the work of the Division of Quality Audit. Various approaches are being used throughout higher education to attempt to ensure that students receive high quality teaching within well planned courses, and a number of these are discussed in this book. Although these will make individual contributions to ensuring the quality of the educational experience, the initiatives need to be integrated in a comprehensive approach to the management of quality of education within an institution. This chapter discusses an approach that was used to try to enhance the quality of a range of different teaching methods used in higher education.

In attempting to achieve a high quality in teaching methods using a quality assurance approach it is necessary first to set standards for the different teaching methods used. These can then be used as the yardstick against which to measure the performance in teaching. Where the performance is lacking then remedial action can be taken. In this exercise standards were developed through a number of groups of staff and students within a faculty examining the most common teaching methods used. The standards developed were distributed to all academic staff in the faculty, who were encouraged to use them to examine and improve their own teaching. As yet there has been no independent assessment of performance against these standards. The approach used to set these standards was an adaptation of the quality circles used in numerous organizations.

Quality circles

Quality Circles are one manifestation of group working. Handy (1985) identified a number of functions that may be carried out by groups, and many of these functions are carried out within quality circles. The functions Handy identified are:

● the distribution of work, i.e. the bringing together of an appropriate set of skills;
● problem-solving and decision-making, i.e. ensuring that the solution of any problem will have all available talents and capacities applied to it;
● information and idea gathering, and also information processing;
● coordination and liaison between individual group members and between groups;
● the management and control of work;
● testing and ratifying decisions, i.e. testing the validity of a decision taken outside the group and ratifying such a decision;
● increased involvement, i.e. to allow and encourage individuals to get involved in the plans and activities of the organization;
● inquest and enquiry into the past.

Quality circles were initially introduced by the Japanese in an effort to improve the quality of their manufactured goods. They are now used in industry and other organizations elsewhere in the world to improve the quality of the product or service of the organization (Hill 1989). They have been defined in numerous ways, some more complex than others. Robson (1982) has described a quality circle as:

> a group of four to ten volunteers working for the same supervisor or foreman who meet once a week, for an hour, under the leadership of the supervisor, to identify, analyse and solve their own work-related problems.

Ferris and Wagner (1985) described them rather more broadly as follows.

> QCs are small groups of employees, usually ranging in size from 3–15 members, that meet periodically to identify and resolve job-related problems. Membership . . . is usually voluntary and the amount of time members spend in QC activities may range from an hour per month to a few hours each week.

The terminology used (e.g. foreman) indicates clearly the industrial setting in which this approach developed and has been primarily used. Within this setting the focus has been on dealing with problems identified by the group and related to the work of the particular group. The members of the quality circle are usually working in the same area or carrying out similar work.

The Japanese (e.g. Ishikawa 1984) discussed the importance of quality circles in terms of human resource development of the first-line supervisors and the shop floor workers. This concept is very different from the Western assumption that problems of quality are due to 'operator indifference, blunder and even sabotage' (Juran 1967). Juran stated that

the Quality Circle concept starts with a different set of beliefs:

● we do not really know the cause of our quality troubles, we do not even know which are the main troubles. Hence,
● we must teach people how to analyze the trouble pattern to identify the main troubles. Also,
● we must teach people how to list the suspected causes of the main troubles, and how to discover which are the real causes. Then,
● we must help people to secure remedies for these real causes. Finally,
● we must teach people how to hold the gains through modern control methods.

(Juran 1967: 335).

Cole (1979) identified some of the key characteristics of quality circles in the industrial setting as including an emphasis on:

● the size, being between three and twenty people, usually from five to ten;
● voluntary membership, autonomy of the group and combined effort of all members of the group;
● the importance of training in the statistical and management methods used in quality analysis and enhancement;
● the application of these methods in problem identification, analysis and solving;
● the ongoing regularity of the meetings of the quality circle;
● the recognition by management of the value of the quality circle activities.

In the activity carried out within the faculty the groups and the methods of functioning did not entirely match the descriptions of the classic quality circle. However, they were an adaptation which suited the task and the method of functioning of higher education. Each of the characteristics described by Cole (1979) can be considered.

1. The size should be between three and twenty people, usually from five to ten. In the faculty exercise the groups matched this characteristic, being made up usually of six to eight people all involved in the business of higher education, either as teachers or as learners.
2. Membership of the group should be voluntary. Functioning of the group should be autonomous and involve the combined effort of all members of the group. In this exercise possible members were

identified and invited to join the group and all who became members contributed to the group's activity. However, while normally the quality circle itself determines the problem it will investigate, in this exercise the circles involved were given a clearly defined task.

3. There should be training in the statistical and management methods used in quality analysis and enhancement. No training was made available before the undertaking of this activity. However, most of the members of the group were knowledgeable about statistical techniques and, as a result of their academic background, had varying degrees of skill in analysis.

4. These methods should be applied in problem identification, analysis and solving. The group members were able to apply their skills in carrying out the task set.

5. The meetings of the quality circle should continue at regular intervals on an ongoing basis. This is the characteristic on which these groups differed the most from the classic quality circle, as the length of time over which these groups met was short. All those involved had numerous other demands on their time and the work was completed in a relatively short time with a small number of meetings.

6. Management should recognize the value of the quality circle activities. There was no formal recognition of the work of those who contributed to this activity. However, the groups were set up by the Academic Courses Committee of the faculty with the full backing of the dean and heads of departments. In addition, the intrinsic reward from involvement in the activity was high.

Setting standards

The concept of setting standards and objectively assessing performance against these standards is one that has become accepted and implemented in many situations. While the idea originated in industry it has been accepted by many professions and used in numerous work settings as a part of their aim to enhance the quality of their services. The approaches within some of the professions are probably a more appropriate comparison with higher education than the use in industry.

The word standard has been defined in various ways, including 'a basis of measurement: a criterion: an established or accepted model: a definite level of excellence or adequacy required, aimed at or possible' (*Chambers Twentieth Century Dictionary*). In the context of quality assurance the Royal College of Nursing, representing one profession that has carried out a considerable amount of work on quality assurance, has defined it as follows: 'A standard is a professionally agreed level of performance appropriate to the population addressed, which is observable, achievable, measurable and desirable' (RCN 1986).

Both definitions contribute to clarification of the objectives of the exercise, with the RCN definition emphasizing the professionalism in-herent within the process. Both definitions highlight the importance of criteria in standard setting. Standards and criteria can be written separately or combined into one statement. In this exercise they were combined into one statement.

Standards can be developed from two very different sources, described by Donabedian (1966) as follows:

> *normative standards* derive, in principle, from the source that legiti-mately set the standards of knowledge and practice; *empirical standards* are derived from actual practice.

Clearly there can be no conflict between these two approaches. The first will identify what is desirable, but this may not be achievable and can lead to disillusionment. The second may simply result in maintenance of the status quo. In practice the standards set are likely to (and probably should) result from a combination of the two approaches, with the idealism of the first tempered somewhat by a recognition of what could be achievable in practice with some (not excessive) commitment of time and resources.

Kemp and Richardson (1990), in the context of setting standards for nursing practice, state that standards should be measurable, realistic, appropriate, desirable, acceptable and unambiguous. These characteristics appear equally appropriate to higher education. The characteristic of measurability does imply that the wording of standards needs to be precise and specific, and should avoid the use of terms that require interpretation.

In attempting to write standards it is valuable to have some sort of structure to guide the work. Donabedian (1969), in evaluating the quality of nursing care, used structure, process and outcome as the framework. This appears equally appropriate to setting standards for teaching methods in higher education. Within this faculty exercise this approach was used by some groups although not by others.

Setting standards for teaching methods

Usually when standards are being set for particular activities in industry the required input in terms of raw materials and the desired outcome of the activity in terms of the product are clearly identified; the reason and necessity for the activity are clear. However, in higher education the input, in terms of the intellectual abilities and the motivation of the entering students, is less easily specified. Among those accepted for a university course, the grades achieved at Advanced level are not a particularly good predictor of success, accounting for only one-sixth of the variance in degree results (Choppin and Orr 1976). Even this is a better predictor than most other factors examined. In addition, the output in terms of specific abilities and knowledge acquired through the course is not always easy to describe, may bear little relationship to success in life and is not inherent in the class of degree awarded.

The activities involved in education can be more readily described in relation to the contact between staff and students and the types of teaching methods used. The most common experience of students is still the presentation of a lecture programme supported by seminars, practicals and tutorials in varying combinations as appropriate to the subject. It is possible to describe and set standards for:

- the contextual factors that relate to the use of a particular teaching method (i.e. the structure);
- the way in which the teaching method is implemented (i.e. the process);
- the effectiveness of the teaching method in achieving the objectives of the particular session or series of sessions (i.e. the outcome).

A key issue in achieving quality in teaching is the selection of methods that will most effectively enhance the learning of the students, taking into account the entry characteristics of the students concerned. One definition of quality is 'fitness for purpose'. Thus, one of the most important issues when considering teaching methods is the appropriateness of the method selected to achieve the objective(s) identified. It is therefore necessary to identify the possible uses of particular methods of teaching to enable staff to select accordingly.

Teaching is an activity that takes place within the total environment of the institution and (sometimes) of other collaborating institutions. The totality of the context needs to be considered if the highest possible quality of teaching is to be achieved. The exercise discussed here involved only the faculty concerned, and while standards were set in relation to externally controlled factors, there was no method for working towards ensuring that these standards were achieved.

The faculty approach

Within the Faculty of Social and Health Sciences at the University of Ulster it was decided to develop a set of standards for the most commonly used teaching methods. A number of members of the Faculty Academic Courses Committee acted as conveners/facilitators and identified members of staff and students from within the faculty to form a group. Each group was to consider and set standards for a particular teaching method allocated.

The groups consisted of the convener, three or four members of staff and three or four students. The staff members were selected from different departments, including staff teaching the more traditional academic subjects such as sociology, psychology or social administration, and staff involved in preparing students for entry to one of the caring professions, nursing, physiotherapy, occupational therapy, speech therapy, community youth work or social work. Similarly, the students asked if they would be prepared to join the group were selected to be representative of the range of student groups within the faculty. They included a representation from those undertaking predominantly academic courses, those preparing for entry to a caring profession, school-leaver and mature students and, when possible, a part-time student (a very large and important part of the student population of the University of Ulster).

The teaching methods selected for examination were:

- lecture;
- seminar;
- tutorial;
- practical;
- placement;
- studies advice;
- research supervision.

It was agreed by the Conveners concerned that in every method of teaching there were three key components which should be considered. These were:

- the environment and other necessary conditions;
- the academic member of staff's contribution;
- the students' contribution.

In relation to each of these the standards that should be achieved would be described. In undertaking this activity it was important for us to retain a grasp of reality. The standards set should be achievable either within existing resources or with a relatively small additional investment in time or money. Unless this principle was adhered to the whole exercise was likely to be somewhat academic and to result in disillusionment among the staff and no improvement in teaching.

Group functioning

The ways in which the groups functioned varied with the conveners involved. None of those in the groups (including the conveners) had been involved in such an activity before and the majority of the students involved had not previously carried out such joint activities with academic staff. Much of this chapter is based on the experience within the group who examined the lecture as a teaching method.

One major similarity was found in the functioning of all the different circles. Within the university environment there are always many demands on time for educational and research activities. It became clear that the exercise had to be effectively completed within as short a period of time as possible if staff were to agree to participate and make the necessary contribution. Thus the groups undertook this exercise with a small number of meetings, usually two or three, with additional work undertaken between the meetings by different members of the groups. The work undertaken then acted as the focus for the discussion at the next meeting.

The first requirement for each group was clarification of the task to be undertaken. This necessitated discussion of the principles of standard setting, what was required in the way of standards to be written and how the groups could work. The convener of the group explained the task and the group decided how it would function to complete this task successfully. Meetings of the groups usually lasted about one and a half to two hours and two or three meetings were usually sufficient to complete the task set.

Brainstorming was the major approach used in the group to generate a wide range of ideas. Hutchins (1990) considers that this is a particularly effective approach to small group working to help identify problems, to help analyse causes and to highlight possible solutions. Everyone in the group proposes ideas relevant to the issue being discussed and all suggestions are recorded uncritically. The ideas proposed are then grouped, discussed further and retained, modified or discarded. In this standard-setting exercise a somewhat modified brainstorming approach was used. The convener acted as chair and ensured that the different areas to be considered were discussed and the points made were noted as they were mentioned. Between the first and second meeting the notes taken were organized into the different aspects to be considered and circulated to all members of the group. At the second meeting this draft was discussed in detail and additions, deletions and amendments were made. Following this the document was revised again. Sometimes the groups met for a third time to finalize the standards written; sometimes this was undertaken by circulating the document and asking for comments to be sent to the convener.

Standard setting

Several of the groups, including that considering the lecture method of teaching, used Donabedian's (1969) framework of structure, process and outcome to guide their work. However, before we began the exercise of actually setting standards, it was found necessary to begin by considering what could be achieved by using a particular teaching method. While stating the reason for undertaking an activity is not usual in standard setting, it was felt to be important in this context as the inappropriate use of a particular teaching method may be highly detrimental to student learning.

Purposes of the teaching method

The appropriateness of a selected teaching method for the goals it is hoped to achieve is a prerequisite for quality. Many academics have used the conventional teaching methods without necessarily considering what can be achieved by any particular method. The students involved in the exercise had tended to accept whatever pattern of the usual lectures, seminars and practicals they had received as normal. In general students may complain about the quality of a lecture but probably rarely consider whether it was an appropriate method to use.

Brainstorming was a valuable method for getting the group to think widely about the reasons why a particular teaching method would be appropriately used. This stage in the exercise sometimes led to the conclusion that the most common reason for using a particular teaching method was not particularly appropriate. In particular the lecture is frequently used to transmit the essential knowledge that the student is thought to need. However, the evidence is that in a straightforward, verbally presented lecture the students' level of arousal falls steadily (Stuart and Rutherford 1978); students may not assimilate much of the material presented. Furthermore, there is recent research (W. N. McPhillimy, personal communication, 1992) that indicates that students do not understand 50 per cent of the words that lecturers identified as ordinary words they used to explain new concepts. Without a dictionary and time to look up the words not understood, students are going to obtain little enlightenment from the lecture. With the development of others methods, such as computer-aided learning for transmitting information, the choice of the lecture for this purpose needs to be reconsidered. However, the group identified a number of purposes for which the lecture may be the method of choice (see Appendix 12.1).

Structure

Structure was considered to be all the contextual requirements for the particular teaching activity to be undertaken to a high standard. This section includes consideration of 'the environment and other necessary conditions' previously identified as one of the key components to be considered. In addition to the physical environment in which the particular teaching method was to be presented, this section included the organization relevant to that method of teaching and competencies within lecturer and student to facilitate the teaching and learning process (see Appendix 12.1).

The physical environment
It was recognized that in relation to the physical environment for teaching the faculty concerned did not have the authority to ensure that the standards set were achieved. However, it was considered valuable to state what was considered necessary as this could then be used in negotiation with the relevant parties within the university.

The standards developed in this area related, first, to the factors that produce an environment conducive to student learning. These include factors related to health, safety and comfort, such as temperature and clean air, as well as those related to the facilities needed by students to participate appropriately in the teaching method used. Individual differences between students need to be taken into account; for example, if chairs with detachable arm-desks are in use, it should be possible to move this to either side for the convenience and comfort of left- or right-handed students.

Second, standards were written that related to the requirements for effective teaching. It was recognized that some of these were not currently available in all teaching rooms but it was considered that such equipment as video players should be readily available in a modern teaching institution.

Organization
This aspect deals with factors that ensure that students are in the right place at the same time as the lecturer, and that the accommodation provided is suitable for the group size and the teaching method to be used.

Lecturer and student competencies
This issue is rather different from the previous two. It was considered that included within 'structure' were the competencies needed by staff and student. The lecturer needs the appropriate skills to plan, present and evaluate teaching. These may be acquired through undertaking a programme such as that discussed in Chapter 16. Students need to have acquired the skills to benefit from the teaching method concerned.

Process

The process of teaching includes preparation, presentation and evaluation of each session and of the programme as a whole. Both lecturer and student have a role to play and 'the academic member of staff's contribution' and 'the students' contribution', the remaining two key components identified, were considered.

Preparation
The effectiveness of any teaching method depends on the commitment of both parties, the staff and the students, to the activity. Unless both undertake their roles effectively, the quality of the learning is likely to be reduced. Different teaching methods require different proportions of contribution from staff and students in relation to preparation. In relation to lectures, most of the preparation is undertaken by the lecturer, although the student still has some role.

The lecturer has to undertake detailed preparation to ensure that the total lecture programme is a suitable component of the course of study and that each individual lecture presented fits into the total programme appropriately. Each lecture planned should take account of work such as that by Johnstone and Percival (1976), who studied the periods of inattention in lectures. When lectures were presented with little variation in style throughout the 50-minute period, they found an initial period of inattention, followed by another 10–18 minutes later, followed by still others. As the lecture progressed the periods of attention became shorter, falling to as little as three to four minutes. Deliberate variation throughout the lecture postponed or even eliminated the periods of inattention. Thus the use of audio-visual aids or other methods of creating stimulus variation should be planned into the lecture.

In some other methods of teaching, such as seminars, students have a greater role to play in preparation. The lecturer is then responsible for ensuring that the students understand the roles they are expected to undertake and that the resources they need for their preparation are available.

Presentation

In the presentation of any teaching session both staff and students again have roles to play and standards were written to specify the expected behaviour for both groups. These include the basic requirements, such as attendance and punctuality, but also the quality of the teaching in terms of audibility and interaction between staff and students.

In the context of presentation of a lecture, the standard includes aspects on structure ('telling them what you are going to say, saying it, and telling them what you said') and pacing to enable students to take appropriate notes. The students' involvement in the lecture to enable them to acquire maximum benefit is also defined.

Evaluation

Evaluation is included as a part of the process stage of teaching methods. In relation to a lecture series, evaluation enables the lecturer to modify the approach or content of the lectures in response to feedback during the programme. Summative evaluation may result in changes for the next group of students.

Evaluation is an essential part of the quality assurance exercise and this section of the standards statement identifies the methods that should be used. Evaluation can be informal or formal and the lecturer plays the major role in undertaking this, although obviously the students provide the necessary feedback.

Outcomes

Outcomes are in many ways the most important aspects to examine. One may ask what it matters if the teaching is poor, the environment is inappropriate and the organization appalling, as long as the outcomes are achieved. Standards in this area need to state in measurable terms what is expected to be achieved. However, while outcomes in relation to student learning through a total course or unit of study may be identified through examination or coursework results, outcomes in relation to a specific teaching method are more difficult to measure. It is not always easy to relate learning outcomes to specific interventions.

Outcomes refer to the learning that has been achieved but, as the student is the consumer of the teaching provided, the outcomes assessed should also relate to student satisfaction with the process. Outcomes in relation to teaching methods may be short- or long-term. It is expected that there will be some formal evaluation of outcomes at the end of the particular unit of study but, as previously mentioned, outcomes may also be examined informally throughout the programme. Students and staff have expectations about the outcomes to be achieved and both groups should be involved in assessment of these.

Measurement of performance

As indicated earlier, the rationale for setting standards is that these then act as a yardstick against which to measure performance. Thus, during the process of writing the standards it was important to consider the feasibility of assessment of the extent to which the standards had been met.

Some standards, which relate to readily observable characteristics in relation to, for example, the physical environment or whether overhead transparencies can be read at the back of the room, can be easily assessed. Other standards, which relate to, for example, the actions of the lecturer in the process of providing lectures, are more difficult to appraise objectively. However, peer and student evaluation carried out using questionnaires or observation schedules that have been assessed for reliability and validity are acceptable. Some of the standards set in relation to the students' involvement can be observed. However, it has to be recognized that there are some standard statements, particularly in relation to work carried out before and after teaching sessions, that it may not be feasible to evaluate. Nevertheless, these statements are valuable because they provide the students with a clear indication of what they are expected to undertake.

As yet, no formal measurement has been carried out of the extent to which the standards are being achieved. It is considered that this will be carried out most appropriately by those most intimately concerned, and course committees have been asked to consider how they will undertake this activity. Some evaluation is being carried out through the student questionnaires discussed in Chapter 6.

Conclusion

This exercise has had a number of beneficial outcomes. It was valuable to the individual members of the groups in that most felt that they had gained through the detailed consideration of the particular teaching method with which they were concerned. The booklet of standard statements circulated to all members of the faculty academic staff has been used by some to provide criteria against which to judge their own teaching. The importance of achieving quality in teaching methods has been highlighted within the faculty. It is hoped that it has been valuable to the students who have been the recipients of the teaching.

It must be recognized that the setting of standards is only one part of the total approach to management for quality that is necessary to ensure that students receive a high quality of teaching, which is appropriate to its purpose, in acceptable conditions, on all occasions. A number of issues arose that have implications well beyond the individual lecturer and his or her students.

The provision of an appropriate environment for all the teaching methods considered was identified as being of considerable importance. This involves collaboration with other departments in the institution and requires a rolling plan for refurbishment of the teaching accommodation and maintenance and replacement of equipment.

The standards set require a level of competence in relation to the selection of an appropriate teaching method and a level of ability in using that method that is likely to be found in very few newly appointed lecturers. It reinforces the importance of encouraging newly appointed, inexperienced academic staff to undertake the Postgraduate Certificate in Teaching in Higher Education, or some similar course (see Chapter 16). Whether or not new staff will undertake such a course will be determined in part by the relative emphases placed by the head of department concerned on teaching and research. In addition, the relative importance placed on teaching and research in promotion of academic staff will have considerable influence.

The lecture is the teaching method that requires least involvement from the student but even here it became clear that students had a clearly defined role. The other methods examined required a greater student involvement. Many students entering higher education will not be aware of what is expected of them in relation to the different teaching methods used to enable them to learn. Some form of preparation to enable them to benefit from the teaching methods with which they come into contact would be of value.

High quality in education will be achieved through an integrated approach to the range of issues discussed in this book, including preparation of students for optimum learning, preparation of staff for their teaching role and coordination of the services that ensure the appropriate environment.

Appendix 12.1 Quality assurance in lectures

Purposes of the lecture

A lecture is a teaching session in which the majority of information is provided by the lecturer, although it may include some discussion and use of videos etc. Lectures are of value in certain circumstances but are often used when there are more effective methods of enabling students to learn. It is considered that lectures are not necessarily the most appropriate method of providing students with the essential knowledge that they require. The use of lectures in teaching needs to be carefully considered when there may be more appropriate methods available.

Aims of lectures

- To provide an orientation to the body of knowledge;
- to provide a structure and appropriate pace for student learning;
- to clarify the subject;
- to impart the most up-to-date research-based knowledge;
- to enthuse the students with the subject.

Because the aims of lectures can vary considerably, it is difficult to be specific in describing the attributes that should be sought. However, the structure, process and outcomes described are applicable to the majority of lectures.

Structure

This involves consideration of the environment, organization, and lecturer and student competencies.

Environment

- The room should be quiet, suitably heated and ventilated, with good acoustic properties;
- seating should be comfortable, arranged so that all students can see the lecturer and writing board etc.;
- a writing surface should be available for each student; if this is a side-arm attached to the chair it should be able to be moved to either side;
- a functional overhead projector with role of acetate and washable OHP pens should be available;
- fixed video replay facilities should be present, sited so that all can see;
- a non-dust producing writing board and materials should be present;
- no-smoking signs should be clearly visible and obeyed.

Organization

- The room allocated should be suitable for the size of the group;
- the timetable and room allocations should be provided to students and staff at least the week before classes commence.

Lecturer and student competencies

- Lecturers should have the opportunity to acquire the necessary skills in preparation, presentation and evaluation of lectures;
- students should have had the opportunity to attend a session on study skills, including note-taking and how to make the best use of lecturers.

Process

The process consists of preparation, presentation and evaluation of the lecture, and the roles of both lecturer and student are described.

Preparation
The lecturer:

- should have a clear idea of why the lecture is being given and have aims and objectives for the whole lecture course and the individual lecture;
- should have a plan for meeting the aims and objectives, including use of audiovisual resources if appropriate, remembering that the attention span is about 20 minutes and there is a need for stimulus variation;
- should prepare hand-outs, including objectives and reading lists, well in advance so that printing can be undertaken economically;
- should prepare acetates for overhead projection using faculty resources for high quality – these should be large and clear enough to be seen at back of room;
- should check that accommodation and resources are suitable and know how to use any equipment;
- should ensure that recommended reading material is available in the library.

The student:

- should do any pre-reading required;
- should have writing materials and paper available.

Presentation
The lecturer:

- arrives on time and completes the session on time;
- should be audible and visible to all, and look at the students;
- clarifies the aim of the lecture and approach to be used (e.g. whether notes need to be taken, student involvement);

- states what is to be covered, presents the lecture, summarizes what has been covered;
- allows time for students to understand and/or copy overheads;
- offers the opportunity for questions and answers them at time or at next lecture.

The student:

- arrives on time;
- does not disrupt the class;
- endeavours to concentrate on the class, taking notes if appropriate;
- participates through answering questions etc. if required;
- asks for clarification if unsure;
- after the lecture, undertakes appropriate reading around the subject and adds to notes taken in class.

Evaluation
Evaluation can be considered as formal and informal.

Informal
- lecturer notes:
  non-verbal cues of attention/inattention, number of students who attend, verbal feedback from students;
- lecturer undertakes a self-assessment of each lecture, considering: whether objectives have been achieved, the general feeling of satisfaction with session;
- the lecturer may ask a colleague to attend the lecture to provide peer review.

Formal
- use of student questionnaire about the unit and teaching methods;
- feedback through:
  course evaluation questionnaires, staff–student liaison committee;
- student performance in coursework and examinations.

Outcomes

Outcomes can be short- or long-term and when possible are measurable through formal evaluation techniques. Formal evaluation of outcomes may be carried out at the end of the unit of study but informally outcomes may be assessed throughout the unit.

The students:

- were satisfied with the environment, organization, presentation;
- found the lectures interesting;
- were clear about what was expected of them;

- felt they had gained in knowledge and understanding of the subject area;
- were able to demonstrate such knowledge and understanding in coursework, examinations and, where appropriate, through application in practice,

The lecturer:

- had achieved objectives set for material to be covered in individual lectures and in the lecture programme or unit;
- met objectives set in terms of student participation;
- identified weaknesses and strengths in content and presentation.

References

Choppin, B. and Orr, L. (1976) *Aptitude Testing at Eighteen-plus*. Windsor: NFER.

Cole, R. E. (1979) *Work, Mobility and Participation: a Comparative Study of American and Japanese Industry*. Berkeley: University of California Press.

Donabedian, A. (1966) Evaluating the quality of medical care. *Millbank Memorial Fund Quarterly*, 44: 166–203.

Donabedian, A. (1969) Some issues in evaluating the quality of nursing care. *American Journal of Public Health*, 59(10): 1833–6.

Ferris, G. R. and Wagner, J. A. (1985) Quality circles in the United States: a conceptual reevaluation. *Journal of Applied Behavioural Science*, 21(2): 155–67.

Handy, C. B. (1985) *Understanding Organisations*. Harmondsworth: Penguin.

Hill, F. M. (1989) An evaluative study of quality circle operation and outcomes in a western context. PhD Thesis, Queen's University, Belfast.

Hutchins, D. (1990) *In Pursuit of Quality: Participative Techniques for Quality Improvement*. London: Pitman.

Ishikawa, K. (1984) Quality control in Japan. In Sasaki, N. and Hutchins, D. (eds) *The Japanese Approach to Product Quality: Its Applicability to the West*. New York: Pergamon.

Johnstone, A. H. and Percival, F. (1976) Attention breaks in lectures. *Education in Chemistry*, 13(2): 49–50.

Juran, J. M. (1967) The QC circle phenomenon. *Industrial Quality Control*, 23: 329–36.

Kemp, N. and Richardson, E. (1990) *Quality Assurance in Nursing Practice*. Oxford: Butterworth-Heinemann.

Royal College of Nursing (1986) *Standards of Care Project: Check List on How to Write Standards of Nursing Care*. London: Royal College of Nursing.

Robson, M. (1982) *Quality Circles: a Practical Guide*. Aldershot: Gower.

Stuart, J. and Rutherford, R. J. D. (1978) Medical student concentration during lectures. *Lancet*, ii: 514–16.

13

Effective Teaching

George Brown

This chapter is concerned with research on effective teaching styles and behaviours. It outlines a framework for discussing the nature of teaching and learning. It provides a review of research on learning and teaching in higher education and it raises issues of the nature of effectiveness and its relationship with quality and values. The chapter does not attempt to review comprehensively all research in higher education. Such an undertaking would be encyclopaedic (Dunkin 1989). Nor is it concerned with the management and leadership of institutions, although clearly their structures and processes have an impact upon teaching and learning. Rather, it focuses upon the question 'What is effective teaching in higher education?'

Learning and teaching

Teaching, in its generic form, is concerned with providing students with opportunities to learn. Before considering the nature of teaching, therefore, it is necessary to consider the nature of learning.

The content of learning may be facts, procedures, skills, ideas and values. The broad goals of learning may be gains in knowledge and skills, deepening of understanding, the development of problem-solving and changes in perception, attitudes, values and behaviour. Last but not least the goal may be the development of capabilities to learn to learn. It is these capabilities that are the foundation of transferable skills and effective life-long learning. Students, of course, may have more pragmatic goals — passing course work, practicals and written examinations.

The content and goals of learning are incorporated in the model given in Figure 13.1. The model itself stresses cognitive learning for the development of thinking, in its broadest sense, which is regarded as a central task of higher education. Such a view does not deny the value of action so much as argue for informed judgement, creativity and action.

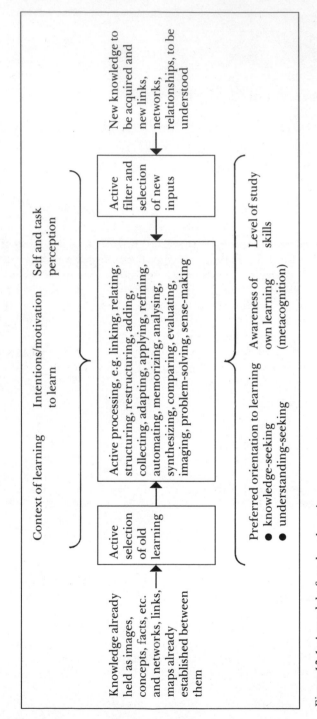

Figure 13.1 A model of student learning.

The model provides the parameters of learning. It includes the pragmatic goals that students may have of passing course work, practicals and examinations. Within this general model there are personal models of learning that influence and shape one's approach to teaching. These models are often not explicit but they may be inferred from a course design, the teaching methods and the assessment procedures in use. Clearly not all learning is dependent on teaching; hence the difficulty of using distal measures of student learning as a sole basis for measuring effective teaching. However, all teaching, regardless of quality, is predicated upon learning.

Teaching

The generic meaning of the term 'teaching' encompasses course design, course management, the methods of face-to-face teaching, the provision of other learning opportunities, assessment and feedback to students. Teaching, in this sense, is an intentional activity and an interactive process involving teachers, students and tasks. Interaction between a teacher and student may be minimal, as in the use of computer-assisted learning or tape slide programmes, but even in these methods, the teacher as designer and manager of the learning environment has an effect. Clearly this definition of teaching implies that there is more to estimating effective teaching than evaluating methods of face-to-face teaching.

The specific meaning of the term teaching is a subset of the generic term. It is the interaction between teachers, students and tasks. These interactions may be classified at various levels and these levels are discussed in subsequent sections of this chapter.

Methods and structures

The most general level is methods of teaching such as lecturing, small group work, laboratory and other forms of practical work, project and research supervision. These methods may be placed upon a continuum shown in Figure 13.2. At one extreme is the lecture, in which student control and participation is usually minimal. At the other extreme is private study, in which lecturer control and participation is usually minimal. It should be noted that, even at the ends of the continuum, there is some control on participation by both lecturer and students. Thus in lectures students may choose what notes to take, whether to ask questions or even disrupt the class. A student's private study is likely to be influenced by the suggestions of the lecturer, the materials and tasks that he or she has provided and the texts that are made available in the library.

Between the extremes of the continuum one may place, approximately, small group teaching, laboratory work and project research and

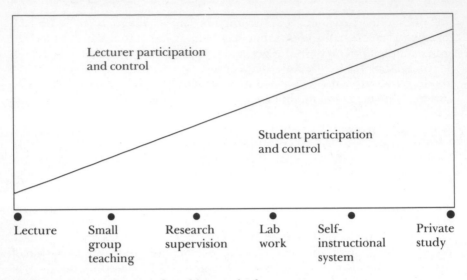

Figure 13.2 A continuum of teaching methods.

supervision. The precise location of these methods of teaching is less easy, for each method of teaching contains a rich variety of structures involving varying proportions of lecturer and student participation. For example, small group teaching may be highly structured and tightly controlled by the lecturer or it may be free-flowing discussion in which the lecturer facilitates occasionally. Laboratory work may be a series of routine experiments specified precisely by the lecturer or a set of guided enquiries in which the student develops hypotheses to test, chooses methods and designs appropriate experiments. A research supervision may be wholly lecturer directed, another may be wholly student directed.

These differences within methods of teaching lead to the second level of analysis: structures. Thus within the method of lecturing one may distinguish between a classical structure that divides a topic into segments that are further subdivided, and the problem-centred structure, which focuses upon different solutions to a problem, such as 'What is the relationship between body and mind?' (Brown 1978). In small group teaching one can distinguish structures such as the mini-lecture, the seminar paper, structured discussions, case studies, question and answer sessions and role play (Brown and Atkins 1988).

There are two implications of these levels of methods and structures of teaching. First, as a researcher, one should be clear what one is comparing. A comparison of two methods may turn out to be a comparison of two structures. Second, broad comparisons of methods of teaching can only provide pointers to potentially effective uses of methods. Small group teaching may be the most effective method of encouraging students to talk and think, but in the hands of some lecturers a small group session may be the most effective way of inhibiting discussion and thinking. To ensure that methods are effective one may have to explore the underlying skills used by lecturers and their styles of teaching.

Skills

In essence, skills are constructs used to describe goal-directed sequences of actions that may be learnt and routinized. All skills have cognitive, perceptual and motor components but the proportions vary across sensory motor skills, cognitive skills and social skills. All three types of skills are involved in teaching, although cognitive and social skills are the most important ones. One should not, however, undervalue the motor skills involved in audio-visual presentation.

The core skills of teaching are:

- preparing and structuring teaching materials;
- the interactive skills of explaining, listening, questioning, responding to students' comments and answers, providing and giving guidance, assessing and providing feedback, monitoring one's own teaching.

These skills do not have a one-to-one relationship with the structures and methods of teaching. Rather they are a personal repertoire of actions that a lecturer may draw upon to shape his or her teaching. Core skills may be subdivided further into subskills and elements or messages. Confusion arises in discussions of the important skills and their relationships. For teaching may be regarded as a skill in its own right or a set of skills. Within teaching the use of questioning is a skill, within questioning the use of probing questions is a skill and within probing questions the use of asking for specific examples may be regarded as a skill. Such confusion may be minimized by recognizing that skills necessarily overlap and be deciding upon the level of an analysis that is appropriate for the task.

Just as student learning has its metacognitive aspects so do the skills of teaching. Indeed it may be argued that the supra-ordinate skill of knowing when to use a skill is as important as the skills themselves.

The construct of skills provides a basis for analysing teaching and for training teachers in higher education. Such approaches enable one to diagnose strengths and weaknesses and to provide appropriate training. However, one should be wary of over-refined analyses or atomistic approaches to training. To give an extreme example, it does not follow that because one can analyse teaching interactions into ten million bits of information – and one can – that this information is useful for analysing teaching or for developing teaching. Rather, one should fit the level of analysis to the tasks and the method of training to the purpose of training, the background of the trainees and, if practicable, their learning styles. Broadly speaking, analyses into meaningful wholes and holistic approaches to training seem preferable.

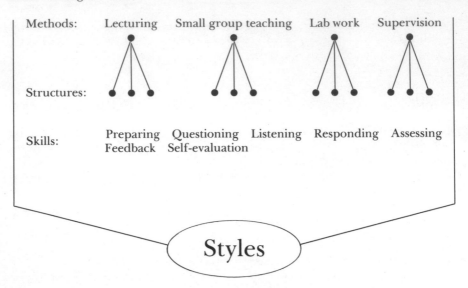

Figure 13.3 Methods, structures, skills and styles.

Styles

Methods, structures and skills provide a general description of teaching. All these are influenced and modified by the salient personal characteristics of the teacher. Usually these characteristics are brought together in the notions of styles of teaching. Styles may be regarded as: 'A characteristic response to situations that are perceived as similar'. Such an approach provides a focus for exploring a person's perceptions and actions within a teaching context. How someone teaches is not necessarily closely related to how he or she behaves in other situations. Styles of teaching are likely to be dependent upon the styles of learning of the lecturer and upon the traditions of the subject that is being taught. It is unlikely that one could ever extract an essence of style that is totally independent of styles of learning and subject, but one can identify and describe broad categories of styles that can then be used to help the lecturer to develop within his or her style – and perhaps to shift or even develop styles.

Figure 13.3 provides a schematic model of methods, structures, skills and styles.

A model of teaching and learning

The framework of teaching and learning described so far is summarized in Figure 13.4. That framework has implications for exploring effective teaching. First, student learning is only partially dependent upon teaching.

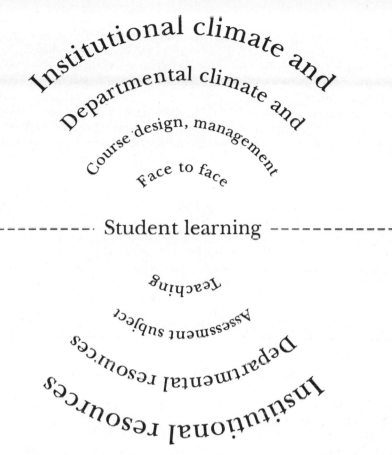

Figure 13.4 Learning and teaching.

The overall quality of the learning environment is likely to have its effects upon learning as well as the learning styles, strategies and motivations of students. Second, evaluations of teaching that rely solely on observations of teaching methods are likely to neglect the crucial variables of course design, management, preparation and assessment procedures. Third, the wide variations of structures within methods suggest that comparisons across methods in any one study need to be treated cautiously. Cumulative evidence or meta-analyses are likely to yield better guidelines.

Research on learning

One strand of the research on student learning has been directed to the effects of personality and motivation on learning (see Wittrock 1986 for a review). This research shows that the way students perceive themselves and the way they account for their academic successes and failures have a strong bearing on their motivation and their performance. Students are likely to initiate learning, sustain it, direct it and actively involve themselves in it when they believe that success or failure is caused by their own effort or lack of it rather than by factors outside their control. Similarly, praise, reward or other positive reinforcements are likely to enhance motivation only if students perceive them to be related to factors over which they have control. Thus building up students' sense of control over their own work, giving them opportunities to exercise responsibility for their own learning, and helping them to develop self-management skills can all help to make them more successful and effective learners.

A second strand of empirical work has been focused on individual skills, strategies, styles and approaches to learning. The results from these studies are pertinent to lecturers since most of the subjects have been undergraduate students engaged on academic tasks. This research is described clearly by Entwistle (1988). Two dominant orientations have been identified: knowledge-seeking and understanding-seeking. Those who have a knowledge-seeking orientation search for facts and information. Their learning may be mechanical and it may be surface learning rather than deep learning. They are not interested in speculating, playing with ideas or searching for deeper meanings. In contrast, those with an understanding orientation are less interested in facts and more interested in searching for personal meaning in what they are doing. They relate what they learn to their earlier experience, they explore potential connections, linkages and discrepancies. They tend to be intrinsically motivated rather than responders to a system. Hence they are likely to be deep problem-solvers and to be creative and independent.

Both reproducers and understanders may have varying degrees of achievement motivation. When achievement motivation is high there is a willingness to switch styles of learning to the one demanded by the system of teaching and assessment. Most students have a predominant style but that style may be influenced by the conditions of learning and assessment. Table 13.1 sets out the characterization of the two orientations.

Perhaps the most disquieting findings are that deeper approaches to study and independent learning decline during many undergraduate courses. The use of multiple choice questions and other forms of tests promotes reproductive styles of learning, whereas projects and open-ended assessments promote independence and deeper strategies of understanding (Biggs 1987). Fortunately, there is some evidence that the use of problem-based approaches and appropriate forms of assessment can promote deeper styles of learning (Newble and Clarke 1987).

It should be borne in mind that style of learning is more likely to be associated with a set of characteristics of a learning environment than with just one characteristic. Hence, to promote a particular style of learning it is necessary to consider the organizational climate of the department or school as well as its use of various approaches to teaching and assessment.

Table 13.1   Orientations to learning

Knowledge seeker
Adds to store of facts, concepts, and so on.
Collects skills, procedures.
Breaks down problems and tasks into separate sub-units
Makes links within units of knowledge.
Uses memorization skills.
Works methodically through logical order of task or problem.
Analyses.
Uses systematic trial and error.
Evaluates data.

Understanding seeker
Tries to relate information or task to own experience.
Makes links to other bodies of knowledge.
Restructures for personal meaning.
Synthesizes.
Likes to work from 'whole' picture.
Searches for underlying structure, purpose, and meaning.
Intuitive use of evidence.
Uses analogies, metaphors.

Ramsden and Entwistle (1981) and more recently Entwistle and Tait (1990) have related these orientations to students' perceptions of their departments. The findings indicate that departments where good teaching was reported were strongly oriented towards personal meaning. Good teaching included such variables as effective lecturing, help with specific difficulties and perceived freedom to learn. Poor teaching included such variables as ineffective lecturing, heavy workload, inappropriate assessment and lack of freedom to learn. In these departments the orientation towards reproductive learning was strong.

There is a tendency to infer that the knowledge seekers produce shallow or superficial learning while the understanding seekers engage in deep processing. The concomitant implication is that the first orientation is inferior to the second. For some subjects and some tasks this may be true but not necessarily for all. The knowledge-seeking domain should not be dismissed out of hand. Knowing that and knowing how are important. For example, a neurologist needs to know the specific neurological function of the optic nerve before he or she can make a diagnosis of a particular patient. A historian needs to know the terms of the Treaty of Versailles before attempting an analysis of Germany's problems in the 1920s.

It seems more helpful, therefore, to consider both the learning for knowledge orientation and the learning for understanding orientation as necessary and useful. Learning can then be conceived as a continuous process of development, backwards and forwards between the two orientations.

Entwistle (1991), in a most thorough literary review on teaching and learning that is relevant to the notion of active deep learning, concludes that

> Where they have been carefully planned and properly implemented, attempts at encouraging active learning have been uniformly rated favourably by teachers and students. There is also evidence that freedom in learning or student autonomy together with good teaching which encourages students to form their own conceptions, will lead to deep approaches to learning which enhance personal conceptual understanding. Such understanding is a necessary first step in being able to apply knowledge in novel context and solve related problems. Adding to conceptual understanding, skills which have been developed through experiential learning (from simulations, projects and work placements) will further strengthen the ability to make these applications. A further step is to use collaborative learning, with its opportunities for developing communication skills and the explicit discussion of the group dynamics involved. These methods seem to foster the social and personal skills so necessary both in working and in everyday life.

The implications of the research on student learning are profound. Commitment to active learning affects course design, assessment, teaching, staff development and the *modus operandi* of departments and universities, yet paradoxically it is a renewal of long-established goals of universities. Indeed it could be said that unless a university is committed to active deep autonomous learning by its students then it is not providing a higher education.

Research on teaching

Most of the research on teaching has been based upon the views of students and lecturers, although the research that compares methods of teaching has also used scores on achievement tests or in examinations. There has been some research on the processes of teaching *per se* but little on the cognitive processes of lecturers when they are preparing materials or teaching. The data collection had ranged from in-depth interviews, semi-structured or structured questionnaires, direct observation of teaching, structured observations of teaching using checklist and rating schedules, and detailed analyses of video recordings and transcripts of teaching and course documents. Anyone who thinks that teaching in higher education cannot be evaluated should look closely at the range of research methods that have already been used.

Comparison of methods of teaching

The cumulative evidence of research provides some broad tentative generalizations on the effectiveness of various methods of teaching. Reviews of this work may be found in Kulik and Kulik (1979), Bligh (1981) and Brown and Atkins (1988).

Lectures are effective, cheap, efficient methods of presenting information and providing explanations. Practical skills are obviously taught more effectively in laboratories but the underlying methodologies and theories may be taught as effectively and perhaps more efficiently in lectures and small group sessions. Small group methods are usually better than other methods at promoting intellectual skills, including problem-solving, and at changing attitudes. They are about as effective as other methods of teaching at imparting information. Small group teaching is clearly not an efficient method of imparting information; its particular strength lies in the interplay of views that develop a student's capacities to think. Comparisons of traditional and newer methods of teaching, such as computer-assisted learning, games and tape–slide programmes, often yield results in favour of the newer methods. However, newer methods are often prepared carefully and evaluated systematically, whereas traditional methods of teaching are rarely subjected to such rigour.

These findings assume that each method is a stable phenomenon. But, as indicated earlier, there is a rich variety of structures within each method and within each method there is potential for both competent and incompetent teaching. As well as comparing broad methods of teaching it may be useful to study each method *per se*, with the intention of identifying the underlying skills involved and their efficacy.

Research on lecturing

The most usual structure of lectures reported in one study are the classical and the eclectic. The eclectic consists of elements of the classical, problem-centred, sequential, thesis and comparative structures. This result may be because many lecturers were unaware of the many ways of structuring various lectures (Brown and Bakhtar 1987). Of the skills of lecturing, explaining has received the most attention. Both lecturers and students value clarity and interest, and evidence from studies that related explaining and student achievement indicates high correlations between clarity and interest and student achievement. The measures of clarity and interest included the uses of signposts, framing moves, focusing statements, examples, metaphors and narrative modes of expressiveness (Land 1985; Brown 1986). There are differences between arts and sciences. Logical structure and clarity is valued more highly by science lecturers and students. Interest, insights and perspectives are valued more highly by arts lecturers and students. This is not surprising given that the role of lecturers is perceived differently in these different subject areas. Arts and science lecturers also differ in their attitudes towards training. Broadly speaking, science lecturers are more likely to believe that training can improve such skills as logical presentation, use of aids and expressiveness (Brown and Daines 1981). The scientists' views are borne out by small-scale studies that demonstrate that short courses of training can produce positive changes in lecturing skills (Brown 1982). In an interesting study of gifted lecturers, Sheffield (1974) concluded that the most important aspect of lecturing was 'To stimulate students to become active learners in their own right.' The group of lecturers and their former students also stressed in their essays and comments the importance of caring for students, love of subject, preparing properly and conveying principles rather than details. The views of lecturers indentified by Sheffield are echoed in the good and bad stories of lecturers told by science students in discussive interviews (Ogborn 1977). Good stories contain descriptions of involvement, enthusiasm, generation of understanding and human interest.

Different styles of lecturing have been identified and these appear to be closely associated with subject content but not with length of experience or status. In one study (Brown and Bakhtar 1987) five styles were identified. These were: the visual information giver; the oral presenter; the exemplary, who used a successful blend of visual and oral approaches; the eclectic, who was less successful at blending visual and oral approaches, who had self doubts, but a strong commitment to his or her subject; and the amorphous, whose main characteristics were vagueness and arrogance. Visual information givers were most common in science and engineering, oral presenters in arts. Both exemplaries and eclectics were found in biomedical sciences and arts. Amorphous lecturers could be found in all departments but were particularly common in science, engineering and medicine.

As hinted earlier, there has been a neglect in research on teaching in higher education of the cognitive processes involved while preparing teaching materials and while teaching. It is likely that preparation of teaching materials is a much messier non-linear process than textbooks on objectives suggest. Stimulated recall techniques do not appear to have been used with lecturers as a method of research. Yet such methods would yield the cognitive processes and so help us to identify differences between novice lecturers and expert lecturers when they are preparing the materials for teaching.

Research on small group teaching

The major theme of research on small group teaching in the past 50 years has been the question of when small group teaching should be used. A review of over 100 studies, which used examination results as the sole criteria (Dubin and Taveggia 1968), suggested that small group teaching is only as effective as other methods of teaching – and more costly. These findings may tell us more about the examinations than the teaching. The reviews by more recent writers (e.g. Kulik and Kulik 1979; Jacques 1991) show that small group teaching is usually better than other methods at promoting intellectual skills and changing attitudes. Kulik and Kulik (1979), in their review, show how the use of questions and open structures can promote discussion skills and thinking. Goldschmid and Goldschmid (1976), in their review of peer group teaching (groups without official tutors), show that such groups when used in conjunction with other methods of teaching increase participation and develop the students' responsibilities for their own learning.

In spite of the potential strengths of small group teaching for developing thinking and discussion skills, there are studies that show that small group teaching is dominated by tutor talk and lower levels of thinking. The skills of questioning and responding are crucial in small group work, yet they appear to be neglected. For example, the level of questions in one study rarely rose above recall (Ellner 1983). Lecturers used students' ideas less than 2 per cent of the time and the proportion of time devoted to lecturing ranged from 7 to 70 per cent (Luker 1988).

There do not appear to be any studies of styles of small group teaching, but Baumgart (1976) in his study identified tasks that were undertaken by tutors. These included instructor, commentator, stage setter, prober and reflexive judge. The reflexive judge appraises a contributor and probes. Baumgart found that students made more thoughtful responses when the tutor appraised and probed. The sessions in which there was more thinking displayed were also the sessions that received more favourable student ratings.

There is still much research required on the structures and methods of small group teaching and its skills and styles. In addition there is a need to explore the feelings and shifts in attitudes that occur in different small group structures. Jaques (1991) offers many suggestions for exploring these issues.

Research on laboratory teaching

The purposes of laboratory teaching are:

● teaching manual and observational skills relevant to the subject;
● improving understanding of methods of scientific enquiry;
● developing problem solving skills;
● nurturing professional attitudes.

If any proof is needed that laboratory teaching can improve technical skills then it may be found in the carefully designed experiments of Yager *et al.* (1969). They demonstrated that technical skills require practice but intellectual skills may be learnt as well in discussion settings as in the laboratory. Other studies show that the acquisition of technical skills requires practice and feedback over long periods but, once they are acquired, they are well retained.

Laboratory teaching fares less well in the development of understanding and methods of enquiry. The results from a comprehensive survey (Garratt and Roberts 1982) were equivocal. Hegarty (1982) concludes from her review that if the development of scientific enquiry is a major goal of laboratory teaching then there are three prescriptions:

1. Students cannot conduct meaningful enquiries in areas in which they have no background. Course planners should design activities that provide for prior learning of the basic concepts and laboratory skills that will be required.
2. If students are to conceptualize the processes of scientific enquiry as conducted by scientists, there must be explicit teaching about what scientists do and the nature of scientific enquiry as well as any implicit teaching that may be embedded in enquiry or discovery-oriented laboratory exercises.
3. If students are to experience the processes of scientific enquiry, course planners must design special learning activities. Laboratory cookbooks are not effective.

Use of the structures concerned with enquiry rather than recipe is also shown to be related to students' interests in laboratory work (Bliss and Ogborn 1977). When a course stresses for education and illustration it seems to promote reproductive learning. Indeed, there is a risk that students in such laboratory courses will resort to superficial rote learning and store the knowledge gained as an isolated unit. Their beliefs and preconceptions are not modified by practical work that is based upon recipes (Tisher and White 1986). However, there is some evidence that the use of self-assessment procedures leads students to a better grasp of what they do and why, even within the structure of verification and illustration (Daines 1986).

It is perhaps the disquieting findings that have led to the development of alternative and augmented methods of laboratory teaching. These methods are, in essence, extensions of enquiry approaches that are used together to develop the full range of capabilities in laboratory work (Boud *et al.* 1986).

The essential skills of laboratory teaching are:

● explaining and presenting information;
● questioning, listening and responding;
● giving directions;
● teaching demonstrators;
● helping technicians;
● preparing a laboratory course.

Each of these skills can be subdivided further. For example, the specific skills of a demonstrator are to know how to do and write up the experiment, *and*:

- observe students at work;
- anticipate major difficulties of understanding;
- recognize major difficulties of understanding;
- give brief, clear explanations of processes and procedures;
- give directions;
- ask questions that clarify difficulties of understanding;
- ask questions that guide students;
- answer questions in a simple, direct and non-critical way;
- offer supportive and encouraging remarks;
- know when to help and not help a student.

The training of demonstrators in these skills may go some way towards reducing the uncertainty that demonstrators experience and the wide variations in quality of help that are reported by students (see Bliss and Ogborn 1977). Daines (1986), in a subsequent study, showed that students' expectations of demonstrators indicated that they valued constructive criticism, clear explanation of errors, written comments on their work, fair marking and listening to students' questions.

Observational studies of laboratory work show that talk is largely centred upon laboratory procedures and low level discussion. Lower level enquiry processes, such as data interpretation or the formulation of conclusions, were detected but uncommon. Even rarer were extended thought questions and discussions of the nature of scientific enquiry (Hegarty 1979; Shymansky *et al.* 1979).

There do not appear to have been any studies of styles of teaching within laboratory classes, although the case studies of Bliss and Ogborn (1977) provide clues on student views of good and bad teaching. Good stories were linked to explicit teaching and demonstration and the provision of freedom to explore within a clear framework. Bad stories centred on the themes of poor laboratory management, chaos and heavily prescriptive regimes. One study has explored styles of learning of students as manifested in experimental design in physical chemistry. Three styles of learning were identified: empiricists, whose methods of scientific enquiry systematically; borderliners, who got to the heart of the problem but by random methods; and dead reckoners, who only developed recipes (Pickering and Crabtree 1979). These styles are almost certainly products of earlier learning strategies and it is likely that well thought out structures and course designs can shift students towards an empirical approach.

Research on project/research supervision

The supervision of projects in undergraduate education and of research students at postgraduate level is the fourth most common teaching method in higher education. While their purposes, complexity and depth of study required are different, there is sufficient commonality to discuss broad common features of effective project and research supervision together. Indeed, project supervision may be regarded as a miniaturized version of research supervision in which a student learns the essential research skills of his or her subject, to work independently and perhaps collaboratively and thereby to gain experience in project planning, time management, oral and written presentation and perhaps the skills of negotiation and persuasion.

Despite the widespread use of projects in final-year courses in most subjects there has been surprisingly little empirical research, but plenty of advice on how to run projects (Adderly *et al.* 1976; Dowdeswell and Harris 1979). In the sciences Hegarty-Hazel's research (1986) indicates that project work is no better than structured experimental enquiries at developing research skills. Obviously projects are intended to do more than develop technical research skills. That they do so is probably true but as yet unproven. Certainly some students value project work highly despite the problems that they report of unclear criteria, inadequate supervision and poor laboratory facilities (Bliss and Ogborn 1977). One study based on students' perceptions of research projects provides a practical set of ground rules for students about to embark upon projects (Gabb 1981). The students reported that their efforts were directed towards getting a good mark rather than using the project as a learning experience. The rules they seemed to work by were:

1. *Supervisor.* A topic must be chosen on the basis of who is supervising it rather than for any intrinsic interest. Important criteria for choosing a supervisor are helpfulness, approachability and friendliness.
2. *Assessment procedure.* Discover as much information as possible on the assessment procedure. It is supposed to be secret but friendly staff members will reveal it if encouraged.
3. *Results.* Most assessors are more interested in results than any other aspect of the project. Results make the projects easy to mark. Advise your supervisor of any results obtained. If no results are forthcoming, don't tell your supervisor until it is absolutely necessary.
4. *Length.* The report should be approximately 30 pages in length. Padding may be necessary to obtain sufficient words but do not exceed the 30 page limit as you will be marked down for waffle.
5. *References.* A long list of references. These can be obtained from abstracting journals, which provide enough information for a decision to be made.

As Heywood (1989) observes in his commentary on this study, 'Once again the power of beliefs about assessment is all too clear.'

There appears to be no research on the supervision of final-year projects, dissertations or theses in the arts subjects. This is an area that is worth exploring given the increasing concern about completion rates in arts research degrees.

Studies of research supervision by Welsh (1981) and Rudd (1985) indicate that many students experience problems in such areas as methodological difficulties, time management, writing up, isolation and inadequate or negligent supervision. Wright and Lodwick's (1989) survey of first-year research students shows that they value these functions of a supervisor: gives critical feedback; checks on progress; academic guidance; provides support and encouragement; allows student to work independently on own initiative some of the time.

In an international comparison of the supervision of science research students, Brown *et al.* (1991) showed that over a quarter of the sample of students across four countries wanted more help in planning, analysing and interpreting results, drafting theoretical models, writing up and publication. Wright (1991) indicates that successful supervisors as measured by completion rates have regular and frequent schedule meetings with their students, set tasks, review progress regularly, comment on drafts and teach their students time management skills. These approaches seem to be more common in the sciences than in the arts.

While there has been no research directly concerned with styles or skills of supervision, the above findings, together with those of Moses (1982) and Hockey (1991), suggest that good supervisors provide expertise, research skills, experience of writing theses and a concern for the personal well being of the students. The least preferred style was cold, aloof and *laissez-faire*. It was also the least successful in terms of completion rates. The study by Brown *et al.* (1991) also indicates that students' preferences change during the course of their projects. In the early and later stages they prefer more direct approaches. In the middle stage they want freedom to explore. However, the overall preferred approach combined professional guidance and personal warmth.

The first prerequisite of effective supervision is probably to be actively involved in research and to reflect upon one's own experiences. The supervisor needs all the skills required by the research student, including project management skills. In addition, interpersonal and teaching skills come into play from the first meeting to the *viva* and even beyond to the first joint publication. Underpinning these skills are the equally important skills of planning, structuring and monitoring.

At the heart of the supervision process is the tutorial. As Moore (1968) said of the Oxford tutorial, it is essentially 'A meeting for work, which usually involves discussion . . . both sides should be at work, understanding, discovering, adjusting.' Rudd (1985) also suggests that supervisors who gave no advance thought to supervisions, preferring to play them by ear, were in part responsible for the failure of their students.

One way of ensuring that supervisions are purposeful working encounters is to consider the structure of an individual supervision. The essential skills involved are:

1. Structuring the research tutorial:
    - questioning, e.g. about progress, problems, results, interpretation;

- listening, including going beyond the information given;
- responding, including decision-making;
- explaining, including demonstration and presentation of argument.

2. Providing feedback.
3. Planning and monitoring the project.

The stages in research supervision are:

1. Opening – rapport established.
2. Review – current context established.
3. Definition – scope and purpose of present meeting.
4. Exploration – problem(s), results and so on.
5. Clarification – decisions taken.
6. Goal-setting – decisions taken, next tasks identified.
7. Conclusion – evaluation, summary, disengagement.
8. Recording – notes on supervision made and filed.

These two lists are based on the work of Shaw (1987), who has designed, implemented and evaluated a short training programme on research and project supervision that demonstrably improves tutors' tutorial and planning skills.

Just as specific training in project and research supervision can help the supervisors, so too can brief courses for students on specific and relevant aspects of research and project management skills. These approaches are used in some departments in universities but no survey has been conducted of the prevalence and efficacy. A course for first-year arts research students has been developed at the University of Nottingham and used with two successive first-year intakes of research students (Brown *et al.* 1991). Student evaluations were overwhelmingly positive but they pointed to the need for supervisors to be more proactive.

Their views point to the underlying tensions in research and project supervision that have yet to be resolved. At least four tensions are discernible:

A scholarship or training?
Original or collaborative?
Independent or team member?
Apprenticeship or employment?

On the one hand there are those that believe a PhD should be entirely the student's original and independent work in an academic subject. On the other, there are those who believe that a PhD is a training ground in which students acquire a repertoire of skills that may be used within and without the academic world. These different orientations lead to different approaches to supervision. Put crudely, if the first position is held, then the supervisor is virtually superfluous and presumably so too are the bulk of the fees! If the second position is held, then the thesis *per se* is an adequate instrument of assessment. Clearly, beneath these orientations are questions of value that need resolving before one can consider the more obvious questions of effectiveness of research supervision.

Perspectives on effectiveness

Shot through the whole of the research on learning and teaching are questions concerning the nature of effectiveness, its relationship to values and to quality assurance. Notions of effectiveness are dependent upon the values, status, purposes and context of the observer. These measures may be based upon publicly expressed values or upon the values in operation in the context. The two are not necessarily identical and are related to the distinctions often made between rhetoric and reality, espoused theories and theories in use. To complicate matters further, reports of other people's approaches to effectiveness are themselves inevitably value-laden. Hence what follows may seem polemical to some readers and too bland to others.

In Britain, the major control of higher education is vested in the government, and in particular in the DES and the newly established HEFC. Given the present economic climate it is concerned to drive down unit costs but to appear to support the drive towards quality assurance. In so doing it runs the risk of moving institutions towards methods of lecturing and assessing by written examinations although some institutions may explore the more radical options of independent learning. Yet the research shows that undue emphasis upon lectures and written examinations is likely to yield passive, compliant, surface learners. If effectiveness measures, in practice, are concerned primarily with cheapness and efficiency, then we run the risk of not providing a well informed, skilled workforce. In contrast, the Department of Employment through its Enterprise in Higher Education initiative is concerned with the production of more active, independent learners who are equipped with high level skills. Their measures of effectiveness are more concerned with the development of social and intellectual skills through project work and work experience. Not surprisingly, this perspective of higher education institutions is influenced by the controllers of higher education. Yet some of the higher education institutions also have a further challenge of demonstrating research activity. Effectiveness in teaching and undergraduate learning in such institutions may be as much concerned with efficiency as it is with quality of learning. The institutional pressures affect academic subjects and departments. Some departments value the use of small group methods and project supervision whereas others prefer large lectures and written examinations – regardless of any external pressures. The espoused values and values in use may not be consonant within departments. There is a need for departments to identify their values, establish their measures and effectiveness and act upon their findings.

As well as institutional pressures there are in some departments the influences of learned bodies, professional associations and employers. All of these have to some extent been influenced by government policy. Their views on effective teaching and learning may differ from those within a department and hence their measures of effectiveness may differ. Within the departments themselves there may be divisions of opinion on whether the primary aim is education *in* the subject or education *through* the subject. Again different measures of effectiveness may be necessary.

To an outside observer, effectiveness is concerned with realizations of the avowed goals of teaching and learning. The key questions are:

● What do you want your students to learn?
● What are they learning?
● How are you teaching?
● How do you know?

This pragmatic viewpoint may look neutral but it is not. For underlying this stance is the view that departments should be free to choose what they teach and in what way. For students, effectiveness is likely to be related to systematic, stimulating and caring teaching that leads to success. Certainly this view is borne out by the research on teaching and learning reviewed in this chapter and elsewhere (see, for example, Cohen 1981). Obviously emphases on these factors will vary across students and subject and each of these factors is, in practice, complex and challenging. Students are being encouraged to see themselves as consumers and this may eventually affect their views of effectiveness. Yet the notion of student as consumer may fit uncomfortably with the notions of students as deep, active processors and generators of learning.

Clearly, questions of values are at the heart of effectiveness and of quality. Effectiveness and quality, however, are not necessarily synonymous or even stable concepts. Their precise relationships are outside the domains of empirical research. Empirical research can inform and illuminate issues of quality, effectiveness and values. This chapter is a modest contribution to that debate.

References

Adderly, K., Ashwin, C., Bradbury, P. *et al.* (1975) *Project Methods in Higher Education*, London: Society for Research into Higher Education.
Baumgart, C. P. (1976) Verbal interaction in university tutorials. *Higher Education*, 5: 301–17.
Biggs, J. (1987) *Student Approaches in Learning and Studying*. Melbourne: Australian Council for Educational Research.
Bligh, D. A. (1981) *Seven Decisions when Teaching Students*. Exeter: University of Exeter Press.
Bliss, J. and Ogborn, J. (eds) (1977) *Students' Reactions to Undergraduate Science*. London: Heinemann.

Boud, D., Dunn, J. and Hegarty-Hazel, E. (1986) *Implementing Student Self Assessment.* Sydney: HERDSA.

Brown, G. A. (1978) *Lecturing and Explaining.* London: Methuen.

Brown, G. A. (1982) Two days on explaining and lecturing. *Studies in Higher Education*, 2: 93–104.

Brown, G. A. (1986) On explaining. In Hargie, O. (ed.) *Handbook of Communication Skills.* London: Croom Helm.

Brown, G. A. and Atkins, M. (1988) *Effective Teaching in Higher Education.* London: Methuen.

Brown, G. A. and Bakhtar, M. (1987) Styles of lecturing: a study and its implications. *Research Papers in Education*, 3: 131–53.

Brown, G. A. and Daines, J. M. (1981) Learning from lectures. In Oxtoby, E. (ed.) *Higher Education at the Crossroads.* Guildford: Society for Research in Higher Education.

Brown, G. A., Smallwood, A. and Brogan Turner, D. (1991) Arts research: a course for research students. Mimeo, University of Nottingham.

Cohen, P. A. (1981) Student ratings of institution and student achievement: a meta-analysis of multisection validity studies. *Review of Educational Research*, 51: 281–309.

Daines, J. M. (1986) Self assessment in a laboratory course on dispensing. Unpublished PhD thesis, University of Nottingham.

Dowdeswell, W. H. and Harris, W. D. C. (1979) Project work in university science. In McNally, D. (ed.) *Learning Strategies in Science.* Cardiff: University of Cardiff Press.

Dubin, R. and Taveggia, T. C. (1968) *The Teaching–Learning Paradox: a Comparative Analysis of College Teaching Methods.* Eugene, OR: Center for the Advanced Study of Educational Administration, University of Oregon.

Dunkin, M. J. (ed.) (1989) *International Encyclopaedia of Higher Education.* Oxford: Pergamon Press.

Ellner, C. L. (1983) *Studies of College Teaching: Experimental Results, Theoretical Interpretations and New Perspectives.* Lexington, MA: D. C. Heath.

Entwistle, N. (1988) *Styles of Learning*, 2nd edn. Chichester: Wiley.

Entwistle, N. and Tait, H. (1990) Approaches to learning, evaluation of teaching and preferences for contrasting academic environments. *Higher Education*, 19: 169–94.

Goldschmid, B. and Goldschmid, M. L. (1976) Peer teaching in higher education: a review. *Higher Education*, 5: 9–33.

Hegarty, E. H. (1979) The role of laboratory work in teaching microbiology at university level. Unpublished doctoral dissertation, University of New South Wales, Sydney.

Hegarty-Hazel, E. (1986) Research on laboratory work. In Boud, D., Dunn, J. and Hegarty-Hazel, E. (eds) *Teaching in Laboratories.* Guildford: SRHE/NFER Nelson.

Heywood, J. (1989) *Assessment in Higher Education*, 2nd edn. Chichester: Wiley.

Hockey, J. (1991) The social science PhD: a literature review. *Studies in Higher Education*, 16: 319–32.

Jaques, D. (1991) *Learning in Groups*, 2nd edn. London: Croom Helm.

Kulik, J. A. and Kulik, C.-L. C. (1979) College teaching. In Peterson, P. L. and Walberg, H. J. (eds) *Research on Teaching: Concepts, Findings and Implications.* Berkeley, CA: McCutcheon.

Land, M. L. (1985) Vagueness and clarity in the classroom. In Husen, T. and Postlethwaite, T. N. (eds) *International Encyclopaedia of Education: Research Studies*. Oxford: Pergamon.

Luker, P. A. (1988) Some case studies of small group teaching. Unpublished PhD thesis, University of Nottingham.

Moore, W. G. (1968) *The Tutorial System and Its Future*. Oxford: Pergamon.

Moses, I. (1982) *Postgraduate Study: a Select Annotated Bibliography*. Brisbane: Tertiary Education Institute, University of Queensland.

Newble, D. and Clarke, R. (1977) Approaches to learning in a traditional and innovative medical school. In Bliss, J. and Ogborn, J. (eds) *Students' Reactions to Undergraduate Science*. London: Heinemann.

Ogborn, J. (ed.) (1977) *Practical Work in Undergraduate Science*. London: Heinemann.

Pickering, M. and Crabtree, R. H. (1979) How students cope with a lab procedures class. *Journal of Chemical Education*, 56: 487–8.

Ramsden, P. J. and Entwistle, W. (1981) Effects of academic departments on students' approaches to studying. *British Journal of Educational Psychology*, 51: 368–83.

Rudd, E. (1985) *A New Look at Postgraduate Failure*. Guildford: SRHE/NFER Nelson.

Shaw, M. (1987) The tutorial: an analysis of skills. Unpublished PhD thesis, University of Nottingham.

Sheffield, E. F. (ed.) (1974) *Teaching in the Universities: No One Way*. Montreal: Queen's University Press.

Shymansky, J. A., Kyle, W. C. and Pennick, J. E. (1979) How do science laboratory assistants teach? *Journal of College Science Teaching*, 9: 24–7.

Tisher, R. P. and White, R. T. (1986) Research on natural science. In Wittrock, M. C. (ed.) *Handbook of Research on Teaching*, 3rd edn. New York: Macmillan.

Welsh, J. (1981) The PhD student at work. *Studies in Higher Education*, 6(2): 159–62.

Wittrock, M. C. (1986) Students' thought processes. In Wittrock, M. C. (ed.) *Handbook of Research on Teaching*, 3rd edn. New York: Macmillan.

Wright, J. (1991) Studies of research supervision. Unpublished PhD thesis, University of Nottingham.

Wright, J. and Lodwick, R. (1989) The process of the PhD: a study of the first year of doctoral study. *Research Papers in Education*, 4: 22–56.

Yager, R., Engen, H. B. and Snider, B. C. F. (1969) Effects of the laboratory and demonstration methods upon the outcomes of instruction. *Journal of Research in Science Teaching*, 6: 76–86.

Part 3

Developing Quality

14
Appraisal Schemes and Their Contribution to Quality in Teaching

Saranne Magennis

The purpose of this chapter is to consider how appraisal can contribute to the enhancement of quality in university teaching. In order to address the question it is proposed to consider three main issues. First, the origins of contemporary debate concerning quality and appraisal of quality in higher education will be discussed. Second, the nature and variety of appraisal schemes and the difficulties that attend them will be considered. Third, the practical experience of North American and Australian appraisal initiatives will be examined. Based upon a consideration of these three elements, that matter of which model of appraisal is most likely to make a worthwhile contribution to the enhancement of quality in university teaching is addressed.

In addressing the issue of quality, this book is right at the forefront of contemporary thinking about university teaching. When the matter of appraisal is addressed, one is not merely at the forefront but at one of those sharp edges of the quality issue where the grand schemes and fine ideals meet the individual human being. This being the case, an underlying assumption must be stated: whatever the origin, or stated purpose, the only reasonable justification for the existence of an appraisal scheme is the enhancement of the quality of teaching. This applies whether the impulse behind the particular scheme or initiative is a concern for the rights of students, the development of teachers, quality assurance or public account-ability. That all of these may be found as the stated reasons for appraisal will be clear from this chapter. That the origin of the contemporary debate may be found in the last of these is the issue to which we may now turn.

The contemporary emphasis on quality: economic roots

To a significant extent the advent of the emphasis on 'quality' in higher education, manifesting itself in the form of an interest in appraisal of performance in research and in teaching, may be traced to the broader emphasis on efficiency and value for money, most particularly public money, that has developed at least partially as a consequence of the oil crises of the 1970s and the global cycle of inflation, recession and unemployment (OECD 1987: 24). One might be forgiven for believing the suggestion that the level of concern for quality has reached such a level as to take on the force of an organizing principle for higher education (OECD 1987: 79). This may be somewhat extreme as a statement of the case but the fact remains that through the 1980s institutions of higher education in many countries have become subject to systems of evaluation of varying degrees of formality, with regard to research, teaching and overall institutional performance.

The terms assessment, appraisal and evaluation, with which we have long been familiar as aspects of our role as teachers in relation to students and their learning, have become progressively more familiar to us as terms that are applied to our own competence in the performance of the tasks that fall to us. The focus of this volume is on the issue of quality in university teaching and within that context the task of this chapter is to address the variety of schemes of appraisal that are documented in the literature, their characteristics and their role, successful or otherwise, in the enhancement of teaching quality.

Problems of definition

The problems that surround any approach towards an understanding of the term quality have been highlighted in preceding chapters. Both Lewis Elton and Roger Ellis, in their contributions to this collection, have offered working definitions: quality is that which gives complete client satisfaction. An amended BS 5750 has been suggested. Fitness for purpose, Christopher Ball's suggestion, from which came the title of his 1985 book, has been put forward. Each, of course, begs questions of an operational or a philosophical nature. The resolution of difficulties concerning the 'fitness for purpose' definition, moreover, takes on a new urgency in the light of its adoption by the Division of Quality Audit, set up recently by the Committee of Vice-Chancellors and Principals to monitor the quality assurance mechanisms of United Kingdom universities.

If we travel the route of client satisfaction we must identify a client, or perhaps establish priorities among a range of clients with interests that do not exactly coincide. If, on the other hand, we choose the route of fitness for purpose this leads to a multitude of questions, though not to many satisfactory answers, concerning the purpose or purposes of universities and the education they provide.

The issue of purpose is, of course, central to any resolution of the problem. Regrettably, the literature on this topic is limited: in fact it comes as a great surprise, in view of the immense changes in the range of disciplines offered, the structure of the institutions concerned and the characteristics of the student population, that John Henry Newman remains among the standard reference points in relation to the nature and purpose of a university.

We might have expected the Committee on Quality in Higher Education, chaired by so eminent a philosopher as Mary Warnock, to have provided answers at least to the philosophical questions. However, this was not to be the case. It appears that we use the term 'quality' as a substitute for the word 'good' and its definition is attended by the same retinue of difficulties that has plagued the philosophers for centuries in an attempt to explain what 'good' means. These include, for example, questions of relative or absolute good, situational determinants versus objective principles, the limited nature of the human mind and the boundaries of individual perception. All of these confuse the issue even when truthful and benign intention are assumed.

The absence of a status quo

It is small wonder that, in the words of Ralph Norman (1990), there is no status quo with regard to the measurement of quality in university teaching. Norman has argued that the development of the movement towards assessing quality has moved through two discernible stages. The first of these is one of experimentation, where single institutions undertake initiatives on an individual basis, as voices in the wilderness. This has given way to a stage of discussion in which these initiatives are shared and compared so that institutions now entering the field have at their disposal a 'toolbox' of instruments that may be adaptable to their particular requirements. What is not yet available, although Norman maintains that it is in process of being developed, is a coherent theory, accepted as status quo within which practical approaches to the appraisal of teaching can be operated and discussed. Such a theoretical framework must include some answers to the unanswerables, some resolution of the problem of the meaning of quality in teaching in higher education.

Philosophical disagreements and practical agreements

While the theoretical framework is still in the making, many institutions and individuals are faced with the necessity of assessing the quality of teaching in higher education. Moreover, they are faced with this necessity in the context not of a single academic community such as Newman might have known, but in the fragmented world of 'continually proliferating subcommunities' in which terms Ronald Barnett described the academic world (Barnett 1990: 201). Furthermore, the chief focus of much of the interest is not whether the process of fragmentation is merely part of a wider cultural disintegration characteristic of contemporary society. It is a practical focus, which asks how we can assess the quality of our teaching now. The number of approaches to the appraisal of teaching in higher education and the developing literature in the field clearly intimate that practical resolutions have been found even if the theorists disagree.

Faced with a problem of this order, where a concept has taken on the status of an organizing principle for an endeavour and yet no widely acceptable agreement can be found on the question of its meaning, one way that is open in the search for a resolution is to enquire whether the question is correctly set. If all the answers are inadequate then perhaps the question is at fault. It would appear that in the case of teaching quality in higher education the question is considerably out of focus.

In order to set the question to rights, I propose to refer to the thinkers who, taken together, probably invented more of the questions that have defined our Western culture than all other thinkers in the tradition, namely Plato and Aristotle. In the Athens of the fifth century BC both Plato and Aristotle were concerned with the best approach to life for man. Plato devoted a great deal of thought to the contemplation and analysis of the concept of the good, to the ideal form of the good. Aristotle, on the other hand, devoted his attention to the more mundane matters of life.

In his considerations of the meaning of good behaviour for human beings, recorded in the *Nichomachean Ethics*, Aristotle starts from an examination of the behaviour, not the good, believing that no other approach could deal adequately with the richness and complexity of human life. To discern the best life open to the human being Aristotle felt that it was necessary to sift and sort among possible actions and qualities and build up from the evidence of real experience a picture of the good life. The result could not be a precise, analytic prescription of what constitutes good behaviour, or the good life for the human being. This, however, is not to cast doubt on the value of the exercise: Aristotle warns us, early in the *Ethics*, that the level of clarity and precision to be sought in a subject is variable. Indeed, he considers it to be 'the mark of the educated man that he brings to each subject only that measure of precision that is proper to the subject' (Aristotle, *Nichomachean Ethics*: 1094a). In discussions of human conduct the level of precision is not at all as great as that required in mathematics. The approach must be a gradual building up from experience, from the trials and errors of life, not a disintegrative analysis from predetermined principles.

Now teaching, like life itself, appears to be a rich and complex form of experience. It is full of challenges, choices and responsibilities. It takes place not in some static heaven of unchanging, perfect forms, but in the rough and tumble of a world of ever-changing relationships, circumstances and people. None of us is faced, come nine o'clock on Monday morning, with the ideal form of 200 students; neither do we attend a meeting with the ideal form of head of department. We meet something more closely approximating 200 bleary-eyed individuals longing for sleep or an overworked head of department, snowed under with paperwork when she would prefer to be in the library of the laboratory. This being the case, Aristotle's mundane, not so precise way towards the good life seems to offer an excellent analogy for our own search for quality in teaching in higher education.

These two strands of thought can be found in the contemporary literature of quality in teaching in higher education. The true Platonists are contemplating the idea of quality. Those born Aristotelian, however, have devoted attention to *teaching* and have set about the task of sifting through the experience of teaching in higher education today in order to understand the distinguishing characteristics of high quality teaching. The intent of this chapter is strongly on the Aristotelian side of this divide and may be summarized in the proposition that if we wish to arrive at a definition of quality in teaching in higher education we will be better served by an analysis of teaching than by an analysis of quality. A number of practical approaches for the evaluation of the quality of teaching in higher education have been developed. It is to these practical approaches that our attention may now be turned.

Characteristics of appraisal schemes

The meaning of appraisal

In order to set a context for a discussion of particular approaches to the appraisal of teaching it is appropriate to consider the meaning of some key terms. To begin with, something may be said about the meaning of appraisal. In the *Oxford English Dictionary* one may read that the words evaluation, assessment and appraisal mean roughly the same thing. Regardless of the fine distinctions and precise shades of meaning that have been attached to them, at base they mean to determine or calculate the value of something. Properly speaking, this is the monetary value of a material thing. Figuratively, it extends to the estimation of any worth, value or quality. In the matter under consideration it extends to the estimation of the quality of teaching.

The appraisal of teaching

There is broad agreement to be found in the literature that the appraisal of teaching is a good thing. This is not, however, reflected in attitudes to the details: regarding the definition and purpose of appraisal, the procedures that may be used, what constitutes evidence, the reliability and validity of the instruments, there is little consensus. Even the theoretical possibility of measurement of quality in teaching is questioned (Gitlin and Smyth 1989: 9).

In practice there are numerous approaches to appraisal. If, in good Aristotelian fashion, we sift through these practical schemes and approaches, there is considerable illumination to be gained. A number of classifications are possible; each clarifies a different aspect of the problem. The varieties of appraisal may, for example, be organized according to purpose. They may, on the other hand, be considered from the point of view of the source of evidence or, finally, they may be considered with regard to the means used to collect the information. These classifications are not mutually exclusive: a particular appraisal scheme or package may belong in more than one class. For the present purpose it is necessary to address the issue from each of these standpoints in turn.

Purposes of appraisal

Within an organization, quality, if it is approached with any measure of seriousness, cannot be the concern of only one individual. In an educational organization, many people will be concerned with and responsible for teaching quality and its measurement. The ongoing necessity of developing their skills and updating their courses gives teachers a major reason for interest in the quality of teaching. The academic administration, deans, heads and course leaders may have different, though related, reasons for interest. The choice of teacher for proposed courses, the use of available skill resources to their best advantage and the assessment of in-service training and recruitment needs can be assisted by an accurate knowledge of the competences of the teaching staff. Students too have their reasons for interest in quality and its measurement. They invest a significant portion of their lives in what is, most probably, a once and once only chance for higher education. That the courses are well taught and stimulating may be of critical importance to their futures. In addition, within the organization, the general administration can find a use for the results of appraisal in the matters of tenure, salary and promotion. This is especially true in the North American context. Finally, for the wider community another set of purposes exists. Businesses, parents, professional bodies and those in charge of the public coffers have reasons for interest in teaching appraisal.

Sources of information

In any attempt to appraise teaching many sources of data are available. Most obvious are those categories of people most involved in the process, namely teachers and students. Others, however, can and do provide data. Heads of departments, deans of faculties and colleagues are in a position to contribute to the appraisal process. Peers from other institutions and, on occasion, external assessors may play a role in an individual appraisal scheme.

Means of appraisal

While the discussion focuses on the purpose of appraisal and the possible sources of information it remains somewhat theoretical and distant from practice. When, however, it begins to focus upon the means that may be used to attain its ends and to collect information from its possible sources, the difficulties multiply. To begin with, if there is any confusion concerning whether *teaching* is appraised or *individual teachers*, it surfaces rapidly when practical methods are discussed. Difficulties related to definitions of teaching and its aims become apparent and uncertainty arises about the way in which reliable and valid criteria for quality teaching may be developed and used.

Despite these difficulties, teaching is appraised in a number of ways. It is appraised by direct or indirect means; that is, either with or without direct observation. The appraisal may be structured or unstructured, with or without predetermined checklists of criteria. Objective measures, such as students' examination results, may also be used in an appraisal. Specific difficulties with regard to the assessment of the quality of teaching appertain to each of these categories. For example, if there is no direct observation then the question of what constitutes our evidence arises; if there is observation it may be argued that the presence of an observer necessarily interferes with the teaching process. If a checklist of criteria is not used then the claim that the data are entirely subjective may be made; if a checklist is used then its origin, validity and reliability must be demonstrated.

Reasons for and against appraisal of teaching

It can give little cause for wonder if there is disagreement concerning the value and propriety of conducting appraisal of university teaching. Equally entrenched positions are to be found on either side of the case, with some supporting appraisal as stridently as others oppose it. Once again, however, sifting through the arguments, both for and against, proves illuminating.

Those in favour of appraisal hold that the evaluation of performance is an essential aspect of professionalism. Setting standards of teaching performance, ensuring that these standards are met, ensuring, as it were, the quality of the product, is, in this view, a necessary part of the job. From the point of view of career development, it is argued, review of perform-ance, building on strengths, eradicating weaknesses and developing potential are both necessary and desirable (see, for example, Donald 1982; Renner *et al.* 1986; Gitlin and Bullough 1987; Rutherford 1987).

Similar arguments are made at the level of departmental organization. Quality teaching is an essential aspect of course quality. Students have a right to expect high quality courses. Those who accept tuition fees have accepted a responsibility to provide such courses. Teaching must, therefore, be evaluated for deployment, training and course development purposes. Without appraisal there can be no assurance that the student receives the service for which he or she has paid. Across a spectrum of attitudes, from academic staff development to a more business-oriented model of keeping the client satisfied, the consensus would appear to be that if links can be established between appraisal and the improvement of teaching performance it is something to be welcomed rather than feared.

Those who oppose appraisal claim that it is divisive. It is argued that it alters relationships among colleagues, setting up systems in which students and staff become surveillance agents, keeping tabs on the other members of their departments, a practice that is both threatening and destructive. Furthermore, it is suggested that, even if the worst excesses of a Brave New Department are avoided, appraisal procedures interfere with the teaching process. The results are not reliable. Moreover, teachers, being human, may find themselves tempted to change their teaching styles to match the expectations of the appraisal scheme. Such changes lead to standardization, loss of flexibility and a decline in creativity. None of this constitutes a recipe for quality teaching.

The opponents of appraisal argue further that in all appraisal the measures are quantitative and cannot give adequate account of the essentially qualitative aspects of teaching. Finally, it is argued that appraisal can only assign a grading, and a spurious one at that, and cannot lead to an improvement in teaching.

A major cause of difficulty

This summary of arguments for and against appraisal makes it clear that many of the difficulties arise in relation to the summative type of appraisal, as opposed to the formative variety. Teachers, in general, favour some type of formative appraisal, which is acceptable because of its developmental emphasis. Formative appraisal is non-threatening because of its focus on identification and development of strengths as well as improvement of weaker points. Even when there has been initial resistance to the idea, formative appraisal has been shown to gain acceptance when it is demonstrated that it is both fair and consistent. Summative appraisal, however, with its emphasis of assigning a grade or ranking for management purposes such as promotion or tenure, meets with greater resistance. It is felt to be threatening because it 'sums up' performance; it is judgemental and seems unconcerned with improvement or development.

Whereas it is highly probable that the distinction between summative and formative appraisal ultimately breaks down, it still serves to highlight those aspects of appraisal that are welcomed and those that are viewed by teachers as unacceptable.

Appraisal in practice

The challenge of establishing procedures for the appraisal of university teaching in United Kingdom institutions, with a view to the enhancement of its quality, is somewhat reduced by the happy chance of late arrival on the field. By virtue of this late arrival there is a considerable body of research to draw upon, especially from North America and Australia. On the basis of the experience of our American and Australian colleagues we are in a position not only to establish the type of evaluation scheme that is most likely to be acceptable to those involved, but also to avoid many of the practical pitfalls that have already been discovered. Therefore, it is appropriate to consider now, in some detail, the practicalities of appraisal as practised by our neighbours.

Agreement among sources

The literature on the evaluation of teaching quality from North America is considerable because evaluation has been a matter of concern there for some decades now. It is a valuable resource in the development of appraisal for the enhancement of quality in teaching both because of the positive approaches that have been tried and because it provides insight into the difficulties that can arise.

In the past, the major emphasis in evaluation, particularly in the United States, has been on student ratings of teaching. Seeking the views of students on the quality of the teaching they have received remains an established part of standard practice in the US higher education system. The system has also been marked by a strongly summative approach to the appraisal of teaching. Decisions concerning tenure, promotion and salary take into account, on a routine basis, the results of evaluation of the individual's teaching.

These evaluations are not exclusively based on students' views. Peers' and administrators' views are also collected, as are the views of the teachers themselves. It is interesting to note the connections among the ratings of teaching provided by the various groups concerned. From Dressel's *Handbook of Academic Evaluation* (1976) to Kenneth Feldmann's 'Assessment and evaluation in education' (1989), little change is reported in the way different groups rate teachers. Administrators, students and colleagues remain the groups among whom some of the highest correlations occur.

On average, these groups were fairly well in agreement in their ratings of teachers.

Teachers' self-evaluations still exhibit the lowest average correlations with the ratings of other groups. There are indications that the gap is closing. The correlation between what teachers say and what the administrators, students and colleagues say is more positive now than in 1976. The change may simply reflect the fact that those involved are becoming more familiar with the process, are becoming 'evaluation wise' so to speak. Another explanation for this, and there is some support for it, is that systematic evaluation has led to an improvement in standards of teaching. Against this, however, the considerable body of literature that exists on the subject of the non-utilization of the results of appraisal would cast a large measure of doubt on so optimistic a view.

The trap of non-utilization has been avoided in a variety of ways. In the United States, numerous investigations of its causes have been reported. Case studies report varying degrees of improvement in teaching when the causes of non-utilization have been identified and overcome (Alkin *et al.* 1979). At least partially as a result of non-utilization studies, the movement now in the United States is towards a more formative type of appraisal, which emphasizes improvement and ongoing development rather than one-off evaluation.

From the experience of the North American evaluators, spanning as it does some decades now, it seems likely that many of their problems may be avoided both at the research stage and at the stage of implementation. One of the major difficulties unearthed by the utilization studies in the United States was that the results of appraisal did not find their way to the people who could implement change, or if they did, they did not do so in a useful, individual but non-threatening form. The challenge to evaluators is to develop systems that do, in practice, overcome these problems and the key to this challenge would seem to lie in a greater measure of involvement of the individual teachers whose work is to be evaluated, at each stage of the process. In this context, recent Australian research is of particular interest.

Linda Hort (1988) describes five principles upon which, she considers, acceptable schemes for the appraisal of teaching may be based. These are:

1. Clearly defined purpose.
2. Multiple scores of input.
3. Careful identification of areas and criteria for assessment.
4. Agreed measurable standards.
5. Flexible, individualized evaluation plans.

At each stage there is involvement of the people who are to be appraised. They are aware of what is being evaluated, of the purpose, the criteria and the standards. Thus many potential threats are defused and the exercise can be a cooperative one aimed at the improvement of the quality of teaching. This approach, of course, begs the question whether the appraisal of teaching can in any circumstances lead to an improvement of teaching quality.

Precisely in this regard the work of another Australian researcher, Ingrid Moses, is illuminating. Moses (1986) suggests that neither self-evaluation alone nor student evaluation alone is likely to lead to an improvement in the performance of teachers when they are evaluated on a subsequent occasion. However, her research indicates that when a combination of these two types of evaluation is used an improvement in performance is discernible. Moreover, the greatest improvement is shown by those who received the lowest ratings on the first evaluation. Geoff Isaacs (1989) used a similar approach to the appraisal of teaching, although he did not study the relationship between the students' evaluations and the teachers' self-evaluations. In his research the second ratings also showed significant improvement.

These findings lead us to precisely the point at which we wished to arrive, namely appraisal and the enhancement of teaching. Having arrived, it is appropriate to draw together the threads of the discussion in order to consider a model for the appraisal of teaching that might suit the context of higher education in our own part of the world.

From the foregoing discussion it may be concluded, first, that teachers in higher education are generally in favour of appraisal if it is developmental in style and fair in its design and implementation. Second, it is clear that an evaluation, if it is to have an impact on the quality of teaching in practice, must have teacher involvement at every level of its design and implementation. This is necessary in order both to draw on professional expertise and to bypass difficulties of non-utilization. Finally, the results that Moses and Isaacs have reported are precisely those to be desired, a method for the assessment of teaching through which the teaching is more highly rated on subsequent assessments.

The question that remains is somewhat biblical: the rich young man asked, 'What then must I do to inherit eternal life?' Our more mundane question is surely: 'What then must we do to enhance the quality of teaching in our university?' Whereas the rich young man was required to give up everything he had, our own task is more likely to consist in doing everything we can. This is to say that one initiative alone simply will not suffice, as keeping the law did not suffice for the young man. If the quality of teaching is to be assured then a great many initiatives are required, beginning with a clear institutional commitment to quality in teaching. The types of initiative that are required are clear from the 'toolbox' that has been developed in the many individual initiatives reported in the literature and known about through the personal and official contacts through which a status quo of teaching is being developed. Fundamental to the endeavour is the establishment of a higher profile for teaching quality within the institution. This can be done in a number of ways. First, by the institution of awards, distinctions and promotional opportunities specifically related to the quality of teaching, the status of teaching as an activity can be enhanced.

Second, support for research into teaching in higher education can contribute to the effort. Provision of training, both initial and in-service, offers a further signal that teaching is taken seriously in the institution. The ongoing monitoring of the teaching performance of each member of staff in an institution is possibly the strongest indication that the institution takes teaching seriously. In identifying good practice and pin-pointing areas for improvement, it states clearly that teaching matters. It also provides the basis for building on strengths and remedying weaknesses.

Quality is the fashionable concept of today and as such is attended by the danger that token solutions to the perceived immediate need to do something about quality may be tried. The key to the endeavour is that tokens are not enough. Enhancing the quality of teaching in an institution is as multi-faceted a task as teaching itself. We are lucky enough to find ourselves in higher education at a crossroads. To take the quality of university teaching seriously, to enhance it, is to expand the concept of a university, to make it grow, better to fit the times in which we live and the people whom we serve. It is to be hoped that, unlike the rich young man, we meet the challenge and do not turn away sorrowfully.

References

Alkin, M., Daillak, R. and White, P. (1979) *Using Evaluations: Does Evaluation Make a Difference?* Beverley Hills and London: Sage.

Barnett, R. (1990) *The Idea of Higher Education.* Milton Keynes: SRHE/Open University Press.

Donald, J. G. (1982) A critical appraisal of the state of evaluation in higher education in Canada. *Assessment and Evaluation In Higher Education*, 7(2): 108–260.

Dressel, P. (1976) *Handbook of Academic Evaluation.* New York: Jossey-Bass.

Feldman, K. A. (1989) Institutional effectiveness of college teachers as judged by teachers themselves, current and former students, colleagues, administrators and external (neutral) observers. *Research in Higher Education*, 30(2): 137–94.

Gitlin, A. and Smyth, J. (1989) *Teacher Evaluation: Educative Alternatives.* London: Falmer.

Gitlin, A. and Bullough, R. (1987) Teacher evaluation and empowerment: challenging the taken-for-granted view of teaching. *Educational Policy*, 1(2): 229–47.

Hort, L. (1988) Staff assessment: the development of procedures for Australian universities. *Assessment and Evaluation in Higher Education*, 13(1): 73–8.

Isaacs, G. (1989) Changes in ratings of staff who evaluated their teaching more than once. *Assessment and Evaluation in Higher Education*, 14(1): 1–10.

Moses, I. (1986) Self and student evaluation of academic staff. *Assessment and Evaluation in Higher Education*, 11(1): 76–86.

Norman, R. (1990) Talk at the Second International Conference on Assessing Quality in Higher Education held at the University of Saint Andrews, 24–27 July.

OECD (1987) *Universities under Scrutiny.* Paris: OECD.

Remmers, R. R., Greenwood, G. and Scott, C. (1906) Responsible behaviour as effective teaching: a new look at student rating of professors. *Assessment and Evaluation in Higher Education*, 11(2): 138.

Rutherford, D. (1987) Indicators of performance: reactions and issues. *Assessment and Evaluation in Higher Education*, 12(2): 94–104.

15

Staff Development and Quality Assurance

Sandra Griffiths

Introduction

Quality assurance and staff development are strongly connected and, in a sense, reciprocal. On the one hand all formal approaches to quality assurance, including total quality management and BS 5750, emphasize that the key determinants of quality are the attitudes and behaviour of staff. A comprehensive and positive staff development policy is essential to help staff deal with changing demands and circumstances. Total quality management may be conceived as a massive exercise in staff development; BS 5750 concludes with a requirement that the organization should make a sustained commitment to staff development and training. It can, therefore, be taken as axiomatic that quality assurance for university teaching requires staff development for university teachers. On the other hand the staff development function itself might benefit from a quality assurance approach. Who are the customers for staff development? What are the critical functions of a staff development unit? What standards should these functions meet? What procedures should be followed to maintain these standards? How is the performance of staff development monitored? What steps does the staff development section take to rectify shortfalls in performance? In other words, how could a function that supports quality assurance benefit from quality assurance?

The major focus of this chapter is a case study of my experience in setting up a new staff development unit in a university. First, however, I would like to consider three aspects of staff development, namely its relation with teacher training, its history in higher education and its amenability to quality assurance.

Staff development and teacher training

Good teaching is becoming crucial, which is good news for students. We want far greater recognition of teaching quality in promotion;

more resources for training lecturers in teaching methods; and greater opportunities for academics to choose mixes of teaching and research at different stages of their careers.

(Warwick 1991)

There has rarely been a more appropriate time to consider the role of staff development in promoting quality assurance in university teaching, as the above quotation suggests. With the demise of the binary line and the prospect of mass participation in higher education, the question of good teaching has become a critical one. The government's intention of opening up higher education to one person in three by the year 2000 (DES 1991) has implications not only for the kind of curriculum, teaching and learning we offer to students but also for the kind of teacher training we offer to staff. Credit accumulation and transfer, reform in the National Vocational Qualification (NVQ), the accreditation of prior learning, year-round teaching, varied entry and exit points, and modularization of courses are but some of the major changes that inevitably will impact on the way students learn and the way we teach. These changes will take place within a climate that emphasizes quality assurance, where the student as customer or client is central.

Despite the current emphasis on the quality of university teaching, and the impending changes in structure and delivery of courses, it has been pointed out by Elton and Partington (1991) that so far the rhetoric outweighs the practice. For example, there is no compulsory teacher training for university lecturers and this is one of the major factors working against the achievement of quality in university teaching. James Meikle (1991) has this to say of the common form of university teaching:

Many outside the walls of Higher Education are amazed that, unlike school teachers, training of academic staff is not compulsory; they simply pass on what they have learned at the feet of similarly untrained staff.

In the past 30 years there have been numerous calls, such as the Robbins Report (1964), for the training of teachers in higher education. Yet the existing system of training relies on an *ad hoc* approach, which for lecturers new to teaching seems largely a matter of chance. In a graphic account of how some lecturers survive their first year in higher education without explicit help, Chris Rust (1991) concludes

At a time when appraisal systems are being established, enterprise training is being funded and the Polytechnics and Colleges Funding Council has given quality of teaching such a high priority, institutions surely cannot fail so many new staff in this way.

At present, the onus to seek teacher training is most likely to fall on the individual concerned. Writing in an insightful article in *The New Academic* (1991), Brenda Wilson (a post-doctoral research officer asked to undertake a brief spell of teaching) says that her personal efforts to seek training in teaching were considered by colleagues to be somewhat bizarre. The dominant view was one of 'Why bother? Dedication to teaching is professional suicide!' For Brenda Wilson this created a role conflict that could only be resolved at moral cost and, in a way, that involved 'trivializing teaching in relation to research'.

Some attempts have been made to redress the lack of teacher training. For example, a Postgraduate Certificate in Teaching in Higher Education has recently been introduced at the University of Ulster and an Accreditation Scheme for lecturers is being set up by the Standing Conference on Educational Development. There are also many examples of good practice in induction courses for new lecturers offered as part of staff development programmes. However, despite these attempts, a system that continues to allow so many of its members to practise without training must surely call into question the very definition of a profession. The Holmes Report (1986) is one of many reports on teacher education that refer to the responsibility of a profession to be concerned about the competence, quality and training of its members.

The absence of compulsory training is not the only factor that contributes to the mixed messages about university teaching. The issue is further compounded by what might be called the prevailing ethos in universities, which, it could be argued, actively discourages teaching excellence. The bleak experience of Wilson (1991) is not at all unusual. Elton and Partington (1991) express the prevailing ethos thus:

> Firstly there is a culture which considers teaching to be a normal duty of all academic staff, while it considers research to be – in a telling phrase – an academic's 'own work' – and administration a 'chore', which at times ought to be rewarded just because it is a chore. In such a culture, staff are expected to be competent in teaching, but to strive for excellence in research, and to accept their share of administrative chores.

The reward structure within universities has reflected this culture, which places a high value on research without a corresponding value being placed on teaching. This in turn puts pressure on staff, who are forced to make a choice that accords with the ethos and reward system, of the university, or face a constant role conflict in trying to afford equal attention to all aspects of the job, knowing that the system perceives and values them differently.

I would argue that teaching deserves at least similar recognition to research in the university reward system. Until such a view is taken, quality in university teaching will remain an aspiration rather than a reality.

The argument that it is difficult to analyse and evaluate teaching systematically does not stand up to the test. In other areas of education (for example, the school and further education sectors) the publication of criteria for analysing teaching is now becoming commonplace. In the further education sector, developments such as NVQ and open/flexible learning systems have introduced the concept of 'competence', and related performance criteria, into the everyday language and practice of the college lecturer. As a consequence, most further education in-service teacher training is now modelling the practice required by college staff in their delivery of vocational education and training for activities other than teaching. Essentially this means that the responsibility for learning is placed firmly in the hands of the 'learner' or student, who is facilitated by the trainer in the development and acquisition of skills and knowledge. The learner is then required to present evidence of competence, which must meet the defined appropriate performance criteria. This means that further education is now grounded in a delivery model that works towards defined, measurable outcomes. It makes sense that this should be mirrored in the structure and form of all in-service training and staff development activities.

In higher education the presentation of evidence of competence in teaching is coming to the fore. Elton and Partington (1991) set out a range of criteria by which an academic's teaching activity might be evaluated and judged. Drawing on work by Prosser (1980), Gibbs (1988) and others, they set out a comprehensive list of criteria and stress the need for training of senior staff, as well as lecturers, in order that the new criteria and procedures might be introduced, and skills for their application developed.

The range of criteria by which an academic's teaching might be evaluated and judged is specified, both within and outside an institution. Preparation for teaching, quality of delivery, volume and range of teaching, innovation in teaching, communications with students, assessment procedures, evaluation of one's own teaching and management of teaching are all aspects upon which a teacher might expect to be judged within the institution. External evidence might include invitations to teach elsewhere, membership of professional groups, service to other universities and organizations, publications on teaching and teaching grants and contracts secured.

As indicated in the quotation at the beginning of this section, greatly increased resources for staff development in the area of teacher training will be necessary in order to enhance the value of teaching. Guildford (1990), in his report on staff development provision in universities of the United Kingdom, notes that the sums of money set aside for university staff development do not compare favourably with commercial organizations, which tend to devote upwards of the equivalent of 1 per cent of their salary bills to the training of their staff. The space afforded to the in-house training rooms, administrative offices and audio-visual facilities is frequently reported as less than adequate by staff development coordinators.

Furthermore, it is not uncommon in staff development in higher education to find one academic staff development coordinator with a remit for providing training support for up to one thousand staff. Clearly this is an impossible task, bearing in mind that the provision of training for teaching is only one aspect of the lecturer's job that must be addressed by the staff developer.

Working in such a culture and climate, with the tensions and constraints outlined above, deflects the professional staff developer's energies away from some of the real and crucial tasks. For example, in-service training for experienced staff, the role of teacher tutor or mentor in a department and specific subject teacher training are all areas deserving more analysis. But they may only be fully addressed in the wake of a total change in the culture and reward system. Before I turn to the reciprocal relationship between staff development and quality assurance it will be useful to trace the recent growth of staff development in a national context.

The emergence of staff development in British higher education

The rapid growth of central units of staff development within universities, in recent years, has largely been brought about by the introduction of schemes of career development and appraisal. A Green Paper of 1985 heralded the way by stating that 'Effective staff development will not happen without a formal institutional framework for evaluating performance and for responding to development and training needs.' The Jarratt Report (CVCP 1985) of the same year recommended that all universities examine their structures and develop plans to meet requirements for the introduction of staff development, appraisal and accountability.

The major emphasis of the schemes in appraisal that were subsequently introduced into universities was on the potential for improvement of professional practice. The question of assessment and hard and fast judgement was somewhat played down. Leaving aside the issue of emphasis, an important point was that this was the first time the concept of quality assurance, linking individual performance to achievements and outcomes, had been introduced into the formal system of British higher education.

Arising out of the introduction of appraisal, there emerged a definition of staff development that supported the notion of meeting both the objectives of an institution, in order to increase its effectiveness, and the personal objectives of the individual to the mutual benefit of both parties. Staff at all levels were to be involved in the design, planning and implementation of training programmes, and there was recognition of the fact that 'leading from the top' would be critical to success in the knock-on and cascade effect. This involvement of staff, and the developing of ownership of staff development by them, was a concept shared by approaches such as total quality management. The ownership would become a reality in a situation where staff saw the emphasis on quality as having something concrete to offer them enhancing their professional practice.

Concentration on the individual client or member of staff was in harmony with the development of a learner-centred curriculum for staff training. This curriculum focused on the identification and analyses of needs, counselling and negotiation, and aimed to translate this into learning programmes that were designed to be practical, relevant and easily accessible.

As a response to the introduction of appraisal and the climate discussed earlier in this chapter, the number of staff working in a staff development capacity has increased greatly in the past seven years. But there is still a long way to go. While growth in staff development has been rapid, the pattern of provision and procedures is somewhat uneven.

The Universities' Staff Development and Training Unit was set up in January 1989, replacing the existing CVCP arrangements for training. This body took over responsibility for the (then) programme of national courses, but its remit differed considerably and included provision for all categories of university staff. From its 'register of contacts' one can see that central procedures for staff development are now in place in a large number of universities. However, these vary greatly in size, scope and the resources allocated, from highly structured well staffed central units, at one end of the scale, to single staff development officers working in a half-time capacity with a university-wide brief, at the other end.

Leaving aside the question of resources it could be argued that the very presence of staff development units signals an important message to staff that management is now placing a greater emphasis on training. The centrality of many of these units to their institutions places upon them an onerous task. To begin with they must act as a mirror and model of good practice, as staff may well be looking to them for guidance and example in setting and achieving their own standards.

In modelling a way of being, staff development units, and their officers, walk a delicate tightrope. They are often required to mirror and reflect institutional objectives and values. But they are also at the forefront of change and this is particularly true in the present higher education climate. This means they must also have the capacity to lead, manage and assist the process of change. As often as not, therefore, they will be confronting and challenging the value system of an institution and asking that objectives be quite fundamentally rethought in a new light. This places staff development in a highly complex role where professional staff developers are preparing staff to work in a system, undertaking leadership and the management of change of that system and preparing staff to work within the changed system.

What would be the characteristics of a high quality staff development service? What would be its critical functions to satisfy the needs and demands of these customers? How would it assure quality? The next section considers a quality assurance approach to staff development.

A quality assurance approach to staff development

The 1980s saw widespread acceptance of ideas on quality assurance and customer services, not only in industrial and commercial contexts, but also in the public sector and, indeed, the world of education and training. It was almost inevitable that this surge of enthusiasm for quality should be reflected in higher education since much of the success of higher education lies in the strong links it has forged with industry, as evidenced by student placements in the workplace, consultancy and the Enterprise in Higher Education Initiative.

This quality revolution not only focused on improved 'end products' of the service and manufacturing industries, but also stressed the importance of developing an organizational culture that fostered positive attitudes to agreed standards of excellence in all aspects of an organization's work. Oakland neatly sums up this emphasis on process:

> Controls and techniques are important, but they are not the primary requirement. It is more an attitude of mind, based on pride in the job, and requiring total commitment from the top, which must then be extended to all employees at all levels. Senior management commitment must be obsessional, not lip service.

What does this focus on process actually mean for the practice of organizations? It means that training and development become priority issues and powerful vehicles as a major part of the process, in creating the new culture of quality assurance thinking, which has pervaded all aspects of economic, government and public service activity.

In the context of a university, it means that in order to ensure the maintenance and raising of standards, everyone within the organization must be made aware of the strategic planning, mission statement and objectives, and how they as individuals play a key part in meeting and shaping such plans and outcomes. Many academics have raised doubts about the wholesale application of BS 5750, and other quality procedures, to education, and point out that an ethos of 'fitness for purpose' and 'product specifications' is likely to be ill-suited to education. This interesting debate raises many major imponderables. The focus of this chapter, however, is not to extend this debate further, but rather to take on board the broad thrust of the movement of quality assurance and see what it has to lend to staff development.

The central thrust of quality assurance, with its client orientation, concentration on identification and meeting of customer need, focus on planning and reviewing the process at every stage, and setting definable measurable outcomes, has much to lend to staff development in British higher education. Indeed it was much of this thinking, and the adaptation of a quality assurance model, that informed the formation of the Staff Development Unit at the University of Ulster as it was beginning to take shape.

The aim of the next section is to examine the objectives and operation of one staff development unit as it grew from a 'green field site' to an established department. It was recognized that the value of using such an approach was that its inherent framework of principles and procedures would allow many of the assumptions, and much of the practice of staff development, to be made more explicit and open to scrutiny.

The achievement of quality in any situation relies on both a well designed system and a culture that encourages and fosters excellence. When a quality framework is being set out the focus will naturally turn towards those parts of the system that can be specified, managed and controlled. This poses a problem for staff development, since by its very nature it places limits on a manager's ability to control quality at all levels, and in all activities. The value of having a framework, however, is that it sets out how things might be done and affords the opportunity of mapping practice against the concepts. It is hoped that some of the approaches will be found appropriate and beneficial while, in other areas, there will be an opportunity to supplement and improve the service. In examining the Staff Development Unit at the University of Ulster it is important to point out that the work is still in its infancy and many of the conclusions are necessarily tentative.

Establishing a staff development unit: a case study

Starting from scratch

In 1988 I was seconded (for a three-year period) to the post of Academic Staff Development Officer in the University of Ulster. At this time little existed in the way of formal training for academic staff. A programme of training in research methods and a well established and well received induction programme were on offer. The previous year senior staff had been introduced to appraisal training at a conference organized to address issues that currently faced them.

My appointment to the seconded post coincided with the proposed introduction of appraisal and the scope of the job was, broadly speaking, to advise across the university on staff development matters for academic staff and stimulate a programme of activities in liaison with faculties and department. The job description (see Appendix 15.1) specified responsibility to the Pro-Vice-Chancellor, who had a remit for personnel matters. On paper there was no other guidance by way of either a policy or a strategy document.

Two university committees, academic and non-academic, presided over the work of staff development, highlighting the perceived separate nature of the training to be given to different categories of staff. This was an area that concerned me right from the start. If equality of opportunity was to be offered in training programmes how was this to become a reality within a structure where there was no equivalent staff development officer seconded to develop training for allied staff? Responsibility for training for allied staff was located with personnel.

Within the university in total there were over 2000 staff members of whom approximately 850 were academic staff. These staff were located on four campus sites at Belfast, Jordanstown, Coleraine and Magee, with a distance of 75 miles between Belfast and Magee. Achieving a reasonable geographical balance and spread of staff development activities would be a major focus.

As one would expect with 850 academic staff, there was a wide range of subject specialisms, backgrounds and diversity in interests and training needs. Somewhat paradoxically, one of the most challenging tasks was the cultivation and fostering of an institutional climate that accepted *in-house* training as a part of lecturer's professional development. While lecturers were accustomed to continuing their professional development through attendance and participation at courses and conferences, outside of their working environment, no such culture existed in-house. This point was brought home to me early on when external training consultants commented on the initial resistance they encountered in presenting workshops to audiences in the university. A year later the same consultants were to comment favourably on the remarkable change in the climate, and corresponding willingness by staff to get involved.

The lack of an environment where training was accepted, the sheer size and diversity of staff interests and the absence of a clear strategy created a job whose scale was challenging, if somewhat daunting. What back-up resources, human and financial, would be forthcoming? Would senior managers 'lead from the top' on staff development? How did lecturing staff view their priorities? Where would I seek guidance on staff development in other universities? Would I be able to bring staff, at all levels, along with me in the complex process? Would others share my commitment and enthusiasm?

One of my first tasks was to persuade the senior managers of the university of the need for adequate resources: physical, in terms of a central office location on one of the main campus sites; financial, in terms of a recurrent budget; and human, in terms of secretarial assistance. Commitment by senior managers to staff development was high and within three months of my undertaking the job a budget was secured, a secretary was in post and I had moved office to be in a more central location on the Jordanstown campus.

It was during this introductory period that I sought the guidance and expertise of others working in the field of staff development. In this respect staff at Loughborough University and the Universities' Staff Development and Training Unit at Sheffield were invaluable to me as a newcomer to the field and assisted in reducing the isolation I experienced while working in a university without immediate staff development colleagues. Links with other universities in the United Kingdom, Ireland and Pakistan were developed during my three-year secondment.

In the very early days I spent quite a bit of energy discussing and debating staff development concepts and principles with staff in the

University of Ulster, directors of other units and professional staff developers. This assisted me to formulate a philosophy (born in part out of my own view of education) that underpinned the strategy I would adopt and the steps I would undertake to achieve it.

How could a quality staff development service be achieved?

A quality staff development service is one that is designed and delivered to satisfy the stated or implied needs and expectations of both the university and its staff. In setting out to achieve such a goal I initiated and implemented a plan of action, the overall aim of which was to set up a credible staff development service. The initiation and establishment of a structure for central staff development involved a number of key steps outlined below. These planned steps did not follow a sequential order, but were part of a natural ongoing process, planned in strategic terms but fluid and dynamic in operational terms.

What were the key steps in the operation?

1. Defining and agreeing the underlying rationale of staff development.
2. Designing and developing a staff development policy.
3. Liaising and negotiating on objectives with senior managers in the university.
4. Prioritizing key areas of work in the light of the university's objectives and individual needs of staff.
5. Planning and implementing a programme of activities on a yearly basis.
6. Marketing the policy and programme appropriately.
7. Evaluating and monitoring the programme, and developing both the rationale and the programme in the light of the experience gained.
8. Reviewing the processes at fixed points to check their effectiveness.
9. Developing links with staff development units and the National Unit of Staff Development and Training.
10. Encouraging research in the field of staff development and the related area of teaching and learning in higher education.

It is not the intention here to give a detailed breakdown of the workings of all these key steps in the operation. Rather, I will look at some selected principles and processes that guided my work and discuss examples of how these principles were borne out in practice.

A model that has been used in other quality contexts permitted me to consider the management of the work within a cyclical framework and assisted the management of the unit in distinct phases. The basic model,

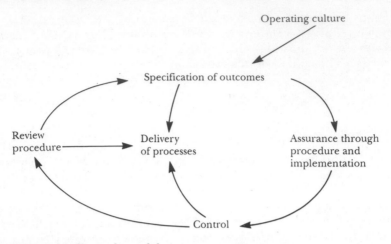

Figure 15.1 A quality cycle model.

shown in Figure 15.1, was adapted and extended to suit the particular purposes of the work in the University of Ulster.

Specification of outcomes

A key imperative in the quality cycle is the specification of outcomes. In the organization of staff development programmes, the intended outcomes guide the style of teaching, the content and the evaluation. For example, foreign language training to support curriculum development on a vocationally oriented course will require that the training should support this aim. But the specification of outcomes will also permeate each phase of the cycle of growth of the work of staff development, including the phases themselves, which will have defined outcomes.

One example will illustrate the use of outcome specification in one of the key steps outlined above. The marketing of staff development programmes is an important function of the service. The purpose of the marketing was clearly defined at the outset. In part, it was to ensure that staff identified with the work of the staff development unit (as it began to form) and used, and contributed to, the activities. An environment had to be fostered, through the marketing process, in order that the operating culture became one that predisposed staff to take up the opportunities built in to the system.

The objective was to produce literature that matched the quality nature of the product on offer, and the value being accorded to the customer's interests. To minimize the risk of poor quality, a specialist firm was employed to assist with the design and production of literature. An imaginative logo was designed as a corporate image to suggest dynamism, leadership, sophistication and worth. In order that staff felt valued by the institution, and in recognition of their right to ownership, it was decided that every member of staff would receive a leaflet for each relevant activity. Another guiding principle was that the advertising material would serve as an educational tool in itself, in that staff reading the leaflets might be encouraged to discuss the concept of the activity with colleagues.

Reaction by staff to the publicity material was swift and very positive, and high uptake of courses continues to be a feature. Feedback about the leaflets suggested that the material was 'setting an altogether new standard', 'breaking new ground' and 'pushing well beyond what is currently on offer'. A further measure of success was the fact that directors of other units within the university sought advice on how they might market appropriately, and the type of publicity material that might be designed.

Now that the literature has been in use for just over three years a full review of the marketing strategies and use of publicity material would be a natural next step, in order for the staff development team to have a detailed analysis of the effectiveness of the publicity in relation to the wide variety of groups and users in the university.

Assurance through procedures: identifying customers' needs

The importance of the customer in the context of quality assurance has been referred to earlier in this chapter. There were a number of sources to draw upon in ascertaining the needs of customers, in this instance academic staff. In drawing on these sources, one was always conscious that the perceived training need of an individual might differ from the real training need or, indeed, the need as perceived by another interested party.

A training survey had been carried out before the establishment of the Academic Staff Development Officer role, and the development of the Unit. This survey identified a number of priorities, which academic staff themselves viewed as important for their professional development. These priorities – supervising postgraduate students, improving lecturing skills, handling meetings effectively and managing time – were among the first priorities in the staff development programme. My previous role as a lecturer in adult and continuing education had taught me the importance of starting where people are at!

An interested party in the definition of the training needs of academic staff is the head of department. Five heads of department were interviewed face-to-face using a semi-structured questionnaire. These same heads of department were also invited to comment on their own training needs. Furthermore, once the appraisal procedure came into operation, six months after my appointment, heads of department were asked to complete a form for staff development, identifying and prioritizing training needs. During all the preparatory sessions for appraisers and appraisees held in advance of, and abreast of, the introduction of appraisal the identification of training needs was stressed.

Perhaps the most important feature of all of this 'assurance' was the creation of an atmosphere where feedback was welcomed, and seen to be utilized in determining future priorities. This atmosphere was in part created by constant reminders to staff that they had a major part to play in identifying and developing their training.

In such a climate, training needs were fed back rapidly, and although the remit of the work was for academic staff, from the start heads of department forwarded requests for training for all categories of staff. I immediately forwarded requests for specific skills training for allied staff to the Personnel Office. In part the wider needs of allied staff were being met by the underlying principle of opening up, where appropriate, all activities to all staff. However, specific job-related training for technicians and secretaries was to go largely unattended until the formal establishment of the Unit in 1991, which incorporated a brief training for all categories of staff.

The rapid identification of training needs shifted the balance of the work from largely proactive in emphasis, to a mixture of proactive and reactive. The issue of prioritizing training needs rapidly became important, as did the issue of expanding the staff resource within staff development to cope with increasing demands. Staff in the Unit increased in 1990 with the secondment of two academic staff on a part-time basis for a three-year period. Two part-time secretaries were also appointed. An office was established at the Coleraine campus, reflecting the emphasis on expanding work on specific campus locations.

My concerns about staff getting involved were quickly laid aside. The climate was ready for training, and commitment, interest and enthusiasm were very much in evidence. Even though some staff showed initial resistance to the workshop methods used, a willingness to change became noticeable once the training was in place, partly owing to the skilful leadership of course tutors.

Devolving ownership to planning groups

In recognition of the vast expert knowledge within the university, and to encourage further ownership of staff development, a network of planning groups was set up to design, implement and evaluate activities based on the identification of training needs. These groups were critical to the success of the programme and have operated on the basis of working within a system which, although designed by central staff development, is receptive to improvement based on the experience of its key users.

In seeking to improve quality, the Staff Development Unit has established a practice that will now be utilized in a more consistent way;

guidelines will be written for planning groups, and might include, for example, 'Guidelines for in-house workshops', 'Conference planning checklists', 'Designing aims and objectives for workshops, seminars, conferences', 'Using small group methods in staff development sessions'.

The planning groups have been the cornerstone of much of the work in the context of teaching and learning. For example, a well established induction programme for new members of academic staff had been in existence at the Jordanstown campus for some 14 years. This programme was planned, taught and evaluated by a committed team of experienced staff, some of whom had been involved with the course since its inception. Part of this programme dealt with the theory and practice of teaching in higher education, and it was much of this experience which informed the planning group that took forward the concept of a Postgraduate Certificate in Teaching in Higher Education.

Quality implementation: delivering the programmes

As a guiding principle, I held the view that quality programmes demand quality implementation by managers, teachers and support staff. However, the processes and activities involved in the delivery of programmes contain inherent variability. In many ways this is desirable as it sustains the view that teaching and learning are not fixed, and methods must be tailored to the needs, level, age and interests of the group, as well as the aims and objectives of the programme. Similarly, one cannot legislate for the effect of different group dynamics or many of the other factors that will have a bearing on the complex learning process, and consequently the outcome. In the quality assurance context the aim was to remove variation in the quality of delivery of programmes, but not the actual variety of delivery itself. Indeed the variety of delivery would offer much to the staff member as learner, allowing him or her to experience first-hand a repertoire of learning and teaching methods.

The means of achieving a concentration on process was not always straightforward, in that individual staff involved in teaching staff development programmes give different weight to the nature and importance of process and method. A number of methods were utilized to attempt to ensure that delivery and process were central to the planning exercise.

In all the planning groups the opportunity was built in to discuss the teaching and learning methods. For example, a large part of the agenda for the language tutors' meetings was given over to a discussion of the usefulness of different teaching techniques. This was backed up by offers of further training for tutors, as and when the need arose. Hence, the training of trainers took place at a number of levels: as part of the agenda of the planning process itself, and more specifically at training events organized with a particular focus. Furthermore, a number of 'training the

262   *Sandra Griffiths*

trainers' events were organized to facilitate staff who volunteered via a 'register of interest' to teach on staff development programmes.

This focus on process has been complemented by the joint programme of activities organized by Staff Development and Enterprise in Higher Education – 'Enterprising Teaching and Learning'. Many of the activities are process-led and some staff participating in these events are contributing elsewhere to the staff development programme. Similarly, on the induction programme for new academic staff, and the Postgraduate Certificate in Teaching in Higher Education, the centrality of process is identified and developed. Indeed, teaching and learning methods used in staff development sessions inform some of the work of the postgraduate course, and vice versa. The centrality of the concept of process is likely to develop in the next few years within staff development in universities, as more emphasis is placed on teacher training of an initial and in-service nature.

Another method of emphasizing process was through a 'Directory of innovations in teaching and learning', which highlighted examples of good learning and teaching practice within the institution. This directory focused on the 'how' as well as the 'what' of teaching, and helped to spread the concept of teachers as reflective practitioners. A resource room providing recent literature on teaching, learning and assessment is currently being set up.

The process of teaching, learning and delivery methods for staff development has also been informed by feedback from participants on courses, who are asked to comment in detail on delivery methods. It is to the way in which the unit developed quality control procedures, through feedback from tutors and participants, that we now turn.

Quality control: checking it out

An operational feature of quality management is control. This is the means by which a devolved activity is managed, maintaining the ability to change or modify the process, intervening when necessary to ensure that outcomes are achieved. From the beginning I introduced two complementary approaches to achieve quality control. These were monitoring and sampling.

Monitoring
This involved collecting information on staff development activities, with the original aim of achieving 100 per cent coverage of all activities. Evaluation forms were designed and used for every staff development event. The planning groups used the evidence contained in these forms to follow up existing work, improve future activities, refine their learning programmes and monitor further training needs.

This simple mechanism proved highly effective for the Staff Develop
ment Unit. Corrective action could be taken immediately if a programme
was not fulfilling its intended objectives. The aim of covering all events was
achieved, until 1991, but as the programme is now extensive, the time
implication of monitoring every event needs to be considered. Furthermore, at some of the activities the return rate of evaluation forms has been
low, rendering the drawing of firm conclusions impossible. Thus, the
question of measuring outcomes still needs attention and must be
considered in the context of the impact on performance in the actual job. A
next step for the Unit is the need to address the issue of the impact of
training on the institution as a whole, possibly by means of follow-up
questionnaires to line managers and individuals on training courses.

Sampling
This process involved selecting key points at which more in-depth
information was sought and gathered. The material gathered was qualitative in nature, in that it involved the direct perceptions of a small number of
staff. For example, staff on the induction courses, research modules and
foreign language courses were asked to provide reports – in each case a
tutor report and at least two participants' views were sought. Obviously, the
method of selecting participants to contribute was important in ensuring
that the sample was random. In the early days volunteers were sought to
write a brief resumé of their view of the course. By the third year of my
secondment the principle of selecting randomly was adopted in order to
reduce bias.

In the light of these methods and in discussion with staff development
colleagues in further education, a number of principles evolved which
underpinned the evaluation of the performance of staff development.
Many of these principles were already in use in further education and a
great deal was learnt from the experience of colleagues working in that
context. At this stage of the Unit's growth, the following are the principles
upon which the work is based.

1. The evaluation should be incorporated into the work of the planning
    group at the initial stage.
2. The overall strategy should be consistent, and fully understood by all
    customers and users.
3. Both formative and summative evaluation should take place through-
    out, and should include the management, design, planning, implemen-
    tation, delivery and impact of staff development.
4. To ensure involvement, and enhance the quality of data, ownership
    should be clearly specified.
5. Judgement should be based on both qualitative and quantitative data on
    efficiency and effectiveness of processes and outcomes.

6. The concept of the self-evaluating practitioner should be encouraged and supported by training in evaluation techniques.
7. Results and outcomes should be immediately fed back to planning groups, acted upon and used to inform decision-making in the future.
8. Integral links with course evaluation and institutional evaluation should be sought and developed.

These principles will develop and change as the extent of the work in staff development grows. A pertinent point facing the Unit at present is the need to review the evaluation strategies themselves.

Reviewing the processes

The final approach in the quality cycle model is that of review. This review is not focused on the outcomes of training, but on the process itself. Such a review provides a formal opportunity at fixed points in the year to modify procedures. To date this approach has not been used as extensively as is likely in the future: the priority has been to establish procedures, define outcomes and begin to consider their measurement. One way of introducing review procedures has been utilized successfully by some planning groups. An experienced practitioner, who has had no input to the planning group, has been asked to cast a rigorous eye over the planned aims and programme prior to their being adopted and implemented. This procedure has the advantage of ensuring that the activities are conceptually sound at the design stage. Clearly, review of the phases of the process will become more important now that the Unit is established. Review of the teaching process itself is an area that is substantially built into the Unit's work, as discussed earlier under the heading of Implementation.

Towards fostering a culture of excellence in teaching

Using the procedures described above, the Staff Development Unit has gained many valuable insights into the developing practice of staff training. One of the many benefits has been that methods of improving the service have been identified at an early stage. However, establishing a quality system in staff development will not in itself guarantee either quality in training or quality in university teaching. As mentioned earlier, quality relies on both a well planned system and the encouragement of a culture that is seen to be striving towards excellence.

In terms of striving for excellence in teaching, the Staff Development Unit has contributed by helping to interweave into the fabric of the university a number of initiatives that recognize and value teaching. Many of these initiatives are discussed in detail elsewhere in this book and include the Distinguished Teaching Award, joint programmes with the Enterprise in Higher Education Initiative, the induction programme for academic staff, the Postgraduate Certificate in Teaching in Higher Education, the 'Directory of innovations in teaching and learning' and the resource room for teaching and learning literature. The Staff Development Unit has contributed substantially to these initiatives by providing expertise, knowledge and resources in support of their management.

Conclusion

The Staff Development Unit at the University of Ulster formally came into being in 1991, three years after my secondment began. The Unit presently comprises a Director of Staff Development, one full-time seconded member of academic staff (in September 1991 I accepted a further three-year term), two part-time seconded members of academic staff, an executive assistant, one full-time secretary and two part-time secretaries. A member of the Personnel Department will increasingly spend more time on the development of training for allied staff and the Equal Opportunities Officer also has a remit for training. As the staff complement has increased so too has the recurrent budget and the physical space allocated to the Unit.

After discussion between the Pro-Vice Chancellor (Personnel) and myself, I presented a policy statement to the Academic Staff Development Committee in February 1991 (see Appendix 15.2). Although this statement is still under review, it represents the basis upon which the university will formulate its future plans for staff development. But the real test of success is that the users have come to recognize and value the work of the Unit. In October 1991 I evaluated the work undertaken and found some recurring themes in evaluation forms and letters. The following comments are typical of a number received.

> You've come a very long way in a short space of time.
>
> I found the programme useful and relevant. Quite an achievement to get such a balance of senior and 'junior' staff involvement.
>
> The level of the course was right. The tutors were superb. They [the tutors] must contribute to the success of the Unit. I have learned a lot from them which I can use in my own teaching.
>
> In the next five years the department will have to sustain the quite remarkable quality of the first three.

This last comment underlines the fact that the Staff Development Unit at the University of Ulster has reached a critical stage. As the Unit has widened its remit to include all categories of staff and as it has grown, quality has been of the utmost concern. In its brief lifetime it has achieved reasonable credibility with its users. The maintenance of quality and credibility will be important during the next phase of development.

So a quality assurance approach has proved beneficial to the introduction of a staff development service. The views of customers, that is the staff and the organization, have been an important determinant of objectives and delivery. Critical functions have been established for the work of the Unit, standards set for these functions and the accomplishment of these standards monitored. Corrective action has been taken where performance fell below standard. However, it is recognized that the approach has been partial and relatively informal; further work will be needed to implement a thoroughgoing quality system. There is no doubt that the university's pursuit of quality for its teaching functions depends crucially on sustained development and training for all its staff. While a good start has been made much remains to be done.

As far as I can tell, my experience in one university reflects that of staff development in the university sector as a whole. While there is general recognition of its importance, implementation at a formal level remains modest and tentative in most if not all universities. Analogously the staff development unit of the CVCP, while admirable in intention and execution, is still a small element of the total system. However, staff do develop their capabilities in all sorts of informal and imperfectly identified and articulated ways. The way ahead is for a more explicit, organized and systematic approach to staff development, which will permeate each institution and the system as a whole. An emphasis on quality assurance for teaching and for staff development should encourage and facilitate this progression.

Appendix 15.1   Academic Staff Development Officer

Applications are invited from members of the academic staff of the university for appointment to the post of Academic Staff Development Officer.

Among the duties of the post will be:

1. liaising with faculties and departments in the identification of training needs;
2. advising the Staff Development Committees on an appropriate programme of training that will give opportunities for staff to enhance their skills and enrich their contribution to teaching, research or management, and, within available resources, planning and monitoring such a programme;
3. assisting faculties to organize the training or retraining of academic staff in the context of the university's academic development plan;
4. coordinating arrangements for the induction of newly appointed staff;
5. devising and mounting appropriate courses, workshops, seminars and other training activities for general or particular purposes.

The post will be for a three-year period but may be renewed. It will be filled by secondment and will carry an allowance above the applicant's existing grade similar to that of head of department.

The person appointed will be responsible to the Pro-Vice-Chancellor (Personnel) and will be expected to contribute to the work of appropriate committees of the university and to undertake such other duties as are thought appropriate.

Appendix 15.2   Policy statement for staff development

1. The university recognizes that staff are a vital and valued asset. It is therefore committed to encouraging and enabling staff to develop their potential in order that they themselves may be enriched and their contribution to the institution enhanced.
2. The provision of staff development will encompass staff at all levels and in all categories throughout the university.
3. Provision for the development of staff will be made both centrally and at departmental level. The central provision, the Staff Development Unit, will be responsible for training of all categories of staff and will report to both the Academic and Non-academic Staff Development Committees. Departments within faculties will mainly be responsible through their faculty to the Academic Staff Development Committee and administrative departments through their head of department to the Non-academic Staff Development Committee.
4. The Director of Staff Development will be directly responsible to the Pro-Vice-Chancellor (Personnel) and will submit an annual report of its activities to the Staffing Committee and the Senate of the university.
5. The Staff Development Unit will:

   (i)   Assist departments and faculties in the identification of training needs; the outcome of the staff appraisal process will be an important information source.
   (ii)   Coordinate, plan and deliver a programme of training, retraining and updating of staff in the context of the university's academic plan.
   (iii) Coordinate arrangements for the induction of newly appointed staff and promote the development of courses aimed at recent appointees.
   (iv)   Offer guidance, consultancy and training to departments wishing to carry out their own programmes of training.
   (v)   Investigate best practice in staff development in other areas of tertiary education in Britain and elsewhere.

(vi) Develop pedagogical methods, teaching materials and learning resources for staff development.

(vii) Encourage research and publication in the field of staff development and related areas.

(viii) Contribute to the work of appropriate committees and working parties of the university.

(ix) Seek to ensure the highest quality of its programmes in terms of content, delivery, teaching methods, evaluation, location and calendar planning.

The work of the Staff Development Unit will be monitored and evaluated at regular intervals.

6. Within departments, heads of department have a managerial responsibility for the personal development of their staff in the context of their respective department's broad aims and objectives. Staff deployment and the allocation and rotation of duties should be planned as a means of personal development, and the granting of study leave, secondments and day release will facilitate the pursuit of research, the acquisition of qualifications and technical updating. Faculties will also be encouraged to arrange conferences, seminars and workshops on relevant topics and immediate training needs.

7. Staff will be encouraged to take responsibility for their own personal development and should be allocated reasonable time and resources for this purpose.

8. Consultations on staff development will take place with the recognized trade unions to ensure that the planned activities of the Staff Development Unit and the opportunities within departments, adequately reflect the needs of all staff.

References

Committee of Vice-Chancellors and Prinicipals (1985) *Efficiency Studies in Universities (Jarratt Report)*. London: CVCP.

DES (1991) *Higher Education: a New Framework*. London: HMSO.

Elton, L. and Partington, P. (1991) *Teaching Standards and Excellence in Higher Education: Developing a Culture for Quality*. London: CVCP Universities' Staff Development and Training Unit.

Gibbs, G. (1988) *Creating a Teaching Profile*. Bristol: Technical and Educational Services.

Guildford, P. (1990) *Staff Development Provision in Universities of the United Kingdom*. London: CVCP Universities' Staff Development and Training Unit.

Holmes Report (1986) *Tomorrow's Teachers*. East Lansing, MI: The Holmes Group Inc.

Meikle, J. (1991) A higher flying Kitemark. *Guardian*, 15 October.

Oakland, J. F. (1989) *Total Quality Management*. Oxford: Heinemann Professional.

Prosser, A. (1980) Promotion through teaching. *HERSDA News*, 2(2): 8–10.

Rust, C. (1991) Surviving the first year. The experiences of new teaching staff in higher education. SCED Paper 65, Learning Methods Unit, Birmingham Polytechnic.

Warwick, D. (1991) Teachers who need a good lecture. *Guardian*, 15 October.

Wilson, B. (1991) Whistling in the dark. *New Academic*, 1(1): 6.

16

Teacher Training for University Teachers?

John Dallat and Gordon Rae

With the exception of the 'oldest profession in the world', university teachers are now members of the only profession in the United Kingdom for which there is no recognized or required course of training.

Although The Report of the Committee on University Teaching Methods, under the chairmanship of Sir Edward Hale in 1964, advocated some form of instruction or guidance on how to lecture and conduct tutorials, particularly for those newly appointed, it did not favour any obligatory or prolonged course of training, primarily on the grounds that it might act as a serious deterrent to the recruitment by the universities of 'men and women whose primary interest was in scholarship and research'. For those of us concerned with improving the quality of university teaching, paragraph 354 of the Report would seem to be as valid today as when it was written:

> A person who adopts the career of university teacher does not do so in most cases because his main object is to teach. A more usual motive is the desire to pursue research in a subject which has engaged his interest as a student, teaching being regarded as a duty incidental to a life of scholarship. And, whatever the motive which first led him to adopt an academic career, he soon realises that it is on his achievement as a scholar rather than as a teacher that his advancement in his profession will depend.

In memoranda to the Hale Committee, the National Union of Students and the Scottish Union of Students both urged universities to provide courses on all methods of teaching for their staff, not simply instruction in the technique of lecturing, and to give greater consideration to teaching ability when appointing and promoting academic staff.

Among the first universities to act upon the recommendations of the Hale Committee were the University of Liverpool and Aberdeen University. The former organized a series of lectures, followed by discussion, on a range of topics, including students as learners, academics as teachers, the lecture, the tutorial and the seminar, and audio-visual aids and pro grammed learning, during the last week of the Michaelmas Term, 1966. In Aberdeen, the first week-long course on university teaching methods was offered by the Department of Education before the start of the 1965–6 session. The course, which was based on the summer school on effective teaching for university teachers of engineering conducted by the Manchester College of Science and Technology, dealt with the preparation of lectures, students as learners, the discussion class, organization of laboratory and practical classes, teaching aids, evaluation of teaching, and examinations. From the outset the course included audio recording and playback of short lectures for criticism but within a few years these were replaced by video recordings. More detailed accounts of these courses may be found in Nisbet (1967) and Blyth (1968).

Although most universities and polytechnics now provide some form of training on teaching methods as part of their staff development programmes, it usually comprises short courses with a very specific focus (for instance lecturing or audio visual aids) and with an emphasis on the practical rather than the theoretical aspects of teaching. Although Piper (1988) acknowledges that short courses of this kind have a role to play in staff development, he argues that, by themselves, they do not make a sound training strategy and can even be a poor investment of time and money. In order to provide a more professional training, the Centre for Staff Development in London's Institute of Education deliberately decided to reduce the number of short courses it offered, and instead developed a two-year award-bearing course for teachers in higher education. Although the Centre has since been closed down, the Institute (through its Centre for Higher Education Studies) still offers a Diploma on Teaching and Course Development in Higher Education, as well as an MA course in Higher and Further Education for administrators and teachers.

During the past few years several other institutions have developed prolonged award-bearing courses for teachers in higher education. In Aberdeen, for instance, Robert Gordon's Institute of Technology has been offering a Postgraduate Certificate in Tertiary Level Teaching Methods by Open Learning on a modular basis since January 1989. Planning is now underway to produce a pack that will enable the course to be run by other Scottish central institutions and to develop a subsequent diploma course, although plans for an MSc course in higher education have been abandoned for the time being owing to lack of immediate support.

The Educational Methods Unit of Oxford Polytechnic also offers a Certificate in Teaching in Higher Education by Open Learning for its new academic staff. The course comprises nine modules (six of which are compulsory and three which are chosen from six optional modules) of 12 hours each and two projects of 20 hours each. The modules include lecturing, audio-visual aids, small group teaching, designing learning packages, evaluating courses and teaching, assessment and course design, and each is supported by a specifically prepared learning package and one set book. As with our own course at the University of Ulster, each student has a mentor for the duration of the programme and each student is expected to keep a reflective teaching diary.

If award-bearing courses of one or two years' duration are to become the norm in higher education, and if newly appointed academic staff are expected to attend such courses as part of their probationary period, then it is more likely to be the result of market forces than any fundamental shift in the attitudes and opinions of academic teachers and senior management. We have little reason to doubt that any attempts to introduce such courses would be resisted just as strongly, and for more or less the same reasons, as they were by the academics who gave evidence to the Hale Committee. However, the UFC selectivity exercise in 1992/3 may focus the minds of some academic staff considerably when they realize that the future of their university or department could depend on its marketing itself as a centre of excellence in teaching, rather than on research, to its potential clientele.

Why has it never been quite the norm, in universities, for newly appointed lecturing staff to possess a teaching qualification or, at minimum, to attend introductory courses in education dealing, say, with pedagogy, psychology or related areas? In contrast, teachers at the opposite end of the teaching spectrum, in the primary sector, have traditionally been required to complete courses of compulsory training, following which they are inspected during a probationary year, and thereafter on both a regular and long-term basis. Not only this, they have been trained and inspected since the earliest days of national systems of schooling, both in Ireland (1831) and England and Wales (1870). Why, moreover, did the University system strive to keep vocational training and the pursuit of knowledge separate from each other?

The answers, we would argue, are deeply embedded historically in the culture and traditions of university life itself. They are also embedded, though perhaps less deeply, in the patterns of educational thought and opinion influencing government policy in education, in Ireland, England and Wales, in the course of the nineteenth and twentieth centuries. For example, much greater importance and status were allocated to the teacher with a university degree than the teacher without. And even more disparagingly, greater importance and status were given to the university graduate without training than the non-graduate with training.

Lest it should be imagined that such thinking was more nineteenth century in origin than twentieth century, it is sobering to be aware of the fact that in Northern Ireland, as recently as 1947, these same distinctions were still being propagated and implemented. Indeed, they were quite a perceptible part of the recommendations contained in the Gibbon Report (1947) on the recruitment and training of teachers in Northern Ireland, the following extract from which illustrates the point we are making:

> Speaking broadly the honours graduate has, by the nature of his course, acquired a capacity for selective reading and independent

study superior to that of the pass graduate ... Again, the honours graduate will be essentially a specialist teacher and, while it is clearly desirable that he should have a knowledge of educational principles and methodology of his own subject, there are many aspects of school work which touch him less closely than the 'form master' and of which he could independently gain the knowledge he requires without a full institutional course of professional training. (Gibbon 1947: para. 84)

Continuing, the Report further recommended that it would be quite sufficient for the honours graduate, rather like the licensed teacher of today, to acquire all the necessary insights on education and schooling as part of the first year of appointment, through the supervision and support offered by the employing school.

This was not a unanimously agreed recommendation, since five members of the Committee were to distance themselves from the majority standpoint quoted above, arguing that the more specialized study of honours graduates was not 'in any sense calculated to make them fitter to grapple with the problems of the classroom' (para. 87). Those putting forward this view believed that it would be 'unfair discrimination' (*ibid.*) in their favour to allow honours graduates to draw salary while still, technically, in training. Even as recently as 1973, in the Lelièvre Report on the initial training and probation of teachers in Northern Ireland, the recommendation was put forward that the period of time then spent on teaching practice by graduates completing a one-year teaching qualification should be reduced (para. 2.13). Expected improvement in the format of the newly qualified teacher's probationary year would, it was argued, render such a reduction feasible. In both the Gibbon and Lelièvre Reports, therefore, the prevailing policy was that university graduates need not spend as much time in training as their non-graduate counterparts. Thus, the better qualified one was, the greater was the likelihood of undergoing the least amount of training necessary. Differing abilities and aptitudes of necessity determined that there were corresponding different needs. What, next, of the universities and their cultural elements? What of the implications of these for professional training on the one hand and the study of education on the other? Why so much resistance to each?

Writing in 1914, in the *Central Educational Annual*, organ of the highly influential Dublin Central Teachers' Organisation, Miss C. M. Mahon, in that year president of the Irish National Teachers' Organisation, had the following to say about the training of teachers in Ireland: 'Next to the reformation of the Educational Administration itself, the reformation of one of its most important functions, namely the Training of Teachers, will demand the imperative attention of a Native Government' (Mahon 1914: 19). The reformation Miss Mahon had in mind was for the universities of Ireland to become more directly involved in teacher training, so that, as she put it, teachers could 'take out a degree', and in so doing, thereby reap the 'inestimable benefits of University education and training' (p. 25). What Miss Mahon found instead, however, was training provided almost exclusively by denominational training colleges and, if not in this manner, through monitorships and pupil-teacherships. Though concerned to see the universities extend their remit to the training needs of aspirant teachers, Miss Mahon was sanguine enough to realize that such provision was rather remote in 1914, and would be strongly resisted.

A root cause of this resistance was the distinction sharply drawn in the universities at this time between the 'pursuit of knowledge' and 'training', in ways implying that the former was the proper concern of the best and higher institutions and its teachers, while that latter was not. As Bell and Grant (1977: 24) point out,

> Professional men and scientists were never expected in England until recently . . . Their schooling and even their university career were meant to be 'gentle' rather than to train them. Training was something to be acquired and pursued 'on the job', in specialist institutions, in teaching hospitals, at the Inns of Court.

Aldrich (1982) makes a similar point when he emphasizes the high premium the universities have traditionally placed on the transmission of knowledge, on students mastering 'closely delimited existing areas of knowledge' (p. 148) as 'a supreme intellectual activity . . . an end in itself' (p. 149). And as Professor Constantia Maxwell reminds us in her *History of Trinity College, Dublin*, referring to Trinity and the Universities of Oxford and Cambridge in the nineteenth century: 'There was . . . no university training for those who wished to enter the professions or the great world of commerce' (Maxwell 1942: 182).

None of this is to deny, however, that the universities were not eventually caught up in the great reforming net which saw them re-examine their curricula and statutes after two commissions on the Universities of Oxford and Cambridge had reported their findings in 1853. According to Aldrich (1982: 148):

> Significant changes occurred in the period 1850–1914. More students were recruited from the middling and lower levels of the middle class . . . In the 1850s dissenters were admitted to first degrees . . . Dons no longer had to be celibate or in holy orders. The curriculum was cautiously broadened. Law and history became separate subjects of study in the 1870s . . . Cambridge forged ahead in its provision of scientific subjects. In 1873 the Cavendish Laboratory was opened where Clerk-Maxwell, Lord Rayleigh, J. J. Thompson and later Rutherford were to lead the world in experimental physics.

These were advances, of course, yet even in the sciences the application of knowledge, through training within a professional-vocational framework, did not materialize. As Professor Brian Simon points out, referring to the British Universities between 1920 and 1940, it was the task of the student to absorb knowledge, 'however indigestibly', not to apply it. And for academics, 'to cultivate their minds, or pursue knowledge for its own sake – a traditional attitude bolstered by the relative lack of demand for new knowledge from a stagnant economy' (Simon 1974: 253).

Moreover, according to Bolgar, the period between 1920 and 1940 was a time when

> Research university laboratories prided themselves on standing aloof from applied science. Historians boasted that History taught us nothing that would be relevant to current problems. Literary critics hastened to claim that aesthetic pleasure provided the main or even the only justification for studying literature. That education might have a purpose outside of itself, that it should be related to the well-being of the community, was a hypothesis few conservative souls were prepared to tolerate. (R. R. Bolgar, quoted in Simon 1974: 253)

Perhaps the analysis is over-stated, since it denies the existence of those who believed that knowledge and training did not have to be mutually exclusive. Yet we are reminded of the problems of credibility and acceptance the study of education has faced in the university sector, as illustrated by the fact that professors of education are a relatively recent phenomenon. At the Queen's University of Belfast, for example, the first professor of education was not appointed until 1914, while already, in 1846 and 1849 respectively, the university had appointed its first professor of Greek and first professor of jurisprudence and political economy.

A further issue is that of accountability or, more specifically, the lack of it in the university sector, though this is changing. In other sectors of education, teachers have historically been held highly accountable in their work situation. Thus, while the Cambridge professor of Latin depicted below might teach in 1870 with great ill-effect, at a similar time teachers in the elementary sector in Ireland were undergoing a different experience. Not only were they rated on a three-point scale of efficiency – highly efficient, efficient, not efficient – they had fees paid to their school on the basis of the examination results of their pupils ('payment by results').

> With his encyclopaedic knowledge and simple-minded enthusiasms for learning combined with a complete absence of any sense of proportion or of what his listeners wanted, he was not a successful lecturer. His method was to dictate long lists of references, unaccompanied by translation or common language, in the hope that his listener would look them up after the lecture. His class would dwindle to one hearer who remained faithful out of kindness, and who might be rewarded after the lecture with a copy of the 'Vegetarian Magazine' or of the reading (of the said professor's) correspondence with the Old Catholic Bishops.

> (Clarke 1959)

The caricature, of course, is universal, reflecting the greater emphasis, at the time, on academic brilliance than brilliant teaching, and begging the question: to what extent is there a contemporary echo?

Although it would be idle to pretend that the University of Ulster is immune from such charges, much has been done in the past few years to enhance the quality of teaching in the university and to accord it the same status as research achievement. These include the introduction of a Distinguished Teaching Award Scheme (discussed elsewhere in this book) and a course of postgraduate study for teachers in higher education lasting for two years. The alternative to the latter, a course of shorter duration, was not favoured for reasons similar to those mentioned by Piper (1988), quoted earlier in this chapter.

The Postgraduate Certificate in Teaching in Higher Education at the University of Ulster

Origins of the course

A certified course in the pedagogical aspects of higher education was identified by the university's Academic Staff Development Committee in 1987 as being an essential facility in the university, and preliminary work on the drafting of such a course was begun by the Department of Adult and Continuing Education. This work was developed further by the university's Working Party on Teaching and Learning and in December 1989 the course, sponsored by the Faculty of Education, was successfully validated. The first intake of participants to the Postgraduate Certificate in Teaching in Higher Education occurred in January 1991. The term 'participants' was deliberately chosen to emphasize that mutually beneficial relationships could be achieved among staff of all ages and experience, regardless of whether they were in the traditional sense course 'students' or tutors. The first cohort consisted of 13 members of staff at the University of Ulster, representing all faculties of the university except education, and one member of staff from the Queen's University of Belfast. Two participants successfully completed the first module of study but failed to register for the second module in October 1991.

Philosophy underlying the course

From the very outset it was agreed that the course should embody a number of cardinal principles. First, while it had been developed primarily for those with little or no experience of teaching in higher education, the course would not be exclusively for them. Second, this was not to be a part-time course that participants took in addition to their jobs; rather it was to be a direct contribution to their normal daily work. Third, as far as possible, the sequencing of the course content should reflect the needs of newly appointed staff during the first two years of their probationary period. Fourth, throughout the course there should be a strong element of theory, which participants should use to inform their practice. Finally, the content of the course would be the same for all participants, regardless of the faculty to which they belonged.

Although, at present, attendance on the course is voluntary it is intended that in future all newly appointed staff who do not possess a relevant teaching qualification will be expected to take the Certificate and that it will be a requirement for successful completion of probation that reasonable progress has been made.

Aims

The aims of the course are:

- to enhance participants' understanding of teaching and learning processes so that they can make appropriate and informed decisions about course design and choice of teaching, learning and assessment methods;
- to provide participants with an opportunity to reflect on their practice and enhance their pedagogical skills, hence improving the standard of teaching and the quality of student learning in their institutions;
- to establish a network of support among participants that will enable them to conduct their teaching duties with a greater degree of confidence, understanding and satisfaction;
- to recognize and enhance the value of teaching in higher education.

Structure and content

The Certificate comprises four modules of study, one module per teaching term. All meetings are organized on one day of the week between 10.00 a.m. and 1.00 p.m. during terms 1 and 2 and a wide repertoire of teaching methods is employed, including lectures, peer teaching, seminars, tutorials, simulations and role play, demonstrations and workshops. Areas covered by the modules include large and small group teaching, planning and conducting laboratory practical sessions or studio work, collecting data to identify strengths and weaknesses in one's teaching, theories of learning and instruction, assessment, final year project and postgraduate supervision, problems encountered by the adult learner, course design and evaluation, and educational, audio-visual and information technology aids.

Assessment of the course

The participant's overall mark or grade for the course is based on *formal assessments* of a portfolio produced for each module of the course and video recordings of their teaching in natural settings in modules 2 and 4. For their portfolio participants are asked to carry out a number of precisely defined tasks arising directly from the content of the module. For example, in module 1 participants carried out five tasks: writing objectives for a unit of instruction and devising valid forms of assessment for these objectives; the production of an audio-visual aids package; identifying from their diary some aspect of their teaching that was problematic, carrying out an action step aimed at reducing the problem and then monitoring the outcomes; analysing and evaluating two practical sessions in the Micro-teaching Centre; and having an observer complete a rating schedule during a lecture or checklist during a small group teaching session and discussing the responses with the course member. Since it is not practical for the participants' pedagogic skills to be observed by their peers or tutors in natural settings (although this will be done by their mentors), video recordings are made of the participants giving a lecture or carrying out a small group discussion with their own students at the beginning and end of modules 2 and 4. The recordings are assessed by the participants, their peers and their tutors. In assessing the participant, consideration is given not only to the final performance but also to the improvement that has taken place.

In addition to the above, participants are also *informally assessed* on a diary kept by them throughout the course and on the microteaching sessions that take place in module 1. Such assessments are considered to be of a formative/diagnostic nature (i.e. they are intended to help participants identify their own strengths and weaknesses) and are *not* taken into account in determining the participant's overall grade or mark for the course. In their diaries participants are required to produce evidence of reflective analysis and evaluation of their own teaching and (where appropriate) the extent of student learning. This includes reference to theoretical issues arising from the module and their relationship to practice, the extent of peer and mentor support in the evaluation of teaching performance at stages during the module, and the value of various evaluative techniques for gaining insight into the effectiveness of their teaching and learning. Assessment of the diary involves the participant only (i.e. self-assessment) and his or her mentor. In the first module participants are also video-recorded during sessions in which they introduce and implement a teaching skill. In addition to improving their pedagogic skills it is hoped that the participants will improve their skills and confidence in carrying out self-assessment and peer group assessment in a relatively non-threatening environment.

Mentorship

The central thrust of our course is to provide participants with the opportunity for reflection on practice, hence improving the standard of teaching and the quality of student learning. This can best be achieved in an environment that is open and honest, where the unique contribution of each course participant is valued – an environment that reflects the andragogical process as outlined by Knowles (1980). This particular process consists of four elements, two of which are of direct relevance here: (a) the learner moves from dependence to independence; and (b) the learner's experience becomes an increasingly rich source of learning.

As previously indicated, participants on the course may come from a diverse range of backgrounds and with great variation in teaching experience. If individuals are to benefit from the course in the manner anticipated a considerable proportion of the teaching must be directed towards the needs of individuals and the experience of participants used as a vehicle for learning.

Crucial to the success of this is the role of the mentor. A mentor can be defined as an experienced person with whom the course participant feels at ease, to whom he or she can speak freely about aspects of his or her work, including personal feelings, and who can also act as an appropriate role model. It is anticipated that the mentor will be a member of staff in the same department (or, if necessary, faculty) as the participant. It is recognized that the mentor needs to possess certain characteristics; for example, to be aware of himself or herself and recognize his or her own feelings, to respond to the feelings of the course participant and to accept the trust of, and empathize with, the course participant. These are the same characteristics as identified by Rogers (1983) when considering the role of a facilitator.

The mentor with regard to this course could be considered to have at least five functions:

1. *Pastoral*, providing personal support and a 'shoulder to cry on' if necessary.
2. *Facilitative*, creating an environment conducive to personal discovery, analysis and reflection, and recognizing the importance of accepting feedback from the course participant about aspects of his or her work that might require attention.
3. *Role model*, allowing the course participant the opportunity to observe teaching sessions and related activities and be prepared to accept feedback.
4. *Assessor*, providing the climate in which the participant can be assessed without feeling under threat, and giving sound constructive feedback.
5. *Supervisor*, joining in teaching sessions as supervisor but without adopting a superior stance, providing feedback as above and acting as a sounding board within the context of the participant's self-assessment process.

As participants on the Course are also colleagues there is a need to produce the right learning environment in which participants feel free to experiment and try things out without fearing the consequences should they go wrong. It is to this end that the process of mentorship is invaluable.

Evaluation of the course

The course was evaluated using a questionnaire administered to participants in the sixth week of the second module. The questionnaire was designed to elicit course members' assessment of the relevance of the course; whether or not it was helping them to look critically at their teaching; whether or not the mentor and departmental colleagues had been supportive; what, specifically, the course participants were discovering about their teaching style; what problems the course was experiencing as a new course; and how, in the light of these problems, the course could be improved. The final question, question 8, afforded the opportunity for further comments. The questionnaire was completed anonymously. Ten course members out of twelve were present on the afternoon the questionnaire was distributed; seven of them were able to remain after class to complete it and two returned theirs some days later through the internal mail. Nine questionnaires in all were therefore returned.

Concerning the relevance of the course, five of the nine respondents regarded it as 'highly' relevant and the remaining four 'relevant in some aspects but not in all'. Significantly, no course participant considered the course irrelevant to his or her needs. Of the five who responded the most positively, the way in which the course has caused them to think critically about their teaching skills was a common assessment. For one such respondent the course had touched on 'almost all aspects' of his/her teaching, while another mentioned the benefits to be derived from linking theory to practice and then monitoring the outcomes. A third respondent emphasized the experiential learning approach, which was described as 'excellent', adding further comment: 'a superb course that builds on previous experiences but lends itself to the developmental and reflective process'. Of the four respondents who considered the course to be relevant in only some aspects, two mentioned that this was so because the structure of the first module was at times vague. Nevertheless, one of these respondents still believed that he/she had been given the opportunity to engage in a valuable reflective exercise in which peer appraisal had played a significant part. Overall, more course participants than not are finding the course relevant to their professional needs, and even those who did not assess it as 'highly relevant' were of the view that it was helping to meet their professional needs.

As to whether or not the course was enabling participants to look critically at their teaching, a majority were of the opinion that it was indeed succeeding in this respect, six respondents being of the opinion that the course was proving 'highly useful', while three considered that it had been 'useful in some respects but not in all'. Of the six course members opting for the first category of response, three made specific reference to the identification of weaknesses and strengths in their teaching. Responses included: 'I have certainly been made conscious of my strengths and weaknesses,' 'Helped to identify gaps and introduced new ideas, concepts and skills,' 'I have begun to critically examine my own methods and experiment in different teaching methods.' Of the three respondents who assessed the course as 'useful in some respects but not in all', one mentioned that time had prevented him/her from taking a really close look at teaching performance, another made no further comment, while the third could still say that thus far the course was proving 'beneficial' to his/her overall performance as a lecturer. Overall, the responses to this section of the questionnaire are most encouraging, none of the course members having stated that the course had not been at all useful as a vehicle for taking a close and critical look at the teaching process.

As already mentioned, the role of the mentor is regarded as a crucial aspect of the course. Yet the opinion of course participants is divided between those for whom mentorship has worked effectively and those who have not found in it the support they would like. The divide is as clear-cut as this. Where the mentor had been supportive, participants were loud in their praise of the value and importance of this. One participant had 'developed a great, informal relationship'. His/her mentor visited classes and provided feedback. Another commented, 'Mine has been excellent,' adding the important comment that being able to choose his/her own mentor had been of crucial importance. Negative comments included: 'Support is minimal,' 'This part hasn't worked for me. The mentor was allocated by my head of department – not my own choice,' 'Advice and help had to be sought for.' The responses in this section of the questionnaire would indicate that there is a close relationship between course participants choosing their own mentor and the subsequent success of the partnership. In contrast, where the course member had been allocated a mentor by the head of department, the partnership had not functioned quite so effectively. This finding is significant.

One very important aspect of question 5, which dealt with course participants' findings about their teaching, is that it is possible to cluster the responses into three main areas: tutor talk, structuring classes and interaction. Regarding the latter, this was observed to dominate at the expense of student participation and interaction with each other. One respondent made the rather important point that what interaction there was in his/her class tended more often to be student–tutor than student–student in character, and this was a cause for him/her to feel concern about his/her interactive effectiveness. The structure of lectures was mentioned as problematic mainly because of the lack of good pacing, not to mention effective planning. Overall, responses indicate that the course participants are thinking about their teaching across a whole spectrum of associated activities and are raising serious questions about such important matters as the value and appropriateness of student note-taking and how effectively they are using their audio-visual aids. Overall, there has been a considerable raising of consciousness about the latter among participants as a whole.

The most serious flaw in the course at present, and on this there is unanimous agreement, is the assignment requirement, eight out of the nine respondents having made specific reference to this. The problem has three related issues: length, timing and extent of tutor guidance. Regarding the first, the course participants generally feel that the first assignment, for the first module, consisting of five individual elements, was much too disparate in nature; they would have preferred to cover one or two discrete areas in depth rather than five in what may have been dubious depth. Comments included 'Too many assignments in Module 1' and 'Heavy assessment in Module 1.' A related issue is that of timing. It is clear that the course members needed more time to prepare their work and that the problem of preparation was compounded by the wide-ranging remit which the tasks for module 1 entailed. There had also been 'lack of information on assignment structure'. One course member made a specific request for 'more clarity about assignments at an early stage'. In view of these assessments, it is clear why, in question 7, which asked for recommendations for improvement, mention should be made of the need for 'better communication' between course tutors and members. Overall, however, there was limited response to question 7, participants having already taken the opportunity, in question 6, to link the problems they observed about the course to recommendations for its improvement.

In the final question, which asked participants to add their own further comment, responses indicated positive support for the course aims and objectives, including: 'I am most satisfied with the course,' 'I am thoroughly enjoying this course. It's not often I attend all classes voluntarily . . . I like them and find them useful – a new experience,' 'Well structured course with lots of variety,' 'The tutors have all been very helpful and understanding.'

In summary, it may be said that the course has been favourably assessed by the course participants. However, there are two aspects that need to be addressed as priority. They are the appointment of a mentor and the assignment requirement in module 1, regarded as much too heavy and wide-ranging, as well as having to be completed without adequate tutorial support. In terms of evaluation it is also worth noting that in May 1991 the National Board for Nursing, Midwifery and Health Visiting for Northern Ireland agreed that the course, together with a supplementary programme of supervision, guidance and support, be approved and recommended to the UKCC as a course of study leading to the recording of a teaching qualification for newly appointed staff in the Department of Nursing and Health Visiting. (In our first cohort four members of staff in that department are enrolled on the course.)

Concluding comments

Although the course has only been in operation since January 1991 we are already anticipating that changes will have to be made to both the content of the course and its mode of delivery. First, with increased student numbers, our participation will require more exposure to the new technologies (such as video-conferencing, interactive videos and computer-assisted learning) and more experience in developing and evaluating self-learning packages for students. Second, as the number of participants on the course increases, we may have to incorporate some element of open learning, along the lines of the Oxford Polytechnic Certificate described earlier.

We have argued in this chapter that, for a variety of complex reasons, universities have generally failed to recognize the value of teaching in higher education and, until comparatively recently, have done little to improve the quality of the teaching that occurs within their institutions. However, we are cautiously optimistic that attitudes will change in the near future, if only as a result of external pressures, and that the 'legacy of apathy' may soon be over.

References

Aldrich, R. (1982) *An Introduction to the History of Education*. London: Hodder and Stoughton.

Bell, R. and Grant, N. (1977) *Patterns of Education in the British Isles*. London: Allen and Unwin.

Blyth, W. A. L. (ed.) (1968) *University Teaching Methods. Report on a Course Held in the University of Liverpool in December 1966*. Liverpool: University of Liverpool.

Clarke, M. L. (1959) *Classical Education in Britain 1500–1900*. Cambridge: Cambridge University Press.

Gibbon, W. D. (1947) *Report of the Committee on the Recruitment and Training of Teachers*. Belfast: HMSO.

Hale Report (1964) *Report of the Committee on University Teaching Methods*. London: HMSO.

Knowles, M. (1980) *The Modern Practice of Adult Education*. Chicago: Associated Press.

Lelièvre, F. J. (1973) *The Education, Initial Training and Probation of Northern Ireland Schools and Institutions of Further Education: Report of a Committee of Inquiry*. Belfast: HMSO.

Mahon, C. M. (1914) University education and the training of teachers. *Dublin Central Review*.

Maxwell, C. (1942) *A History of Trinity College Dublin*. Dublin: Dublin University Press.

Nisbet, J. (1967) Courses on university teaching methods. *Universities Quarterly*, 21: 186–98.

Piper, D. W. (1988) Staff development in universities: should there be a staff college? *Higher Education Quarterly*, 42: 238–52.

Rogers, C. (1983) *Freedom to Learn for the 80s*. New York: Merrill.
Simon, B. (1974) *The Politics of Educational Reform, 1920–1940*. London: Lawrence and Wishart.

17

Quality in Teaching and the Encouragement of Enterprise

Ann Tate

Given the overall theme of this book, i.e. quality in university teaching, it is not surprising that the title of this chapter reflects a particular emphasis on *teaching* as the primary impetus for change. However, I wish to argue that in order to assess the ways in which teaching may encourage the development of enterprise competencies in students, we first of all need to look carefully at the relationships that may exist between teaching and learning *per se* – and in particular at the research which suggests that the form that teaching takes affects the quality of student learning. Indeed, it may be the case that the reverse relationship to that of the title may be more appropriate, i.e. that enterprise, or rather a focus on enterprise, can encourage teaching. However, in order to substantiate such a claim, we need to explore why the relationship between teaching and learning is enhanced by the introduction of what at first glance appears to be an extraneous variable, something more in tune with issues marginal to the educational process rather than germane to it. Thus, I wish to discuss in this chapter the meaning of 'enterprise' (as it relates to university education) and what it is about 'enterprise' that so influences teaching that it has an impact not only on learning but on the quality of teaching itself.

The chapter is divided into four main areas.

1. A description of conventional or traditional university teaching, and the consequences of learning.
2. The effects on teaching and learning of a change in focus towards the development of enterprise competencies.
3. The consequences of this changed focus for the teacher, the student, the course and the institution.
4. The implications of such changes for the quality of teaching.

It has become customary over the years, whenever university teaching has been discussed (and attempts made to evaluate it) to focus the attention on the person and the process, and to treat the object of that process as given. Thus we may discern many learned debates surrounding teaching styles, content, organization and presentation, appropriate use of props, mode of delivery and peer appreciation. Yet lurking in the shadows we may discern a rather pathetic and passive creature, more often victim than instigator of actions, object rather than subject, who seems destined to be increasingly harangued by teacher with that burning question, 'How was it for you?' (which as a mechanism of feedback leaves much to be desired). Our supporting, silent character is, of course, 'student', without whom the role of teacher is essentially unplayable.

Traditionalist views of university teaching assume a simplistic relationship between teacher and student in which teacher imparts knowledge to student, who receives it and replays it as learning. This is a view that is *teacher-centred*. Lewis Elton encapsulates this characteristic when he suggests that, in universities, teaching and learning are rather separate activities carried out by different people – students receive knowledge from their teachers and excellent learners are those who receive it best (Elton 1990b). Teachers for their part are not motivated to change for they have learned by experience that this is how it is done – given that learning by experience is the primary form of training for university teaching. Neither does the rewards system in university life encourage much effort. This view of university teaching has been graphically reinforced by Brenda Wilson's account of her first year as a lecturer, in which she says

> I was invited to display *indifference* to teaching. The University culture pressured me to see students as empty vessels to be filled, to ignore that they had unique personalities and aspirations. I had to internalise the contradiction of the high status of research and the low value placed on teaching and suffer the role-conflict – a kind of moral schizophrenia – that resulted.
>
> (Wilson 1991; emphasis added)

It has been suggested that this traditional teaching suffers from the 'tyranny of content' (Jenkins and Pepper 1987), in which the major method of teaching is the lecture and staff-led seminar. These methods reflect a preoccupation with the lecturer's knowledge of content, despite statements from governing bodies, mission statements and official reports that stress that the purpose of higher education is to develop in students a range of higher order intellectual skills and capabilities. The CNAA *Handbook* 1989, for example, says that

> a primary aim of any programme of studies must be the development of the students' intellectual and imaginative skills and powers; their understanding and judgement; their problem-solving skills; their ability to see relationships within what they have learned and to perceive their field of study in broader perspective.

In a similar vein, the Mission Statement of the University of Ulster states, *inter alia*: 'The University's educational programme seeks to . . . emphasise creativity and a problem-solving approach as valid alternatives to more conventional academic and intellectual pursuits; encourage inter-disciplinary and, so far as possible, inter professional perspectives.' In practice, it would appear that the lecturer is the only one whose skills in these areas are being encouraged and developed. It is, in these circumstances, somewhat paradoxical that, as Susan Weil points out, 'Teachers have learned experientially to teach traditionally' (Weil 1990).

It is worth noting at this point that while I shall in general be critical of this situation as far as the development of enterprise is concerned, it is an approach that many students find comfortable – especially the students who come to university directly from schools where the notion of autonomous and active learning is incompatible with the drive to achieve the necessary 'A' level scores.

Such an approach to learning on the part of the student has been characterized as a 'surface' approach, in which learning is characterized as acquiring facts, increasing knowledge and memorizing (Gibbs 1990). This reproductive approach, Gibbs argues, has been brought about by a particular style of teaching (which he calls 'closed') in which the teacher does all the work and makes all the decisions. However, such a disabling approach to learning is not immutable. It can be changed, but in order to understand how change can be brought about we must take a different view of the student; rather than seeing her as a passive recipient of teaching, we must view the situation and the teacher–student relationship from her point of view.

Studies of occupational socialization – notably those of nurses – have shown that there is a sense in which students are active and organizing: they have motivation, goals and values; they develop and adopt strategies for coping with this situation; they learn and interact with the norms and values of a student culture (Olesen and Whitaker 1968). Superficially, then, students may appear to be passively listening and display rapt attention to the tutor, but this may simply reflect the fact that they have learned that this is the correct front to display to meet the tutor's expectations of them. If they have interpreted the situation as one in which the teacher is 'in authority', their task becomes one of learning what is in the teacher's mind rather than an enquiry into knowledge itself. Other clues to the active and interpretative basis for student behaviour may be found in the negative comments often made by teachers about students: students don't attend, don't participate, don't read round their subject, etc. Such overt inactivity may be seen as a strategy for coping with an overburdened timetable or with the threats to self-esteem posed by seminar participation. Students are, therefore, behaving rationally in these circumstances, which Becker *et al.* (1968) refer to as the 'social structured conditions of student perform-ance'. Becker's study shows that within an overall condition of subjection (to the demands of the institution and teaching staff) students collectively calculate appropriate courses of action that will fulfil a variety of personal and academic goals. They say:

Students do not respond to the teacher alone, or to the lure of his subject matter. They respond to him only after they assess what a reasonable course of action vis a vis him would be, given other demands, academic and extra-academic, made on them and given the definitions and understandings about academic achievement current among their peers.

(Becker *et al.* 1968)

They go on to suggest (in a similar vein to the argument proposed by Gibbs) that in an institution in which the students perceive the pursuit of grades to be the dominant priority of faculty (teaching staff), this becomes a major obstacle to the adoption of a more scholarly approach by students. In other words, a surface approach to learning is a conscious and rational strategy, adopted by students in response to institutional demands to achieve grades at the expense of intellectual growth. In failing to recognize that our students are actively engaging with the world rather than simply absorbing it, we have failed, until now perhaps, to capitalize on the best learning resource at our disposal – the student. By seeing the student simply as audience, consumer or client, we miss out on the fact that he or she is also a player on the stage, exerting an influence on the learning outcome, which we have not directly identified but must do so if we are to focus on the relationship between teaching and learning. As Ramsden reminds us, 'only by finding out about how students learn what we expect them to learn, can we help them learn better' (Ramsden 1987).

Enterprise and teaching

The new focus on the development of enterprise competencies in our undergraduate population brings the student into the limelight of centre stage rather than relegating her to the ranks of supporting players. In order to understand how and why this is the case, we need to rehearse, briefly, what is meant by enterprise in this context.

The Enterprise in Higher Education Initiative is a programme initiated by the (then) Manpower Services Commission in 1987 and has two broad aims:

1. Every person seeking a higher education qualification should be able to develop competencies and aptitudes relevant to enterprise.
2. The competencies and aptitudes should be acquired at least in part through project-based work, designed to be undertaken in a real economic setting, which should be jointly assessed by employers and the student's higher education institution.

The Initiative arose from a widely shared concern with the extent to which institutions of higher education were providing for their students the kinds of educational experience that would enable them to make a positive and effective contribution to the world beyond the university. It was not really a question of knowledge or academic standards, more a question of empowering students to put that knowledge into action via the development of generic competencies – or personal transferable skills. In a statement issued by the NAB and UGC in 1985 they assert:

> The abilities most valued in industrial, commercial and professional life as well as in public and social administration are the transferable intellectual and personal skills. These include, the ability to analyse complex issues, identify the core of a problem and the means of solving it, to synthesise and interpret disparate elements, to clarify values and to make effective use of numerical and other information, to work co-operatively with others and above all, to communicate clearly, both orally and in writing. A Higher Education System which provides its students with these things is serving society well.

This very much echoes the objectives of the CNAA described above, but implicit in this statement is the criticism that institutions of higher education have not been conspicuously successful in achieving these objectives. The notion of competence is, of course, drawn extensively from the kinds of management theories that were coming to prominence in the 1980s, in which competence is defined as 'an underlying characteristic of a person which results in effective and/or superior performance in a job' (Boyatzis 1982). In such studies, specialized knowledge *per se* did not account for the difference between average or superior performance, and past performance. Rather it would seem that specialized knowledge is best considered to be a threshold competency, i.e. it is necessary for performance. If, however, enterprise or personal transferable competencies are to be developed as an integral part of the HE curriculum then the role of knowledge itself, and its assessment, must be recast. (For an interesting discussion on the issues involved in this process see Fleming (1991).)

If such competencies are to be developed, then they must be practised in a relevant and meaningful context – relevant and meaningful not only to the competence, but also to the aims and objectives of the academic programme or course of study that the student is engaged in. Hence the emphasis is on employer involvement in the curriculum.

Depending on the definition of enterprise adopted, one may envisage different – and not necessarily exclusive – implications for the education process. These may be summarized as: learning for enterprise; learning about enterprise; and learning through enterprise. Learning for enterprise is probably best illustrated by the various courses offered by, for example, the Small Business Institutes and Business Schools, where the key objective is to provide students with the skills and knowledge they will need to start their own business, or be most effective in business.

The Graduate Enterprise Programme is a good example. Learning about enterprise is the concept that underpins the government concern about teaching economic awareness as part of the new National Curriculum. However, learning through enterprise underpins Enterprise in Higher Education, for the effective delivery of the enterprise competencies relies on the development of a new strategy for teaching, learning and assessment. Through a focus on these competencies, the whole process of learning itself is radically altered. Or, as Gibbs (1990) suggests, the approach to learning becomes a 'deep' as distinct from a 'surface' approach.

This focus – on the outcomes of learning – has been alluded to in Chapter 13 by George Brown, and the skills he outlined (as possible learning outcomes) are those personal and transferable skills that form the focus of enterprise competence development. He argues that measures of teaching effectiveness are predicated on a prior understanding of the learning outcomes of such teaching – thus a focus on enterprise competencies as learning outcomes directly affects measures of teaching effectiveness and thereby its quality.

If we look for a moment at the enterprise competencies adopted by the University of Ulster's EHE programme, we can identify a range of underlying characteristics here that could immediately lead to superior and effective performance – *as a student initially*, regardless of career orientation. The competencies underpinning the programme are:

1. Communication – the ability to express one's thoughts concisely and coherently both orally and in writing; active listening and questioning; making presentations.
2. Leadership – adopting appropriate style for achieving group objectives, monitoring and evaluating their work, showing vision and inspiration, developing skills and competencies of subordinates.
3. Teamwork and followership – the ability to work in a team, formal or informal, specialist or interdisciplinary, long-term or project-based; being supportive of others and promoting the group towards the task.
4. Negotiation and persuasion – use of deliberate strategies to influence or persuade others.
5. Problem analysis and solving – logical thought, ability to identify key issues and create solutions.
6. Decision-making – generating sufficient information to assess various alternatives and to make a high quality decision based on perceived outcome(s).
7. Creating opportunities – seeing and acting on new opportunities and seizing unusual opportunities.
8. Achievement drive – setting and achieving realistic goals.
9. Risk-taking – being prepared to take risks.
10. Self-awareness – knowledge of one's limitations and capabilities.
11. Coping with and managing personal stress and stressful situations – ability to eliminate stressors through time-management or restructuring of work.
12. Dealing with conflict – understanding the dynamics of the situation and the options available through bargaining, controlling and/or confrontation.
13. Flexibility – not being rigid in one's beliefs, views or ideas.

14. Proactive – disposition towards taking action to accomplish something, initiative, persistence.
15. Numerate – feeling comfortable in working with numbers.
16. Computer literate – understanding computers and their use.

These competencies are not simply technical or instrumental, or knee jerk reactions to the demands of industry. Rather they are a real attempt to put into action the broad statements of intent referred to earlier. In other words, they present a worthwhile undertaking in relation to the values of higher education regardless of their utility for the immediate demands of industry. As Ronald Barnett has argued,

> Improved powers of insight, analysis, evaluation, communication, self-presentation and toleration ought to result from all higher education courses, simply by doing justice to their intrinsic educational aims. And these educationally-based abilities will do much to improve the graduate's value and usefulness in the world.
>
> (Barnett 1989)

Peter Wright, Higher Education Adviser to the Training Employment and Education Directorate, argues that enterprise has always been part of the academic curriculum, but in a rather covert and implicit fashion. He suggests that EHE is about rendering enterprising practices more explicit and measurable; it is about making that practice more related to the actual and practical experiences of students and to working life; and it is about making enterprising qualities one of the central outcomes of the teaching process rather than one of its by products (Wright 1989a). From the point of view of teaching, then, the emphasis is on process rather than content, or, as Lewis Elton says, on the how rather than the what (Elton 1990b), which in turn shifts the emphasis in responsibility for learning from the teacher to the student – or from teacher-centred to student-centred learning. Student-centred learning was not invented by Enterprise in Higher Education, but EHE does provide a clear rationale for a movement across all courses in this direction, and, more importantly, because EHE draws on experience of the development and assessment of competence derived outside the university or academic environment, different models of learning and assessment are available for evaluation in this setting.

In order to clarify what the implications of this change might be for teaching and learning, we could (following Pennington 1988) set up two models or ideal types that represent two rather extreme positions along a continuum.

Teacher-centred	*Student-centred*
Focus on content.	Focus on process.
Emphasizes knowing that.	Emphasizes knowing how.
Students work as individuals, often in competition with each other.	Students work in groups and teams, collectively and cooperatively.

Teacher-centred	*Student-centred*
Students highly dependent.	Students work independently.
Learning objectives imposed.	Objectives negotiated.
Assessment by written exams.	Assessment varied.
Knowledge is handed down from subject to novice.	Students actively generate and synthesize knowledge from many sources.
Lectures predominate as mode of curriculum delivery.	Teaching sessions flexible and not always classroom-based.
Teacher role is that of expert.	Teacher is facilitator and a resource for students in a learning partnership.

I should add that moving from the left to the right of the continuum has ramifications that transcend the interaction between teacher and student, and focus attention on the nature of the institutional climate in which such a movement may best occur – I shall return to this later.

In moving along the continuum in this way, we are tapping into the idea that students are not passive recipients (however strongly that image may come across in the traditional side) but learn through constructing, interpreting and reinterpreting their world. Teaching that encourages students to develop their enterprise competencies must harness this by providing structured opportunities for students to reflect and capitalize upon their own learning experiences in their course.

What does this mean in practice?

The style of curriculum development and delivery

One of the consequences of a focus on enterprise competencies in curriculum development is a shift in emphasis from inputs to learning outcomes. Many courses in my own institution are described primarily in terms of syllabus content, modes of teaching and methods of assessment. The standard of attainment expected is rarely described – rather it is implied by where it occurs in the programme (first year, second year etc.) – and neither are those other widely accepted outcomes of a university education: problem-solving, decision-making, the ability to make judgements etc. An emphasis on learning outcomes describes what the student is expected to know, and be able to do, as a result of a unit or course of study. Outcomes can be subject-based knowledge, with attendant processing skills, and personal, such as interpersonal and intrapersonal skills. (An excellent example of an attempt to identify learning outcomes for a range of disciplines and subject areas is currently the focus of a Unit for the Development of Adult and Continuing Education project; UDACE 1990.) There are clear advantages in this approach from the point of view of developing varied and more independent approaches to learning, but perhaps more importantly from the student's point of view the process of self-evaluation and assessment can be developed when there is a coherent set of outcome criteria, which identify the purpose and level of perform- ance. Moreover, if employers are encouraged to participate in curriculum development (as envisaged by the EHE) then the language of learning outcomes will be one with which they are already familiar, and communi- cation between the academic world and the employment world will be better facilitated.

In relation to curriculum delivery, the shift in emphasis is from teacher to student-centredness, from imparting knowledge to discovering it. There is an obvious central role here for groupwork and teamwork methods of delivery, as these can open up opportunities for the development of a range of related competencies. Groupwork emphasizes cooperation rather than individualism; it provides exemplars of teamwork in action; it can facilitate peer tutoring and mentoring skills; and it can provide opportuni- ties for creativity and innovative solutions to problems. (For an excellent exposition of the strategies most likely to foster a student-centred 'deep' learning approach see Gibbs 1990.)

It follows that lectures will take a much lesser role in the delivery of the curriculum. As Jenkins and Pepper (1987) point out, 'Teachers and students should treat them like cigars, as pleasurable now and then, but dangerous if taken in large doses.'

Coupled with the emphasis on learning outcomes, the negotiation of learning contracts between teacher and students is enhanced when the criteria for good performance are made explicit. Naturally, when ideas such as these are raised, staff are concerned about content: 'How can I cover the syllabus if "teaching time" is reduced in this way?' There are many answers to this dilemma, not all of them solutions it must be said. One cannot avoid the problems, however, and conscious decisions must be made about whether all the 'content' is absolutely necessary and, if it is, whether it must be covered by the teacher.

It should also be pointed out that questions of this kind raise larger policy issues that cannot be solved by teachers alone. Professional accreditation bodies, professional subject associations and validating authorities must all be involved in these broader policy issues (I shall return to these 'institutional' implications later). Nevertheless, despite such deeply held reservations among university teaching staff, there is evidence, at least in many universities, that staff are responding positively to the opportunity that EHE offers for curriculum development with a focus on student- centred, problem-based learning. The Academic Audit Unit (1991), for example, notes that:

> the Enterprise in Higher Education Initiative operated by the Depart- ment of Employment is, for many of those Universities which have EHE programmes, providing a challenging opportunity to develop

approaches to teaching and learning which go well beyond the traditional expectations of the British Honours degree.

Placement and work experience

One of the key aims of the EHE initiative is the encouragement of project-based work in real economic settings outside the university. In the vast majority of programmes associated with the initiative, placement and work experience carry a large measure of the responsibility for furthering this aim. However, one of the evident problems for courses where placement exists is the interrelationship between the placement experience and the 'formal' or 'taught' curriculum. In too many instances the experience, from the student's point of view, is a disjointed one where the progress made during placement is inadequately reflected in the subsequent academic programme. Similarly, preparation for placement takes the common form of awareness-raising for the student and general advice about how to behave in an organizational environment. What we may in fact have in the student experience are two worlds in which the student must learn sometimes quite contradictory responses and behaviours (see Davis 1990).

With the enterprise focus in teaching, placement can be seen as an opportunity to extend the development of the key competencies, which in turn may make the learning experience in placement settings much more coherent from the student point of view. The placement has enormous learning potential, but it must be structured, and related to the overall learning outcomes of the course of which it forms part. Where placement is located within a course that emphasizes student-centred learning, explicit criteria for good performance and the establishment of clear learning objectives, then its potential is maximized. Where students are already confident about managing their own education, the placement experience can provide an excellent opportunity to put this into practice in a less safe environment than the academic cloister. Furthermore, on their return from placement, the course team will be able to have a much clearer idea as to how well the student has developed in relation to the course objectives, and utilize this development in the final academic phase of the course. (An example of the kinds of learning objectives for placement that may be identified is given by Nixon (1990) in a discussion of assessment issues in placement.) It follows from this that the supervision of placement and its assessment is primarily part of the teaching process, rather than an administrative task.

Assessment

One of the most common problems raised by teachers who are comfortable with the 'traditional' model in contrast to more student-centred learning is that of assessment. A traditional assessment scheme with which we are all familiar is characterized as summative (it occurs at the end of a course or unit for the purpose of grading) and it is norm-referenced (it ranks individuals in relation to each other). Many exam board spread sheets reflect this system.

Ramsden has suggested that this form of assessment fails to test quality in students' work. He says 'all too often what we really test is not changes in how students understand the world, but something that is an invalid proxy for such changes . . . The fact that students are aware of this leads them to adopt strategies at variance with their teachers' aims' (Ramsden 1987). We do so because we are afraid to do otherwise, and we are concerned about standards. Yet, in this system, we can produce doctors who are qualified to practise by virtue of achieving a place in the top 50 per cent of their course – they might be licensed but have got, say, only half of everything right. Would we allow someone to drive a car on the roads who could perform only half of the necessary operations? If the driving test were norm-referenced, then people would obtain licences by being in the best group from all those who had taken the driving test on that day – irrespective of whether any of them could actually drive a car or not.

Teaching with an enterprise focus involves assessment that is formative (it is used as a learning instrument) and is criterion-referenced (assessment is based on how well a person has performed independently of how others have performed). It is based on the establishment of performance criteria in the form of outcomes, i.e. this person is able to . . . In such a system, feedback becomes a crucial component, for it is an opportunity to learn rather than an indicator of rank.

The use of feedback can also help students to develop their capacity for self-evaluation if the criteria for good performance are made explicit – whatever the *form* of assessment. It is also helpful, in this context, if the students have been involved in setting the criteria for a good performance, in, say, giving a seminar presentation, so that when they have to give their own presentation they have some measure of how they are performing. One of the objectives of any assessment process with an enterprise focus is that students may be able to make judgements about themselves in relation to a set of standards, rather than by comparison with peers. The ability to self-assess, to appraise one's own performance, is an intrinsic part of the learning process. Many of the enterprise competencies outlined earlier presuppose the effective development of self-assessment skills. They also presuppose a much wider set of assessment instruments being utilized, in addition to the more traditional essay and three-hour unseen examination paper.

Self, peer and group assessments play an important role here, as do case studies and projects. In teaching for enterprise, then, assessment forms part of the learning experience, where reflection on experience is a key element. Such reflective ability, in itself, is an important competence. However, there is perhaps an additional, if unintended, consequence of such a change in the approach to assessment in higher education courses – a consequence that has profound implications for the quality of teaching. For, if students become more expert in self and peer assessment, if they become more confident about and competent at evaluation, then the process of student evaluation of teaching (an integral part of quality assurance mechanisms) will become a more reliable measure of teaching quality and effectiveness than it is at present. The question 'How was it for you?' will have a much improved chance of eliciting feedback that can genuinely be used to improve teaching performance. (Presumably the question becomes, 'what did I do (or not do) that made it better/worse for you?')

Roles of teacher, student and employer in the learning process

The consequences for teaching and learning of a focus on enterprise outlined above have considerable implications for the roles of those involved in the process. For the teacher, the new role is one of facilitator, organizer and resourcer – someone who is *an* authority without necessarily being *in* authority. In research at the University of Chicago, Charles River Consultants utilized the Job Competence Assessment instrument (used in the identification of management competencies) to identify the characteristics of a student-centred teacher. These were:

- has positive expectations of students;
- is aware of students' concerns;
- places a high value on the learning process;
- views specialized knowledge as a resource;
- works to establish mutuality and rapport;
- holds students accountable for their learning interests;
- diagnoses problems and prescribes actions;
- structures processes to facilitate active learning;
- links pedagogy to student concerns.

To my knowledge, such a staff profile has not been developed in the UK context, but it at least provides a starting point for what the 'enterprising teacher' may look like. The role of student is to become more active, autonomous and responsible: a manager of her own learning; an organizer of her resources; a partner in the learning process.

In EHE a clearer role emerges for employers – not just a provider of placement, sponsor of events and presenter of talks about careers in industry. Rather the employer is someone cognizant with curriculum objectives and the way they relate to the development of the enterprise competencies that recruiters say are most important in graduates.

Such changes in role give rise to considerable training issues – for staff crucially, but also for students. One cannot demand that students develop enterprise competencies without affording training opportunities. For example, students need to practise groupwork skills in a safe learning environment before being set tasks that involve groupwork on which they are to be assessed.

The environment

Both the physical and the cultural environment are important in the encouragement of enterprising learning. Such learning is facilitated by 'user friendly' spaces, with comfortable seating that can be rearranged to suit the purposes and that allows for eye contact between participants. Attention needs to be paid to resources that support learning and the accessibility of these to students. But perhaps more important than the physical environment is the cultural climate – the ethos, values and style – that characterizes the institution in question. Learning must be clearly emphasized as a value. This seems odd in a context where universities are characterized as 'institutions of learning' but careful attention needs to be paid to the consequences – perhaps unintended – of policy decisions for learning. For example, in an institution where class contact hours are the measure of teaching and learning effort, the development of the autonomous learner may be undermined. Where the results of three-hour unseen examinations are taken to be the only realiable and valid indicator of student achievement, student-centred learning is unlikely to flourish. Where the quality of courses is measured in relation to the entry and exit qualifications of students, the added value of enterprise competencies may be ignored. In many instances enterprise teaching and learning can be enhanced *only* by larger organizations, such as the university itself or the professional body taking a general policy decision, e.g. to reduce the number of units of study per year without increasing class contact hours per unit, to focus on outcomes and competencies required for professional accreditation, rather than content or syllabus coverage.

In a recent article, Leftwich (1991) has raised serious doubt about the extent to which teaching quality can be enhanced, given the absence of interest in universities (and outside) in providing significant additional resources for the support of pedagogic innovations. He suggests that while the EHE initiative may be a step in the right direction, the money available in relation to the overall average recurrent budget of universities is too small to effect any real and lasting cultural change. While there is much in his article that an EHE director could (and indeed should) take issue with, notably that a reorientation of university values towards teaching and learning can *only* be achieved with significant additional resources, Leftwich does focus on a very deep concern in relation to the institutional climate, i.e. that the system of rewards and incentives in universities supports and promotes research and publications at the expense of teaching – a perception that Brenda Wilson (1991) had acquired very early on in her university career. Leftwich concludes:

> In the last few years, there have been one or two shuffling steps in the direction of regarding teaching proficiency as a criterion for promotion from the lecturer to the senior lecturer grade (but not beyond that) at some institutions. But it still remains the case that all the main benefits, prestige and job advancement or mobility prospects depend primarily on research output and quality. In some institutions, now, the 'prize' for steady research output is *having to teach less*.
>
> (Leftwich 1991)

Enterprise and the quality of teaching

The argument presented so far has postulated that a shift in emphasis from content to process in relation to teaching and learning requires a fundamental shift in the attitudes to teaching on the part of the teacher and the university, together with a change in both the nature and provision of staff development for teaching. All of this has considerable implications for both the quality of university teaching and the process of quality assurance.

In the context of a general discussion on what is meant by quality in higher education teaching, Clive Colling (1990) has argued that 'the acid test of good quality teaching is in what students are capable of doing as a result of it.' He goes on to argue further that the essential 'capability' in this context is that of life-long learning. Thus, in line with the argument presented in this chapter, Colling suggests that the measure of quality (in teaching) lies in the learning outcomes in students. Raising awareness of the importance of learning outcomes for students focuses attention on the relationships between the standards and parameters set by the teacher and the measured competencies of the learner in a far more explicit way than has hitherto been the case in the 'traditional' model of university teaching and learning outlined above. Moreover, the establishment of more explicit 'learning contracts' between teachers and students, which make clear the rights and responsibilities of each of the contractors in relation to the achievement of stated outcomes, provides a context within which the achievements of the teacher can be evaluated.

The assessment of the teacher's performance is much more than the checking off of achievements against standards or outcomes set. Enterprising assessment is initially formative rather than summative and this applies to the assessment of teaching as well as the assessment of student performance. In an environment where students are trained and competent in peer and self-assessment they can feel more confident in assessing or evaluating the performance of their teacher or facilitator. In fact, I would contend that *until* students are competent in making judgements and evaluating the work of others, the appraisal of teaching by students will be at best a haphazard affair. Enterprising evaluation of teaching is for improvement and enhancement; it is criterion-related and focuses on the quality of the learning experience as well as the role of the teacher. Encouraging teachers and students to reflect together on their common experience of the learning process, and to offer mutual feedback in constructive and trusting environments, enhances and improves each aspect of that process. Perhaps above all, it is the impetus that EHE gives to innovation and creativity in the teaching and learning relationship that ultimately may be the best vehicle for the promotion of quality in university teaching. For the subsequent feedback on the outcomes of such innovations promotes the active engagement of the teacher in the whole learning process (in much the same way that he or she would *engage* in research) and raises the status of teaching as an integral element of the professional activities of university staff. Undoubtedly the time is now right for change and innovation in university teaching.

As Peter Wright argues,

The increasing involvement of the Manpower Services Commission (now the Training Commission [*sic*]) in higher education has begun to provide the basis for new definitions of higher education and, indeed, the funds to support them.

(Wright 1989b)

It is these competing ideologies and definitions of the purposes and practice of higher education that ultimately challenge the traditional approaches to teaching and learning in universities, which have underpinned the edifice of the professional expert. Enterprise in Higher Education reflects this challenge, and the process of meeting it can only be good for the enhancement of the quality of university teaching.

References

Academic Audit Unit (1991) *Annual Report of the Director 1990/91*. London: AAU.
Barnett, R. (1989) Responsiveness and fulfilment: the value of higher education in the modern world. *Higher Education Foundation Paper*, September.
Becker, H., Geer, B. and Hughes, E. (1968) *Making the Grade: the Academic Side of College Life*. New York: John Wiley & Sons.
Boyatzis, R. E. (1982) *The Competent Manager: a Model for Effective Performance*. New York: John Wiley & Sons.
Colling, C. (1990) In pursuit of (good) quality teaching. *Bulletin of Teaching and Learning*, 4: 26–8.
Davis, L. (1990) *Experience Based Learning in the Curriculum*. London: ASET and CNAA.
Elton, L. (1990a) Criteria of excellence in teaching and learning and their appraisal. *Bulletin of Teaching and Learning*, March (3): 6–7.
Elton, L. (1990b) Teaching excellence and quality assurance. Paper given to SRHE Conference, December.

Fleming, D. (1991) The concept of meta-competence. *Competence and Assessment*, 16: 9–12.

Gibbs, G. (1990) Briefing paper – Improving student learning project. Oxford: CNAA/Oxford Centre for Staff Development.

Jenkins, A. and Pepper, D. (1987) Enhancing employability and educational experience for students. SCED Paper no. 27.

Leftwich, A. (1991) Pedagogy for the depressed: the political economy of teaching development in British universities. *Studies in Higher Education*, 16(3): 227–90.

Nixon, N. (1990) Assessment issues in relation to experience based learning on placement. In Bell, C. and Harris, D. (eds) *World Yearbook of Education*. London: Kogan Page.

Olesen, V. and Whitaker, E. (1968) *The Silent Dialogue*. San Francisco: Jossey-Bass.

Pennington, G. (1988) *Teesside Polytechnic Enterprise Newsletter*. Teesside EHE Unit.

Ramsden, P. (1987) Improving teaching and learning in higher education: the case for a relational perspective. *Studies in Higher Education*, 12(3): 275–86.

UDACE (1990) *What Can Graduates Do?* A consultative document. Leicester: Unit for the Development of Adult and Continuing Education.

Weil, S. (1990) Education for capability. *RSA Newsletter*, no. 3.

Wilson, B. (1991) Whistling in the dark. *New Academic*, 1(1): 6.

Wright, P. (1989a) Enterprise in higher education. *Bulletin of Teaching and Learning*, May (2): 2–3.

Wright, P. (1989b) Who defines quality in higher education? Reflections on the role of professional power in determining conceptions of quality in English higher education. *Higher Education*, 18: 149–65.

Glossary

This glossary contains terms in current use in or of potential applicability to higher education.

Academic Audit Unit   Previous title of Division of Quality Audit of Higher Education Quality Council.

Accreditation   The award of credit to individuals, groups or organizations that meet specific standards. Recognition that a course meets standards usually with regard to its capability to assess performance of students. Process of subjecting individuals, groups or organizations to quality appraisal and awarding those who meet standards a certification of achievement.

Aim   A statement of intention usually referring to a goal or desired outcome. Less specific than *objective*.

Appraisal   Comparison of performance or events with *standards*. System for regular review of employee performance to determine strengths and weaknesses and plan for future development.

Audit   Process of observing and recording events or scrutinizing records for comparison with standards. Standards may be for the records or for the events themselves. Comparison of actual events with predicted or implied events as in audit of university mechanisms for quality assurance.

British Standards   Standards set by the British Standards Institution for both products and the management of their production. Standards for products cover a wide range of goods which can be awarded the *Kitemark* indicating that they *conform* to relevant standards. BS 5750 covers standards for the management of quality. Comparable organization is ISO (International Standards Organization); whose equivalent to BS 5750 is ISO 9000. BS 5750 may be applicable to university quality assurance and management but there is no British Standard as yet for university teaching itself.

Code of Practice   Broad indications of appropriate practice. Generally associated with level below which standards should not fall. Also disciplinary code produced by professional organizations which includes sanctions for failure to conform to code of practice.

Company Wide Quality Control (CWQC)   Japanese approach establishing quality control in all aspects of company activity including those only indirectly associated with production. Often involves *quality circles*.

Competence   A specified repertoire of skills, knowledge and attitudes deemed sufficient for a particular job or profession (e.g. the competence of the university teacher). Alternatively the particular skills, knowledge and attitudes of an individual.

Competency/competencies   Single specific skill, knowledge or professional value; a component of overall *competence*. Alternatively, narrow area or small group of related skills within a broader repertoire.

Conformance   Meeting standards; state of having met standards. Also the behaviour of patient or student who follows instructions.

Consumer   Recipient of product or service. In education normally implies students but employers, professions also so described. Can be external (e.g. student, employer) or internal (e.g. teaching staff are consumers of secretarial and administrative services).

Cost-benefit analysis   An approach which identifies and equates inputs with outcomes for a particular process. Costs of inputs are typically easier to measure than benefits of outcomes.

Credit accumulation and transfer   *Credit* is given for assessed learning; credits *accumulate* to lead to awards; and students may *transfer* credits from one university to another. Implies establishment of common standards of achievement and compatible units, courses and patterns of organization.

Criteria mapping   System for selecting cases for review from medical records. Screening uses maps or algorithms which outline sequence of decisions which should be taken and action which should be initiated during progress of care. Cases with more than a threshold number of wrong or absent decisions are selected for review. Major application in health care but could apply, for example, to student records or course reviews.

Criterion   Specification of expected or desirable quality of a product or service. Can be more or less specific than related term *standard*.

Criterion-referenced test   Test designed to facilitate comparison of individual performance with specified criteria; often leads to simple pass/fail categorization. Does not facilitate detailed comparison of individuals with each other but can be used to compare teachers or facilities dealing with similar students (cf. *norm-referenced test*).

Customer   Recipient of product or service who exchanges money for it. Can be external or internal (see *consumer*).

Distinguished Teaching Award (DTA)   Award given in recognition of excellence in teaching as judged by students, ex-students and peers. Well established in the USA but an innovation in the UK.

Division of Quality Audit   Division of Higher Education Quality Council responsible for audit of universities' quality assurance mechanisms.

Economy   Avoidance of unnecessary expenditure or waste in the consumption of resources to achieve objectives.

Effectiveness   The extent to which something achieves its aims. For example the extent to which goods are fit for their purpose or teaching is successful in modifying student knowledge, skills, attitudes or values.

Efficiency   Producing maximum goods or delivering maximum services with minimum expenditure of resources.

Equity   Treatment based on relevant distinctions. In education the fair distribution of resources for teaching and learning; ensuring fairness and lack of discrimination in access to education.

Evaluation   Comparison with *standards*; alternatively attribution of a number, literal grade, or verbal description to permit comparison with other instances of similar phenomena. (Also see appraisal; *formative evaluation* and *summative evaluation*.

Feedback   Knowledge of results used to modify future performance. Knowledge of results of *quality appraisal* used to inform *quality action*.

Formative Evaluation   Evaluation undertaken or used to inform or modify a continuing process (e.g. teaching and learning; delivery of care or other service). Often more specific but less comprehensive and less rigorously controlled than *summative evaluation*.

Guideline   Broad indication of appropriate practice or procedure. Less specific than *standards* or *criteria*.

Health Accounting   System of cost-benefit analysis in health care in which quality is determined by balance of benefits of specified treatments or procedures over their costs. Involves health currency of psychosocial goods or utilities which are accounted against financial costs. Comparable calculations could be carried out in education.

Indicator   Aspect of product or service taken as representative of set of like instances and selected for attention and possibly measurement during quality appraisal (see *performance indicator*).

Inspection   Process of scrutiny to determine conformance with standards. Often refers to goods after production when defective goods may be scrapped or recycled (see *quality control*). In education inspection may be of student performance, teaching, curricula, institutional management and facilities; and is usually carried out by external groups often government instigated.

Inspectorate   Expert groups charged to appraise and report on performance of individuals and organizations including schools, colleges and universities. Membership, relationship with government and role in higher education all currently matters of debate.

Kitemark   Mark or logo which can be displayed for goods, services or procedures which *conform* to standards.

League Table Statistics   Statistics purporting to compare universities with regard to indicators (e.g. degree classifications awarded; admission qualifications; application to place ratios).

Manufacturing Industry   Industry in which the production of physical goods is the primary aim. Will also have external and internal service functions (e.g. sales, finance).

Monitoring   Observation and recording of events over time. Implies concurrent or subsequent comparison with standards.

Norm-Referenced Test   Test designed to facilitate comparison between individuals by identifying differences in performance with a range of scores; not necessarily related explicitly to any predetermined standard of performance (cf. *criterion-referenced test*).

Objective   Goal or desirable outcome. In education usually short term, specific and measurable. Less general than *aim* and easier to use as a *standard* or *criterion* in *quality appraisal*.

Occurrence Screening   System for selecting cases from records for subsequent review. Systems use lists of *criteria* (often adverse occurrences) for selection. Major application in health care but could be used in review of educational events for example student progress records, course reviews or service schedules.

Outcome   The end result or effect of a service, for example student learning as a function of teaching. Impact of service on consumers. Related expression 'outcome quality' is the quality of service outcomes.

Patient Satisfaction   Extent to which patients express positive attitudes to specified treatments or to care in general. Often determined by administration of patient satisfaction questionnaires (see *student evaluation questionnaire*).

Peer Review   Technique for appraising quality of service (e.g. teaching, health care) by individuals selected for their similar status and common interests to groups being appraised.

Performance   Observable behaviour; what a teacher, student or organization actually does.

Performance Indicator   A measurable entity taken as representative or indicative of overall performance.

Process   Organized series of activities or events which comprise production of goods or delivery of service. In education comprises all components of teaching delivery and its support including selection, curriculum design, face to face teaching, facilitation of independent study, assessment, pastoral care, provision of leisure facilities, educational and careers guidance.

Process Control   Systems and procedures for ensuring that production and service processes do not vary beyond predetermined limits. Most frequently employed in manufacturing industry and in areas of education where material objects are processed or produced (e.g. reprographic services, catering).

Process Control Chart   Chart displaying specified limits of variation with which actual variation (in products or services) can be compared. Excessive variation leads to modification of the processes of production or delivery.

Product   Manufactured object.

Protocol   Organized list of activities and events specified as necessary for delivery of particular aspect of service so as to meet minimum or desirable standards of care.

Quality Action   Action taken to identify and implement procedures for *quality improvement* or *quality enhancement*. Usually follows *quality appraisal*. Second half of *quality cycle*.

Quality Activity   Any event or series of events designed to improve quality of goods or services.

Quality Appraisal   Series of activities including standard setting, measurement, and interpretation of measurements to determine extent to which products or services meet standards. Usually followed by *quality action*. First half of *quality cycle*. Related term is *quality assessment*.

Quality Assurance   Process by which confidence in consistent quality is established. Emphasis on standard setting, monitoring and recourse to consumer as arbiter of quality.

Procedures and systems designed to maintain quality of goods or services. Emphasizes attention to *processes* of production or delivery, *company wide* systems, and prevention of error and excessive variation from standards. Can be represented in *quality cycle*.

Quality Audit   Scrutiny and review of *quality systems* to determine whether they meet standards. In current higher education primary task of *quality audit division*.

Quality Circle   Technique for solving problems using small groups of employees and relying on participation and creativity.

Quality Control   Systems of product *inspection* and *process control* designed to minimize variation from standards.

Quality Culture   Organization wide ethos and value system which stresses importance of quality of products and services and effectiveness of quality assurance. Quality values are often formally articulated in statement of mission and reflected in commitment of time and material resources to quality activities.

Quality Cycle   Sequence of related activities comprising *quality appraisal* and *quality action* carried out iteratively in a process of continuous *quality improvement* and *quality enhancement*.

Quality Documentation   Records used in the process of *quality assurance*. Alternatively, records describing *quality systems* and procedures.

Quality Enhancement   Process of continuously setting and achieving higher standards. Implies quality is already high but can still be improved.

Quality Improvement   Process of continuously setting and achieving higher standards. Implies identification of areas of poor quality and solution of quality problems.

Quality Initiative   New quality activity or system.

Quality Management   Process of continuous planning, implementation and evaluation to assure quality. Implies emphasis on human factors including motivation and development of *quality culture*.

Quality Manual   Compilation of *quality documentation* including procedures, standards and responsibilities.

Quality Mission   Formal statement of quality ethos and values which underpin *quality culture*. Can include indication of *quality strategy*.

Quality Plan   Operationalization of *quality strategy*. Includes specification of *quality structures*, *quality systems* and possibly *quality procedures*. Includes a designation of quality responsibilities.

Quality Procedure   Statement of who does what to whom when in order to satisfy customer needs.

Quality Strategy   Broad indication of organization's aims and intentions for quality assurance. Usually produced at a relatively high organizational level. Often includes indication of quality structure and designation of senior responsibilities.

Quality Structures   Organization-wide arrangement of working groups, reporting responsibilities and accountability for quality assurance. Designed to facilitate operation of *quality system*.

Quality System   Arrangements for exchange of information and liaison between components of *quality structures*. The way structures are expected to function.

Reliability   The extent to which a measuring instrument measures consistently (cf. *validity*).

Review   Process of retrospective quality *appraisal*. Can also involve determination of *quality action*. Also reconsideration of appropriateness of any aspect of *quality assurance* or *quality management*.

Service Industry   Industry in which the primary aim is the effective execution of a series of interactions between people, i.e. in which one group of people does things for, to or with other groups. Component activities can include production or processing of physical objects e.g. food in catering services, documents in financial or legal services. Teaching may be conceived as a service and education as a service industry.

Standards   Specification of expected or desirable quality of a product or service. Can be more or less specific than related term *criterion*.

Student Evaluation Questionnaire   Questionnaire designed to elicit student views on specified episodes of teaching or on units, courses or institutions in general.

Summative Evaluation   Evaluation undertaken or used at the end of a specified process (e.g. a course, unit or programme of instruction). Comprehensive and rigorous but often less specific than *formative evaluation* and less likely to provide pointers for improvement.

Total Quality Management   A management philosophy which emphasizes the personal involvement and accountability of all, the inseparability of customer needs and business goals and the establishment of company-wide structures, systems and procedures.

University Statistical Record   Statistics complied by UFC across all UK universities providing a basis for detailed analysis and comparison.

Validation   Process of *appraising* quality of curriculum and resources (including staff) for specified units, courses or programmes of study.

Validity   The extent to which an activity accomplishes what it claims. Of a measure the extent to which it measures what it purports to measure (cf. *reliability*).

Variation   Deviation from a specified standard.

Zero Defects   An approach to quality control and quality management which stresses the prevention of error and variation. Related expression is the 'right first time' approach.

Author Index

Subject Index

The Society for Research into Higher Education

The Society for Research into Higher Education exists to stimulate and coordinate research into all aspects of higher education. It aims to improve the quality of higher education through the encouragement of debate and publication on issues of policy, on the organization and management of higher education institutions, and on the curriculum and teaching methods.

The Society's income is derived from subscriptions, sales of its books and journals, conference fees and grants. It receives no subsidies, and is wholly independent. Its individual members include teachers, researchers, managers and students. Its corporate members are institutions of higher education, research institutes, professional, industrial and governmental bodies. Members are not only from the UK, but from elsewhere in Europe, from America, Canada and Australasia, and it regards its international work as amongst its most important activities.

Under the imprint *SRHE & Open University Press*, the Society is a specialist publisher of research, having some 55 titles in print. The Editorial Board of the Society's Imprint seeks authoritative research or study in the above fields. It offers competitive royalties, a highly recognizable format in both hardback and paperback and the worldwide reputation of the Open University Press.

The Society also publishes *Studies in Higher Education* (three times a year), which is mainly concerned with academic issues, *Higher Education Quarterly* (formerly *Universities Quarterly*), mainly concerned with policy issues, *Research into Higher Education Abstracts* (three times a year), and *SRHE News* (four times a year).

The Society holds a major annual conference in December, jointly with an institution of higher education. In 1992, the topic was 'Learning to Effect' with Nottingham Trent University. In 1993, it was 'Governments and the Higher Education Curriculum: Evolving Partnerships' at the University of Sussex in Brighton, and in 1994, 'The Student Experience' at the University of York. Future conferences include in 1995, 'The Changing University' at Heriot-Watt University in Edinburgh.

The Society's committees, study groups and branches are run by the members. The groups at present include:

Teacher Education Study Group
Continuing Education Group
Staff Development Group
Excellence in Teaching and Learning

Benefits to members

Individual

Individual members receive:

- *SRHE News*, the Society's publications list, conference details and other material included in mailings.
- Greatly reduced rates for *Studies in Higher Education* and *Higher Education Quarterly*.
- A 35 per cent discount on all Open University Press & SRHE publications.
- Free copies of the Precedings – commissioned papers on the theme of the Annual Conference.
- Free copies of *Research into Higher Education Abstracts*.
- Reduced rates for conferences.
- Extensive contacts and scope for facilitating initiatives.
- Reduced reciprocal memberships.

Corporate

Corporate members receive:

- All benefits of individual members, plus
- Free copies of *Studies in Higher Education*.
- Unlimited copies of the Society's publications at reduced rates.
- Special rates for its members e.g. to the Annual Conference.

 *Membership details*: SRHE, 3 Devonshire Street, London, W1N 2BA, UK. Tel: 0171 637 2766
Catalogue: SRHE & Open University Press, Celtic Court, 22 Ballmoor, Buckingham MK18 1XW.
Tel: (01280) 823388